THE NEW
COCKTAIL
HOUR

The Essential Guide to Hand-Crafted Drinks

André Darlington & Tenaya Darlington

Photography by **Jason Varney**

RUNNING PRESS
PHILADELPHIA

Running Press
Hachette Book Group
1290 Avenue of the Americas, New York, NY 10104
www.runningpress.com
@Running_Press

Printed in China

First Edition: April 2016

Published by Running Press, an imprint of Perseus Books, LLC, a subsidiary of Hachette Book Group, Inc. The Running Press name and logo is a trademark of the Hachette Book Group.

The Hachette Speakers Bureau provides a wide range of authors for speaking events. To find out more, go to www.hachettespeakersbureau.com or call (866) 376-6591.

The publisher is not responsible for websites (or their content) that are not owned by the publisher.

Print book cover and interior design by Joshua McDonnell
Drink Stylist: Keith Raimondi
Prop Stylist: Kristi Hunter
Hand-drawn Cover Type: Rachel Peckman

Library of Congress Control Number: 2015958577

ISBNs: 978-0-7624-5726-7 (hardcover), 978-0-7624-5727-4 (ebook)

1010

15 14 13 12 11 10 9 8 7 6

CONTENTS

"The American cocktail is nothing if not forward-looking and optimistic."

—William Grimes, *Straight Up or On the Rocks*

PART ONE

WHO'S THIRSTY?

INTRODUCTION

We're not bartenders . . . we're lushes. We are siblings and journalists who have covered the food and drink beat for over a decade. (You could say we're drinkers with writing habits.) In that time, we've also become serious home enthusiasts.

We became enamored of mixing drinks in our early twenties, at the onset of the craft cocktail boom. As brother and sister, we often celebrated milestones by inventing special drinks for one another in our apartment kitchens—the Demoted Freelancer, the First Gray Hair—and eventually we traveled around the country in search of transportive sips at new cocktail meccas. Our wild passion, combined with our journalistic inclination to take notes and do research, has resulted in the book you now hold in your hands.

What you have before you is a com-pendium of exquisite drinks from the last two hundred years, with flavor notes, food pairings, and historical context. We don't know of any other cocktail resource that has been curated in quite the same way. Most books present cocktails in alphabetical order or group them by spirit, making it impossible to grasp how drinks have evolved. When we began organizing recipes by era, fascinating flavor patterns emerged. For example, we saw how sweetness exploded after Prohibition and how bitterness could be traced to early medicinal elixirs—a taste that faded, only to become beloved again today.

We also love to cook, and as we delved into cocktails we naturally began to play with food pairings. We took a shine to fixing citrus drinks alongside oysters, thanks to cocktails like the Pimm's Cup (page 171)—which was invented at a British oyster bar—and we discovered how well tiki drinks riff off spices in Thai and Indian cuisines. Throughout these pages, we offer our flavor notes and pairing suggestions so that you can experiment, too.

The craft cocktail movement has restored the cocktail as an American rite. Today's challenge is to incorporate its lessons and recipes into daily use at home. There has never been a better time to do so. The explosion of small-batch tonics, artisan bitters, craft spirits, and resurrected liqueurs means that home mixology is more exciting than ever. Our goal is to make it accessible. What we pass on to you are the things that we have discovered to be essential—about mixing balanced drinks, about stocking a liquor cabinet, about preparing your own syrups and shrubs. We also chose drink recipes that reflect a contemporary sensibility, emphasizing seasonality and unrefined sweeteners. Whether you're a cocktail-scene veteran or a thirsty new-comer, we hope that this collection—like a good cookbook—becomes *your* house-hold cocktail guide. Dog-ear the pages, spill rum on the spine, and scribble notes in the margins.

It's time to take matters into your own shaker.

HOW TO USE THIS BOOK

If you're hunting for a specific drink by name or looking for drinks by base spirit, flip to the index in the back. If you're wondering which bottles to buy at the store, we offer recommendations for each recipe along with flavor notes in our Booze Glossary (page 271).

Here are a few things that separate this book from the colossal list of great literature on the subject of mixed drinks:

Tasting Notes

Every drink in this book includes flavor descriptions—something we yearned for as we combed through recipes over the years, licking our lips but also scratching our heads as we tried to imagine how an unknown drink might taste. If you love citrusy cocktails or herbaceous drinks, you can easily find them by scanning the tasting notes for each recipe.

Pairing Ideas

We suggest food for each cocktail so that you have some idea which drinks pair well with, say, sushi, barbecue, pasta, spicy foods, or dessert. We also provide some general pairing guidelines in What to Eat with What You Shake (page 18).

Chronological and Occasional Organization

Part Two of this book is organized by era so you can experience the evolution of the American cocktail. Note that we've taken the liberty of placing some drinks in the time period in which they became widespread, not necessarily when they were created. Part Three is organized by seasons and special occasions, so you can quickly find a brunch drink or a dessert cocktail. This section also includes a chapter on tiki drinks, along with a final chapter on no-proof cocktails, for designated drivers and non-drinkers.

Curated Drink Lists

Flip through this book and you'll find conveniently curated lists in each chapter to help you find the right drinks for exploring and entertaining.

In the back, you'll find recipes for syrups, shrubs, and more (Part Four), along with techniques for making impeccable drinks and garnishes (Parts Five and Six), followed by a glossary of the booze we like to use (Part Seven).

We hope this book inspires you to fall in love with a signature drink, explore recipes from different eras, and host your first, second, or hundredth cocktail party—complete with fresh juices, quality spirits, and stunning garnishes.

ANATOMY OF A
CRAFT COCKTAIL

So what is a craft cocktail exactly? It's a mixed drink in which all of the elements—from spirits to mixers and garnishes—have been selected with care to create visual appeal, seductive aroma, balanced taste, depth of flavor, appropriate mouthfeel, and above all, some pizzazz. The great ones even have a good story. Like a bespoke suit or a handmade bag, the final product transcends the ordinary. It sings. It embodies inspiration, quality, and skill. Does this mean you need to begin an in-home ice program and invest in a sous vide appliance? No. With a little creativity and a few tips, you can craft fine drinks at home without a lot of fuss or special equipment.

CRAFT COCKTAIL ELEMENTS

• Fresh ice, made from filtered water

• Seasonal inspiration (herbs, fruit, spices)

• Chilled glassware

• Homemade syrup, made from raw sugar (page 241)

• Freshly squeezed juices

• Garnish

• Technique (page 260)

FIVE TIPS FOR MAKING A COCKTAIL TONIGHT

A great cocktail is made in the details. In Part Five (page 253) you'll find information about tools, glassware, specific pantry items, and techniques that are key components of successful cocktailing. Here are the five most important things to know when you're getting started:

1. USE QUALITY SPIRITS

In the words of bon vivant Charles H. Baker, Jr., who penned a book on exotic cocktails at the turn of the century, "We can no more build a fine cocktail on dollar gin than Whistler could paint his mother's portrait with barn paint."

2. PREP BEFORE YOU MIX

Bartenders, like chefs, call this setting up a *mise en place*. Once you've read through the recipes, set out your bottles and cocktail tools (page 254). Then, squeeze your juices, and cut any garnishes. You don't want to finish making drinks, and then have to dig through kitchen drawers for a peeler.

3. PREPARE THE GLASS

It takes five minutes to completely chill a glass in your freezer. If you skip this step, your drinks will turn lukewarm within minutes and taste less than crisp. If you don't have room in your icebox, drop some ice into the glass, swirl it around, and let it sit while you are mixing the drink. For hot drinks, warm a mug with boiling water.

4. MEASURE YOUR INGREDIENTS

A drink should be multi-dimensional. You want to taste all of your ingredients without any one component over-powering the others. To get your proportions right, use a jigger (we like OXO). Then, measure out your cheapest ingredient first—it may be lemon juice, or it may be vermouth. That way, if you make a mistake and need to start over, you won't have to toss out precious spirits. Remember to always taste before serving (dip in a straw if the drink is for someone else) to ensure the drink is balanced.

5. REMEMBER THE GARNISH

A twist, a flamed peel, or a wheel of citrus doesn't just add to the visual appeal of the drink, it also contributes aromatics and flavor. That first sip is all about smell—a whiff of lime, a hint of cucumber. For more on garnishes and to learn how to make them, see page 264.

HOW TO HOST A PARTY WITH THREE BASIC BOTTLES

We know it can be daunting to flip through pages of recipes, trying to figure out how many different bottles you'll need before you host friends. Don't panic. A bar should grow like a library, which is to say a few bottles at a time. If you're just starting out, here's a trick we use when we throw open our doors for cocktail hour: pick two star recipes—one crisp, the other brooding. The first recipe will satisfy drinkers who simply want something light and refreshing (read: clear spirits). The second recipe will appeal to those who favor something a bit richer (read: brown spirits).

Gin

Bourbon

Campari

Once you have your two recipes, fill in around the edges with soda water, vermouth, and some bubbly. These can also be used to build additional drinks. The French 75 and the Boulevardier are two of our favorite party drinks. Once you buy gin, bourbon, and Campari, you only need a couple of additions (sparkling wine, sweet vermouth, and lemons) to get started. From two featured drinks you can make many more—see the list below. For example:

French 75 (page 60): 1 ounce gin, ½ ounce lemon juice, ½ ounce simple syrup (page 241), 4 ounces Champagne

Boulevardier (page 88): 2 ounces bourbon, 1 ounce Campari, 1 ounce sweet vermouth

HOW TO PLAN DRINK PORTIONS

• Plan on roughly three drinks for each guest (guests typically consume two drinks in the first hour, and one drink each hour after).

• Each 750-ml bottle of alcohol will yield about fifteen cocktails.

• For ice, plan on two pounds per guest.

POSSIBLE SHOPPING LIST ADD-ONS TO MAKE MORE RECIPES

Add powdered sugar and soda water to make a Gin Fizz (page 42).

Add ginger beer and Angostura bitters, and you can make a Kentucky Buck (page 176).

Add Angostura bitters and sugar cubes for a bourbon Old Fashioned (page 28) or a Champagne Cocktail (page 205).

Add maraschino cherries, and you can make a bourbon variation on a Manhattan (page 41).

Add tonic water and lime for a Gin and Tonic (page 167).

Add orange wedges, and you can make a Negroni (page 91) or Americano (page 33).

Add honey to make a Bee's Knees (page 85).

Add mint, and you can make a Mint Julep (page 171).

Add an egg, and you can serve a Whiskey Sour (page 129).

For more, see our index of drinks based on specific spirits (page 271).

WHAT TO EAT WITH
WHAT YOU SHAKE

We like to drink cocktails with food, or before or after a meal. This runs counter to much of the traditional wisdom that says cocktails fatigue the palate. We beg to differ. In fact, there may be no better way to whet the appetite. Whenever we fix a few drinks, we inevitably set out a few nibbles and start cooking. Here are a few tips we've learned about sloshing and noshing.

Pair acidic food with citrusy cocktails. Acid likes acid. In other words, if you're serving a salad with vinaigrette, pair a bright, lemony cocktail alongside it.

Bold cocktails offset other bold flavors. Try a Toronto (page 117) and a hunk of Stilton. The intensity of the drink and the cheese stand up to one another and round each other out.

Beware of rich on rich. We've been to cocktail-pairing dinners where there's a sumptuous cognac-based cocktail paired with foie gras. It's just too much richness together. Take the opposite tack, and contrast the richness of duck liver with a crisp fruit- or citrus-forward drink.

Work the herbaceous flavor bridge. Try serving an herb-heavy cocktail alongside a dish that contains complementary herbs. Common kitchen garden herbs like rosemary, basil, and mint can meld food and drink to form mutually enhancing flavors. For instance, serve pesto with a Gin Basil Smash (page 142).

Don't upstage the food. At a dinner party, consider choosing low-proof cocktails (page 231) made with wine, sherry, or beer. They will be enchanting background sippers for a wide selection of foods.

GREAT COCKTAIL AND FOOD PAIRINGS

Gin-based cocktails work beautifully with meat-and-cheese boards or other starters. Herbaceous notes cleanse and refresh the palate, making a Martini (page 46) a lovely alternative to wine when you're snacking on fatty foods. Next time you serve charcuterie or pâté, try the Hi Ho Cocktail (page 103).

Bright, citrusy drinks love seafood. Next time you're serving grilled fish, ceviche, or a plate of oysters, pick a cocktail with plenty of lemon or lime. Whip up a Bramble (page 178) with seafood paella.

Big brown liquor-based drinks with flavors of caramel, raisins, and toffee go with roasted meats and can work with grilled vegetables, especially those on the sweet side (yams, acorn squash, etc.). Try a Saratoga (page 41).

Sweeter cocktails offset the intensity of salty and spicy foods. Try a Cuba Libre (page 109) or an Old Fashioned (page 28) with bar snacks or a Reuben sandwich. Make a Rum Runner (page 188) with Thai green curry. Check out our Tiki Takeout cocktail list (page 191).

Bitter drinks, such as those containing amaro or Campari, are versatile aperitifs and digestifs—perfect for complementing or contrasting flavors. Explore them with melon, meats, sandwiches, even dessert. Also, consider drinks with a touch of bitterness when serving greasy and salty foods, such as a burger and fries.

A NOTE ON THE CONTEMPORARY COCKTAIL PALATE
(& HOW WE CHOSE BRANDS)

Tastes have changed over the centuries of cocktail-making, and in keeping with modern practices we've updated many of the recipes in this book to reflect a contemporary palate.

Sugar has been reduced or eliminated completely when it has been feasible to do so. When we do use it, we like to use unrefined sugars or honey. See specific sweetener notes on pages 256 and 257.

Base spirits are emphasized, not just fillers. With today's high-quality artisanal liquors, cocktailers want all the flavors and elements to be detectable. For instance, see our re-balanced Last Word (page 85) and Negroni (page 91).

Bitter is in, thanks to artisan bitters, amari, Aperol, and Campari. For an alluring gateway to this flavor profile, fix an Intro to Aperol (page 165), and check out our bitter-forward list of cocktails (page 228).

Drink portions are manageable. As chef Thomas Keller argues, there's a law of diminishing returns to every dish—the more bites you take of it, the less exciting it becomes. Same with drinks. Many of the recipes in this book are 3 to 4 ounces. Make a few of them, rather than one gonzo cocktail. Beware that many kitchen stores still sell oversize martini glasses. See our glassware recommendations (page 255).

We list specific brands for our cocktail recipes, not as an endorsement but to provide recipes that work. There are just too many options on today's market to not be specific—note that if you use different bottles, recipes may need adjusting. We arrived at our choices through research, recommendations, and trial and error—always searching for good value bottles in each category. We do not have relationships with any of the brands we mention. While we strongly encourage you to seek out small, handcrafted liquor made in your state, we opted for quality brands with wide distribution.

PART TWO
HERITAGE COCKTAILS

EARLY DRINKS
& THE GOLDEN AGE

Drinking has always been a part of American culture, from communal punches served in colonial taverns to Gold Rush bars and tobacco-stained saloons in which mixed drinks blossomed. During the second half of the nineteenth century, innovation drove the cocktail—advances such as refrigeration, carbonation, and water filtration spurred creativity and ushered in a world of novel, made-to-order libations. Hotel bars like New York's Hoffman House offered sumptuous seating and a lineup of seventeen bartenders furiously shaking drinks to the entertainment of customers. Americans fell hard for tinkling player pianos, handlebar mustaches, and elaborate menus filled with exotic names: the Bijou (page 51), Moral Suasion (page 34), and the East India (page 44).

The first cocktail book, *How to Mix Drinks: Or, the Bon Vivant's Companion*, appeared in 1862—a handy tome penned by a relentlessly enterprising bartender named Jerry Thomas. His drinks featured fresh citrus and seasonal berries, along with notes on proper technique. This uniquely American phenomenon, which combined ice and new implements such as the straw and shaker, raised eyebrows throughout the world.

As you drink your way through this chapter, you'll discover the first drink to use fresh citrus, the appearance of the straw, and the creative presentation of cocktails such as the feathery Ramos Gin Fizz (page 43) and the bejeweled Knickerbocker (page 32).

BITTERS

Originally concocted as medicinal tinctures, bitters flourished in the early nineteenth century, when it was common to step into an apothecary for a tipple. They are potent additions to cocktails—a little goes a long way—but they bring balance and complexity to a drink. Think of them as the cocktailer's spice cabinet.

Over the last decade, there's been a resurgence in artisan bitters, with brands such as The Bitter Truth, Bittermens, Bittercube, Dram, and Bittered Sling Extracts appearing on liquor store shelves and in bars. Serious bartenders, many of whom are closet mad scientists, often concoct their own bitters by macerating plant materials in alcohol, especially for seasonal drinks that might benefit from a touch of rhubarb, blood orange, or winter mint. See our bitters master recipe (page 252).

For a quick stomach soother, add a few drops of bitters to a glass of sparkling water after a large meal or before bed.

Commonly used bitters and their flavor profiles:

. . . .

ANGOSTURA: Grapefruity, smoky, and herbaceous with holiday spice notes, especially clove. Dark brown in color.

. . . .

PEYCHAUD'S: Sweeter than Angostura with notes of cherry, anise, nutmeg, licorice, and clove. Bright red in color and used in classic New Orleans drinks, like the Sazerac (page 37).

. . . .

ORANGE BITTERS: Regans' Orange Bitters No. 6 are widely distributed and are dry and astringent with a honeyed-orange flavor. Nearly neutral in color.

BRANDY CRUSTA

Citrus, caramel, spice

- -

With its sugared rim and eye-catching garnish, this is a fetching conversation piece for an intimate gathering or formal affair. The orange and caramel notes here play beautifully off of grilled meats, especially barbecued ribs.

Lurching out of the past with elegance and ornament, the Brandy Crusta is one of the few drinks that is fully garnished before the cocktail is completed. This is the first cocktail made with fresh citrus juice—and it changed everything. Before the Crusta, only citrus rinds were used in fashioning drinks. It speaks across time of craft and class, elements that are hallmarks of today's drink-makers who emphasize proper pours and a touch of panache. Jerry Thomas picked this one up from a fellow bartender in New Orleans. Many recipes call for the addition of maraschino liqueur, and we think it's better this way, adding depth.

Note: The Crusta's grandchild, the Sidecar (page 60), emerges around WWI.

$2\frac{1}{2}$ ounces (75 ml) brandy (Pierre Ferrand 1840)

1 teaspoon orange curaçao (Pierre Ferrand)

1 teaspoon maraschino (Luxardo)

$\frac{1}{2}$ teaspoon fresh lemon juice

Dash of Peychaud's bitters

1 teaspoon granulated sugar, for garnish

Lemon Twist, for garnish

Prepare a small wine glass with a sugared rim. In a mixing glass, stir the ingredients with ice. Strain into the prepared goblet. Garnish.

OLD FASHIONED

Rich, spice, aromatic

- • -

We love an Old Fashioned alongside bacon-wrapped appetizers or even cassoulet. With wild game? Glorious.

The word "cocktail" first appeared in 1806, in a New York newspaper: "*Cock-tail* is a stimulating liquor, composed of spirits of any kind, sugar, water and bitters—it is vulgarly called a *bittered sling.* . . ." From this specific definition, the word became shorthand, over time, for all mixed drinks.

The Old Fashioned is the cocktail from which all others sprang. Originally, this drink was a mix of water, sugar, whiskey, and bitters. Over the years, it (d)evolved into a sticky-sweet concoction with muddled orange and a maraschino cherry. In Wisconsin, where the Old Fashioned "survived" Prohibition in this form with a base spirit of brandy instead of whiskey, the cocktail is synonymous with supper clubs and fish fries. Nowadays, cocktail purists fret over any fruity additions, and we omit them here.

2 ounces (60 ml) whiskey or brandy

1 Demerara sugar cube

2 to 3 dashes Angostura bitters

1 teaspoon water

Orange peel, for garnish

Place the sugar cube in a chilled rocks glass. Dash in the bitters and muddle, coating the bottom and the sides of the glass. Drop in a large cube of ice, then add spirit and water, and stir. To garnish, twist the peel over the surface of the cocktail to express the oil. Drop the peel into the drink.

WHISKEY SOUR

Lemon, woodsy, frothy

— • • • • —

Try serving this versatile vintage drink with a classic baked chicken dinner or a lemon-herb pasta. It's also divine with brown-butter gnocchi or steak.

The venerable whiskey sour, which appears in Jerry Thomas's 1862 *Bartenders Guide*, had a terrible tour through the twentieth century, when it was abused with pre-made sour mix and rail booze. Returned to fresh lemon juice and quality bourbon or rye whiskey, it is a magnificent revelation of spice and tartness in perfect harmony. We prefer the frothy, mellowing effect of the egg white, but it can be omitted. Sours are a family of drinks containing a base spirit, citrus, and a sweetener—think daiquiris and the Jack Rose, among many others (see our cocktail taxonomy, page 54).

    2 ounces (60 ml) bourbon or rye whiskey

    1 ounce (30 ml) fresh lemon juice

    ¾ ounce (22 ml) simple syrup (page 241)

    ¾ ounce (22 ml) egg white

    Dash of Angostura bitters

Dry shake your spirit, lemon juice, simple syrup, and egg white to emulsify. Then shake with ice and strain into a chilled coupe glass. Dash the bitters on top.

COFFEE COCKTAIL

Creamy, dark fruit, spice

— • • • • —

This drinks almost like a dark beer. Try it with a blue cheese (Stilton) and a plate of gingersnaps.

A frothy nightcap from 1887 that tastes faintly like figs, this is an unexpectedly sumptuous drink with a silky mouthfeel, thanks to the addition of a whole egg. It's full-bodied and vaguely holiday-ish, given the nutmeg garnish. Serve it in place of eggnog, or drink it like a boozy smoothie on a cold morning. It's verve-y and just a little purple. In its day, this was the fashionable after-dinner drink choice.

    3 ounces (90 ml) ruby port (Niepoort or Warre's Warrior)

    1 ounce (30 ml) brandy (Pierre Ferrand Ambre)

    1 teaspoon simple syrup (page 241)

    1 small fresh egg

    Freshly grated nutmeg, for garnish

Dry shake port, brandy, simple syrup, and egg together to emulsify. Add ice and shake, then double-strain into a chilled goblet or cocktail glass. Garnish with grated nutmeg.

SHERRY COBBLER

Mint, citrus, fruit, plum

● ●

A glamorous drink with a delicate sweetness, pair it with oysters, crab cakes, or smoked salmon. It's an impressive garden-party starter or patio sipper.

Named for the "cobblestones" of ice that were produced when bartenders pounded down larger blocks in a sack, the Sherry Cobbler takes its place in the pantheon of drinks as the reason we today consume beverages through straws. Made with sherry and elaborate fresh fruit garnishes over crushed ice, patrons required a straw—at first a wooden reed—to get to the liquid at the bottom. Later, the reed evolved into a special metal straw with a little spoon on the end. The invention of the Cobbler was also an important milestone in the development of the cocktail shaker. As one of the first drinks that needed straining, the drink gave rise to the common three-piece cocktail shaker, properly called a cobbler (a bottom shaker, a top with a built-in strainer, and a small cap).

Note: You can use any combination of seasonal berries as garnishes here. The more festive the presentation, the better. We love to serve this with metal straw, but any straw will do.

4 ounces (120 ml) dry sherry (Amontillado)

1 teaspoon sugar

1 orange slice

Mint sprig, for garnish

Seasonal berries (blueberries, raspberries, blackberries, and strawberries), for garnish

Shake ingredients with ice and strain into an ice-filled highball glass or metal tumbler. Garnish with mint and berries.

SHERRY FLIP

Dried fruit, spice, brown sugar

— • • • • —

A round of flips are festive and comforting on a wintery afternoon. Serve them alongside nuts, olives, and charcuterie.

In centuries past, it was common for fellow travelers to share stories around a roaring fire when staying at roadside inns. The innkeeper would provide a sherry-based drink that was brought to a rolling boil by inserting the fireplace poker—called a loggerhead—into the mug. The drink was dubbed the Sack Posset, and if guests had a few too many and began to fight, which apparently happened often, they were said to be "at loggerheads." The Sherry Flip is a distant, although not too distant, grandchild of these old drinks, appearing in the second edition of Jerry Thomas's book in 1887. Charles Dickens mentions the libation as a curative in his novel, *Little Dorrit*, and, in fact, used it as a restorative on his American reading tour. We like to add a dash of cayenne pepper on top, along with freshly grated nutmeg.

2½ ounces (75 ml) oloroso sherry

½ ounce (15 ml) simple syrup (page 241)

1 small fresh egg (preferably organic)

Cayenne pepper, for garnish (optional)

Freshly grated nutmeg, for garnish

Dry shake sherry, simple syrup, and egg to emulsify. Then, shake with ice and strain into a goblet. Garnish with a dash of cayenne pepper and nutmeg.

KNICKERBOCKER

Citrus, berries, vanilla, spice

— • • • • —

A quick-to-fix beauty studded with raspberries, this drink is unfussy but glamorous. Serve it on the patio with ceviche, grilled shrimp, or fish tacos.

Here's a cocktail that reads like the precursor to all later tiki drinks, but it appeared at least as early as the 1860s. This drink was probably named for New York's Knickerbocker Boat Club, and is an early sailing party classic. The mix originally calls for raspberry syrup, and purists are correct that homemade syrup cannot be surpassed. The addition of a spent lime half in the bottom of the glass is unexpectedly rustic.

2 ounces (60 ml) gold rum (Appleton Special)

½ ounce (15 ml) orange curaçao (Pierre Ferrand)

1½ teaspoons raspberry syrup (page 242)

1 ounce (30 ml) fresh lime juice, plus spent lime half

2 to 3 raspberries, for garnish

Drop the spent lime rind into a shaker. Then, add ice, lime juice, and spirits. Shake, then pour the contents—ice and all—into a chilled rocks glass. Garnish with raspberries.

JAPANESE COCKTAIL

Almond, lime, spice, caramel

— • • • • —

For a sophisticated dessert, serve a round of Japanese cocktails after dinner with a plate of sliced fresh pineapple and oranges, or with dark chocolate truffles.

....

Orgeat (pronounced OR-zsat, or Or-zsa in French) is the star in this early drink concocted by Jerry Thomas for the Japanese commission to the United States in 1860. Their translator, "Tommy" Noriyuki, was a reputed ladies' man and cocktail quaffer, hence this honorary libation. This drink is often cited as the first known cocktail to eschew a functional name for a fantasy one, although nothing about the drink is particularly Japanese. Orgeat is an almond-based emulsion that appears later in island drinks like the Mai Tai (page 185), as a bridge between rum and spice. See the recipe for homemade orgeat (page 244), or you can find artisan brands at the liquor store or online.

2 ounces (60 ml) brandy (Pierre Ferrand Ambre)

½ ounce (15 ml) orgeat (page 244)

½ ounce (15 ml) fresh lime juice

Dash of Angostura bitters

Lime wheel, for garnish

Shake ingredients with ice and strain into a chilled coupe glass. Garnish with lime.

AMERICANO

Orange, bitter, aromatic

— • • • • —

Serve this bitter aperitif with antipasti, like olives, hard cheese, and cured meats.

....

Think of this drink as the great-grandfather of the Negroni, minus the gin and with sweet vermouth. *Amer-* means "bitter" in Italian, so this drink may have less to do with America and more to do with the bitter liqueur Campari, created in 1860 by Gaspare Campari. The Americano originally hails from the 1860s, and was sold in bottled form by Martini & Rossi in the 1890s. On a hot day, the bracing bitterness—tempered by sweet vermouth and soda—helps take the edge off. It's a real thirst quencher, one that settles the stomach and whets the appetite, especially before a big meal.

1½ ounces (45 ml) Campari

1½ ounces (45 ml) sweet vermouth (Cinzano)

3 ounces (90 ml) club soda

Orange wheel, for garnish

Pour Campari and vermouth into a highball glass filled with ice. Top with soda, then garnish with an orange wheel on the side of the glass.

MORAL SUASION

Floral, candied citrus, honey

• •

We love to serve this decadent drink with white butter-cream cupcakes. It's perfect for showers and birthdays.

Consider this a revenge cocktail. It was created in the 1840s by Boston bartender Peter Bent Brigham in response to a temperance zealot, who publicly condemned his "fancy drinks." Brigham ran the bar at the Boston Concert Hall, and his drinks—seven kinds of punch, juleps, and cobblers—were the height of fashion. He added this powerful cocktail to the list as a jab to moral crusaders. We adapted our recipe from an update that appeared in *Imbibe* magazine, bumping up the lemon juice to offset the peachy sweetness. It utterly captures the old timey flavors of candy shop sweets, like lemon drops and rose pastilles.

2 ounces (60 ml) peach brandy (Mathilde)

1 teaspoon maraschino liqueur (Luxardo)

1 teaspoon orange curaçao (Pierre Ferrand)

1 teaspoon honey syrup (see page 242)

3 teaspoons fresh lemon juice

½ teaspoon rosewater

½ ounce (15 ml) brandy float (Pierre Ferrand Ambre)

Half orange wheel, for garnish

Half lemon wheel, for garnish

Add ingredients—except for the brandy float—to a shaker filled with ice. Shake and strain into a rocks glass filled with crushed ice. Float brandy on top by pouring it over the back of a spoon. Garnish with citrus wheel halves on the side of the glass.

IMPROVED HOLLAND GIN COCKTAIL

Citrus, licorice, malt, brine

◦•◦•◦

Try serving this at brunch with eggs Benedict. It's smashing with Hollandaise, since the citrus cuts through fat.

....

Malty genever, the precursor to modern gin, is given a glorious boost with absinthe and bitters, making for an aromatic cocktail with oomph. Pale pink and not the least bit sweet, this is a lovely brunch cocktail for those who want an elegant eye-popper. The recipe appears in Jerry Thomas's 1887 guide as a variation on the Gin Cocktail—replacing curaçao with maraschino and adding absinthe. An improvement indeed.

2 ounces (60 ml) genever (Bols)

½ teaspoon maraschino liqueur (Luxardo)

⅛ teaspoon absinthe

¼ ounce (7 ml) simple syrup (page 241)

2 dashes Angostura or Peychaud's bitters

Lemon twist, for garnish

Stir ingredients with ice. Strain into a chilled coupe glass. To garnish, twist the peel over the surface of the cocktail to express the oil. Drop the peel into the drink.

MARK TWAIN COCKTAIL

Smoky, citrus, aromatic

◦•◦•◦

This drink makes a smashing aperitif at a literary salon, and its smoky edge pairs well with hearty appetizers like aged cheese, nuts, deviled eggs, and smoked fish.

....

In 1874, Mark Twain wrote to his wife from London: "Livy my darling, I want you to be sure & remember to have, in the bathroom, when I arrive, a bottle of Scotch whisky, a lemon, some crushed sugar, and a bottle of Angostura bitters. Ever since I have been in London I have taken in a wine glass what is called a cock-tail (made with those ingredients) before breakfast, before dinner, and just before going to bed." This is essentially a Whiskey Sour (page 29) with Scotch. For an updated version, try using Art in the Age Snap—a ginger-flavored liqueur made with blackstrap molasses. While Twain used a wine glass, we prefer a rocks glass.

2 ounces (60 ml) Scotch (Dewar's or Famous Grouse)

¾ ounce (22 ml) fresh lemon juice

1 ounce (30 ml) simple syrup (page 241)

2 dashes of Angostura bitters

Lemon peel, for garnish

Shake ingredients with ice and strain into an ice-filled rocks glass. To garnish, twist the peel over the surface of the cocktail to express the oil. Then, drop the peel into the drink.

SAZERAC

Spirituous, anise, rich, prickly, aromatic

• •

With lingering flavors of rye and licorice, this kissing cousin to the Old Fashioned is husky and complex. Pair it with pâté or spicy red beans and rice.

This iconic New Orleans mix was originally made with a French brandy (cognac) called Sazerac de Forge et Fils, and the name of that brand rubbed off on the drink. But after the phylloxera outbreak in the 1860s, which wiped out France's grape vines, cognac became well nigh impossible to procure. In 1873, there was a switch to rye whiskey. Frequently cited as one of the oldest cocktails, the Sazerac is also sometimes ascribed to Antoine Peychaud, an apothecary, who, legend has it, served the drink in a little egg cup called a *coquetier*—thus, the alleged origin of the word "cocktail." While a nice story, the word "cocktail" appears in print long before the Sazerac existed.

2 ounces (60 ml) cognac (Pierre Ferrand 1840) or rye whiskey (Sazerac)

1 Demerara sugar cube

2 dashes Peychaud's bitters

Dash of Angostura bitters

Absinthe, to rinse the glass

Lemon peel, for garnish

Wash a rocks glass with absinthe, discarding any extra. In a mixing glass, drop in the sugar cube, followed by the bitters, and a splash of whiskey to help the sugar dissolve. Add spirit, stir with ice, and strain into the prepared rocks glass. Twist the lemon peel to express the oil over the drink, and drop it into the drink.

VERMOUTH TASTING

Vermouth is a fortified, aromatized wine originally developed for medicinal purposes. The name comes from the German *Wermut*, translated as "wormwood," an herb (scientific name *Artemisia absinthium*) used for the treatment of intestinal parasites. With the birth of the cocktail in the nineteenth century, vermouth became a staple in many mixed drinks, appearing first—according to common belief—in the Manhattan around the 1870s or '80s and then later in the Martini. Of important note for those interested in historical accuracy, the first vermouths available in the United States were only the Italian sweet variety—it would take until the 1890s for French dry vermouths to make inroads in the U.S. market. Thus, when Jerry Thomas lists "vermouth" as an ingredient, he means the sweet Italian variety. Today, it is often agreed that sweet vermouth goes best with brown liquors, and dry vermouth with clear ones—but this wasn't the case during the cocktail's initial development.

Today, vermouth is experiencing a full-blown renaissance with new artisan producers and renewed interest among enthusiasts. Here is a list of flavor notes for vermouths found in this book, along with sample drinks in which to try them.

CARPANO ANTICA: A high-quality Italian sweet vermouth based on an old recipe, Carpano is outstanding in Manhattans and many other cocktails. Drinkable on its own.

Flavor notes: vanilla, clove, caramel, burnt marshmallow

Sample drinks: Manhattan (page 41), Martinez (page 46), Hanky Panky (page 73)

VYA: The first small-batch vermouth in the United States (California), Vya was released in 1999 and has garnered much praise for its complex balance of bitter and sweet. Try it over ice with an orange twist.

Flavor notes: candied fruit, caramel, bitter marmalade

Sample drinks: Rob Roy (page 52), Leap Year (page 73), Manhattan (page 41)

MARTINI & ROSSI ROSSO: This sweet, widely available vermouth can balance intensely bitter cocktails. Delicious alongside a classic American rye whiskey, like Wild Turkey, where its strong oregano and black olive flavors shine through. Its herbaceousness will make you want pizza!

Flavor notes: oregano, fig, raspberry, black olive

Sample drinks: Americano (page 33), Manhattan (page 41)

CINZANO ROSSO: Originally developed by the Cinzano brothers, who ran an herbal shop in Turin back in the 1700s, this sweet vermouth pairs well with Campari—no surprise since the Campari Group now handles its production. It tastes much like tawny port with a bitter finish.

Flavor notes: dried fruit, herbs, quinine, caramel

Sample drinks: Americano (page 33), Manhattan (page 41)

NOILLY PRAT DRY: The innovator of the dry French style, Noilly Prat was created in 1813 in Marseille and was the first dry vermouth to reach American soil. Even though it's "dry" in style, it's still rather sweet. It sports a pale golden color with a nutty apricot nose.

Flavor notes: oak, chamomile, lemon peel, stone fruit (apricot pit)

Sample drinks: Negroni (page 91), Marguerite (page 47), Kangaroo (page 123)

DOLIN DRY: One of three styles of vermouth made by the French company Dolin, based in the Savoy region and now the last remaining producer in Chambéry. Dolin is favored by bartenders not only for its quality, but because it is clear and clean, while other dry vermouths can be yellowish and hazy. It's drier than Noilly Prat, and has a pleasant smell of fresh thyme and yeast.

Flavor notes: bright, clean, crisp, lime, thyme

Sample drinks: Gibson (page 102), Salomé (page 69)

DOLIN BLANC: Blanc is a distinct vermouth style. Clear with a slight golden cast, Dolin Blanc has spearmint on the nose. Sweet and brightly herbaceous.

Flavor notes: spearmint, tarragon, minerals, citrus

Sample drinks: Martini (page 46), Bamboo (page 51), Bijou (page 51)

CARPANO BIANCO: By the same makers as Carpano Antica, this blanc vermouth has a pronounced floral nose and lingering vanilla flavor. It became available in the United States in 2013.

Flavor notes: floral, vanilla, citrus, orange, lemon, spice, bitter

Sample drinks: Bijou (page 51)

PUNT E MES: A bitter style vermouth, which is paradoxically both quite sweet and very bitter.

Flavor notes: bitter herbs, balsamic, prune

Sample drinks: Red Hook (page 135), Negroni (page 91)

IMBUE BITTERSWEET: An American vermouth from Oregon, Imbue was designed to pair with new American gins. It's noted for its mellow quality and fine balance of bitter and sweet. Highly sippable on its own.

Flavor notes: vanilla, tangerine, lemongrass

Sample drinks: Obituary (page 48), Metropole (page 48)

MANHATTAN

Aromatic, woodsy, smooth

• • • •

Try a Manhattan with all things pork or anything caramelized—roasted root vegetables, steak, even crème brûlée.

Probably hailing from the Manhattan Club in the 1870s, this is believed to be the first drink to sport vermouth. In fact, this is the king of vermouth drinks, the ultimate marriage of grain and grape. Originally, it would have been made with rye whiskey and Italian sweet vermouth, although it works with bourbon as well. With great simplicity comes great responsibility; like unaccompanied Bach, the Manhattan is the cocktail pared down to bare essentials, a naked revelation of flavor and the mixer's skill. Early proportions would have been 1:1, but here we relate a modern 2:1 take. We enjoy using high-proof rye whiskey, such as Rittenhouse, or a rough-around-the-edges classic, such as Old Overholt.

- 2 ounces (60 ml) rye whiskey
- 1 ounce (30 ml) sweet Italian vermouth (Carpano Antica or Vya)
- 2 dashes Angostura bitters (or other aromatic bitters)
- Cherry, for garnish

Stir ingredients with ice and strain into a chilled coupe glass. Or, serve in a rocks glass with a large ice cube. Garnish with a cherry.

SARATOGA

Aromatic, citrus, woodsy

• • • •

The combination of brandy and rye whiskey is ideal alongside charred meats and vegetables. Serve a round while you grill.

This mahogany drink from the 1880s is spectacularly aromatic, a wonderfully complex departure from the Manhattan. Although the original recipe from Jerry Thomas calls for Angostura bitters and a lemon slice, we find this drink is lovelier with orange bitters and a twist of orange rind. It likely originated in the town of Saratoga Springs, New York, which was a hot bed of casinos, horse racing, and mineral spring spas.

- 1 ounce (30 ml) brandy (Pierre Ferrand Ambre)
- 1 ounce (30 ml) rye whiskey (Wild Turkey or Rittenhouse)
- 1 ounce (30 ml) sweet vermouth (Carpano Antica)
- 2 dashes orange bitters (Regans')
- Orange twist, for garnish

Stir ingredients with ice and strain into a coupe glass, or serve in a rocks glass with a single large cube of ice. To garnish, twist the peel over the surface of the cocktail to express the oil. Then, rest the peel on the side of the glass.

THE BIRTH OF THE FIZZ

Carbonation took off in the nineteenth century as the technology became available to produce bubbles artificially. The first soda fountains appeared at apothecary shops, where fizzy water was added to syrups or mixed with medicinal herbs. It was bottled soon after, and the first "soda" was likely sparkling lemonade.

The alcoholic version is the fizz: any drink with liquor, a citrus element, and carbonated water. The most famous of these is the Gin Fizz, a drink associated with New Orleans. The recipe is below, but note that there are a number of versions: Royal Fizz (whole egg added), Silver Fizz (egg white only), Gold Fizz (egg yolk only), Diamond Fizz (no egg and sparkling wine added—also called a French 75), and a Green Fizz (crème de menthe).

GIN FIZZ

Effervescence, lemon, juniper

Think of this as a fancy boozy lemonade. Pair it with celery and dip, pretzels, and other salty fare.

Fizzes enjoyed a heyday in the early 1900s, when teams of bartenders, called "shaker boys," took turns preparing these cocktails for their fashionable patrons. We like to use mineral water for livelier bubbles, but club soda works as well. It's worth noting that a drink called the Gin Punch appears in the 1862 edition of Jerry Thomas's *Bon-Vivant's Companion* with these same ingredients, plus maraschino liqueur. By the 1887 edition of the book, the combination becomes the famous gin fizz (although Thomas curiously spells it "Fiz").

2 ounces (60 ml) Old Tom gin (Hayman's)

½ ounce (15 ml) fresh lemon juice

1 teaspoon powdered sugar

3 to 4 ounces (90 to 120 ml) soda water or mineral water

Lemon wheel, for garnish

Shake the gin, lemon juice, and powdered sugar with ice. Strain into a highball glass. Top with mineral water and garnish with a lemon wheel on the side of the glass.

RAMOS GIN FIZZ

Lightly floral, citrus, cooling

* · *

Ripe sliced melon is a terrific accompaniment to this delicate drink. Or, serve it after a spicy meal of Creole cuisine.

Also called the New Orleans Fizz, this drink by Henry Charles Ramos gained such popularity that bars employed fleets of "'tenders" to shake them. You'll understand why once you see a Ramos Gin Fizz in action. It requires a long shake in order to emulsify all of the ingredients, and once it goes into a tall highball glass—in one long feathery pour—it looks downright regal. Add a splash of soda and it foams up like a root beer float. This is one of the more difficult and time-consuming drinks to shake, but it's worth the effort. An exquisite showpiece, especially when served with an orange slice and a straw.

2 ounces (60 ml) Old Tom gin (Hayman's or Plymouth)

1 tablespoon (15 ml) simple syrup (page 241)

½ ounce (15 ml) fresh lemon juice

½ ounce (15 ml) fresh lime juice

¾ ounce (22 ml) egg white

½ ounce (15 ml) half-and-half

3 drops orange flower water

Splash of club soda

Orange wheel half, for garnish

Dry shake ingredients except the club soda. Then, shake with ice and strain into a highball glass. Top with club soda until the glass foams up to the top. Garnish by twisting an orange wheel on top of the glass. Serve with a straw.

EAST INDIA COCKTAIL

Citrus, exotic fruit, spice

— • • • • —

With its pleasing sweetness and acidity, this drink pairs well with a variety of light foods. Try lettuce wraps, turkey salad, or cold noodles.

We love getting transported to the exotic climes of Britain's nineteenth-century trade areas of Burma, Malaysia, and Singapore—and imagine that the original imbibers of this drink did, too. It was reputedly a favorite sipper of British expats living in East India, according to Harry Johnson, who first penned this recipe in his 1882 *Bartender's Manual*. Truly a global fusion, the ingredients include French brandy, orange curaçao from the Caribbean, tropical fruit, and spices from the spice trade.

2 ounces (60 ml) brandy (Pierre Ferrand Ambre)

½ ounce (15 ml) orange curaçao (Pierre Ferrand)

½ teaspoon (15 ml) maraschino liqueur (Luxardo)

1½ ounces (45 ml) fresh pineapple juice

Dash of Angostura bitters

Freshly grated nutmeg, for garnish

Stir well with ice and strain into a chilled coupe glass. Garnish with nutmeg.

FANCY VERMOUTH COCKTAIL

Raisin, citrus, tea, bitter herbs

— • • • • —

We love this drink with a plate of figs and prosciutto. In fall, it's glorious alongside spiced desserts, like pumpkin pie.

This low-proof concoction demonstrates how vermouths can be more than just modifiers and are worthy of playing a central role in mixed drinks. We like to use Carpano Antica or other high-quality vermouths, like Vya or Imbue, to highlight complex flavors and aromatics. While it seems like this would be a stirred drink, we follow the lead of Jerry Thomas here and shake this cocktail with cracked ice. This enlivens it considerably.

3 ounces (90 ml) sweet vermouth (Carpano Antica)

¼ teaspoon maraschino liqueur (Luxardo)

2 dashes Angostura bitters

Lemon peel and lemon wheel, sliced extra thin, for garnish

Shake ingredients with ice and strain into a chilled coupe glass. To garnish, twist the lemon peel over the surface of the cocktail to express the oil and discard. Float a thin lemon wheel on the surface of the drink.

EVOLUTION OF THE MARTINI

The Martinez, the Martini, and the Marguerite exhibit the rapidly changing tastes at the turn of the twentieth century. Italian sweet vermouth was on the way out, at least as paired with gin, and dry vermouth was on the way in. This culminates in the Gibson (page 102), a much drier form of the Martini than previous versions. The combination of sweet vermouth and gin, now rather contrary to modern American taste, endures as the Lone Tree Cocktail. A similar drink survives in Britain as the Gin 'n' It, often three parts gin to one part sweet vermouth.

For a fascinating flavor comparison, serve a flight of these three cocktails together: the Martinez (page 46), the Martini (page 46), and the Marguerite (page 47).

MARTINEZ

Rich, malty, fruity, aromatic

— • • • —

An excellent aperitif to enjoy with a dish of fresh cherries or smoked almonds.

Derived from the Manhattan, the dark origin of the martini lies in this combination first printed in 1884. Many recipes use Old Tom gin, but the drink may have been made with an even older gin style, genever, which is recreated here. More of a style than a single recipe, the Martinez is a delightful combination of malty Holland-style gin and Italian vermouth that, legend says, first appeared in the California town of Martinez, where it was served to a gold miner in 1874. Majestic, smooth, and robust, it mimics the color of a shiny mahogany bar.

> 2 ounces (60 ml) Italian sweet vermouth (Carpano Antica)
>
> 1 ounce (30 ml) genever (Bols)
>
> 1 teaspoon maraschino liqueur (Luxardo)
>
> Dash of Angostura bitters
>
> Cherry, for garnish (optional)

Stir ingredients with ice, strain, and pour into a chilled coupe glass. Garnish with cherry.

MARTINI

Acidic, fruity, herbaceous, thyme

— • • • —

Few things are better than a martini served with a dish of olives and a hunk of aged pecorino.

The martini replaces the genever of the Martinez with Old Tom gin and pairs it with white vermouth. Light, acidic, and seductively fruity—thanks to the orange curaçao—this clear, peach-tinged beauty is aromatic and astonishingly drinkable. Far from a freak footnote in the development of the classic dry martini, this cocktail could be the best of both worlds—a touch sweet with enough aromatics to pair with a wide variety of foods. Or, a go-to aperitif to ease into the hours after work.

> 1½ ounce (45 ml) Old Tom gin (Hayman's)
>
> 1 ounce (30 ml) white vermouth (Dolin Blanc)
>
> 1 teaspoon orange curaçao (Pierre Ferrand)
>
> Dash of Angostura bitters
>
> Lemon peel, for garnish

Stir ingredients with ice, strain, and pour into a coupe glass. To garnish, twist the peel over the surface of the cocktail to express the oil. Drop the peel into the drink.

MARGUERITE COCKTAIL (DRY MARTINI)

Crisp, orange, juniper

• • • •

Try serving this faintly briny martini with a plate of anchovies, or play off the orange bitters with a dish of walnuts and slivers of candied orange peel.

Those who enjoy a bone-dry martini will be seduced by the touch of orange here. This original dry martini harkens back to an 1896 book, *Stuart's Fancy Drinks and How to Mix Them.* A sophisticated drink, light in taste and pale, pale yellow, it differs from the martini and the Martinez—its sisters—by including dry gin. Sweet vermouth would still have been in wide use, so for an interesting variation—called the Lone Tree—try Carpano Antica.

2 ounces dry gin (Plymouth)

1 ounce (30 ml) dry vermouth (Noilly Prat)

Dash of orange bitters (Regans')

Lemon peel, for garnish

Stir ingredients with ice and strain into a chilled coupe glass. To garnish, twist the peel over the surface of the cocktail to express the oil. Then, drop the peel into the drink.

TUXEDO COCKTAIL

Dried cherry, juniper, aromatic

• • • •

A worthy drink for a formal affair, especially alongside seafood stew or grilled lamb.

As its name suggests, this red-curtain sipper was designed for a certain diamonds-and-cummerbunds set, namely those dwelling in a "planned community" called Tuxedo Park, outside of Jersey City. In 1886, the town's Tuxedo Club hosted its first autumn ball, attracting a few young bucks who had chopped off the tails of their suit coats—a fashion statement that imitated the prince of Wales. Thus, the tuxedo of proms and weddings was born. The drink was a popular after-work cocktail at the Waldorf-Astoria bar in New York, which catered to "tuxedo-ites."

2 ounces (60 ml) gin (Plymouth)

1 ounce (30 ml) fino sherry

Dash of orange bitters (Regan's)

Lemon peel, for garnish

Stir ingredients with ice and strain into a chilled coupe glass. To garnish, twist the peel over the surface of the cocktail to express the oil. Then, drop the peel into the drink.

OBITUARY COCKTAIL

Anisette, grassy, herbaceous

· + · + · ·

With its ghoulish glow, this is the perfect cocktail for Halloween or a Day of the Dead party. As if by black magic, it pairs well with sushi—it loves wasabi—as well as vinegary dishes like salads and escabeche.

An eerie martini made with absinthe, this drink is the signature cocktail of Lafitte's Blacksmith Shop in New Orleans, the oldest continuous bar in the United States. While some recipes call for Herbsaint or Pernod, absinthe is more traditional. Typically, the Obituary is served straight up, but we prefer it in a rocks glass over a single monster cube. The added ice melt releases grassy notes.

2 ounces (60 ml) gin (Plymouth)

¼ ounce (7 ml) white vermouth (Dolin)

Absinthe, to rinse the glass

Lemon peel, for garnish

Rinse a rocks glass with absinthe and add one large ice cube. Stir the ingredients with ice. Strain into the prepared rocks glass. To garnish, twist the peel over the surface of the cocktail to express the oil. Then, discard the peel.

METROPOLE

Citrus, aromatic, woodsy

· + · + · ·

Elegance and refinement define this cocktail, a natural pairing for mushroom bruschetta, steak, barbecued brisket, or desserts with toasted nuts.

At the turn of the twentieth century, New York's first hotel to feature running water in the rooms was the Metropole, just off Times Square. It was a classy place with a bar that attracted—shall we say—a lively clientele? Here, the house cocktail served to late-night lovers, dreamers, and gamblers was essentially a Manhattan or Martini with brandy instead of whiskey or gin. Many recipes for this drink call for equal parts brandy and vermouth, but we alter the ratio a bit so the drink is brandy-forward.

2 ounces (60 ml) brandy (Pierre Ferrand Ambre)

1 ounce (30 ml) dry vermouth (Dolin)

2 dashes Peychaud's bitters

Dash of orange bitters (Regans')

Orange peel, for garnish

Stir ingredients with ice and strain into a chilled coupe glass. To garnish, twist the peel over the surface of the cocktail to express the oil. Then, drop the peel into the drink.

ALABAZAM

Spice, orange, caramel

A sexy nightcap, best enjoyed by a roaring fire with a meerschaum pipe in hand.

This bitters-forward cocktail can be traced back to Leo Engel of the Criterion Bar in London, the spot where Sir Arthur Conan Doyle first imagined Sherlock Holmes and Dr. Watson meeting. The recipe appears in Engel's book, *American and Other Drinks*, in 1878 with the instructions: "Use tumbler. One tea-spoonful of Angostura bitters; two tea-spoonfuls of orange Curaçao; one tea-spoonful of white sugar; one teaspoonful of lemon juice; half a wine glass of brandy. Shake up well with fine ice and strain in a claret glass." Cocktail sleuths will note how close this drink comes to the later Sidecar (page 60). Because of the minimal lemon juice, we stir this drink instead of shaking it, as recommended by Jamie Boudreau, the bartender who revived this classic.

1½ ounces (45 ml) brandy (Pierre Ferrand 1840)

½ ounce (15 ml) orange curaçao (Pierre Ferrand)

1 teaspoon Demerara sugar

1 teaspoon Angostura bitters

¼ ounce (7 ml) fresh lemon juice

Orange peel, for garnish

Add sugar to a mixing glass and top with bitters and lemon juice. Stir to dissolve. Add the spirits. Stir ingredients with ice and strain into a rocks glass over a single large ice cube. To garnish, twist the peel over the surface of the cocktail to express the oil. Then, run the peel around the rim of the glass and drop it into the drink.

BIJOU

Crisp, mint, juniper, bitter herbs

— • • • • —

A lovely drink to serve with big, briny oysters or nothing at all.

....

This dazzling opaline drink emerged as a favorite in the 1890s but is mentioned as early as 1882 by Harry Johnson, author of the first *Bartender's Manual of How to Mix Drinks*. He specifically called for Plymouth gin, which we agree melds well with Chartreuse, an aromatic, naturally green liqueur made by Carthusian monks. Many recipes call for a sweet vermouth, like Carpano Antica, but this turns the drink a sad, muddy brown. The drink shouldn't be called the "jewel" made that way, so try a colorless vermouth, like Dolin Blanc or Carpano Bianco, and be rewarded with a cocktail as wondrous to behold as it is astonishingly herbaceous to sip.

1½ ounce (45 ml) gin (Plymouth)

¾ ounce (22 ml) green Chartreuse

1 ounce (30 ml) sweet vermouth (Dolin Blanc)

2 dashes orange bitters (Regans')

Stir ingredients with ice and strain into a chilled martini glass.

BAMBOO

Dried cherry, herbaceous, crisp

— • • • • —

This is an exquisite drink for tapas, featuring Spanish sheep's milk cheeses, cured meats, olives, and almonds.

....

Named for Bob Cole's 1902 song, "Bamboo," one of the first songs to chart written by an African American—and a classic that's still music to our ears—the Bamboo calls for dry sherry and blends it with two types of vermouth to add complexity and smoothness. We like to use a quality fino and serve this as a party starter, alongside old records and lots of nibbles.

1½ ounces (45 ml) dry sherry (La Gitana)

¾ ounce (22 ml) white vermouth (Dolin Blanc)

½ ounce (15 ml) dry vermouth (Dolin)

Dash of orange bitters (Regans')

Orange twist, for garnish

Stir ingredients with ice, and strain into a chilled cocktail glass. To garnish, twist the peel over the surface of the drink to express the oil, and then rest the peel on the side of the glass.

ROB ROY

Smoky, woodsy, herbaceous

• - •

Try serving this at a game dinner with pheasant or venison. Thanks to its smoky complexity, it's strangely delicious with Chinese takeout, especially anything with plum sauce, like moo shu pork.

A Manhattan prepared with Scotch whisky, this smoldering cocktail was created by a Waldorf-Astoria bartender and named after the highland outlaw Rob Roy MacGregor, a Robin Hood–like figure among the Scots. As with many early drinks, this one was created to honor an event, the premiere of an operetta loosely based on Roy's life. Victorian opera lovers might have sipped it over their high collars before or after the show. At Chicago's famed bar, Aviary, the cocktail is dramatically served on a charred plank covered with a transparent, smoke-filled pillow, which is then cut open tableside. We have a hard time imagining it without some similar touch of added depth, and achieve it with a dash of tea syrup featuring smoky Lapsang Souchong.

2 ounces (60 ml) blended Scotch (Dewar's or Famous Grouse)

½ ounce (15 ml) sweet vermouth (Carpano Antica or Vya)

¼ ounce (7 ml) Lapsang Souchong syrup (page 243)

Dash of Angostura bitters

Lemon peel, for garnish

Stir ingredients with ice and strain into a chilled coupe glass. To garnish, twist the lemon peel over the surface of the cocktail to express the oil. Then, run the peel around the rim of the glass and drop it into the drink.

SIX MUST-TRY FORGOTTEN
HERITAGE COCKTAILS

Many early American cocktails survive, or even thrive, on bar menus and in homes to this day: the Old Fashioned, the Manhattan, the Rob Roy, the Ramos Gin Fizz. And a few that were obscure, like the Martinez, have reappeared. We'd like to turn your eye toward cocktails that receive less attention but are crucial to understanding the evolution and diversity of mixed drinks in the nineteenth century. The French gastronome Anthelme Brillat-Savarin once said that the "discovery of a new dish confers more happiness on humanity than the discovery of a new star"—we like to think the same can be said about the rediscovery of vintage cocktails!

The drinks listed below are either dazzling to behold, or they combine ingredients in ingenious ways to create novel flavors. Explore these for their sheer delight and pairing potential. Trust us, if you make them once, you'll be hooked.

Coffee Cocktail (page 29)

East India Cocktail (page 44)

Improved Holland Gin Cocktail (page 36)

Bijou (page 51)

Moral Suasion (page 34)

Knickerbocker (page 32)

THE FIRST COCKTAIL PARTY

The first "cocktail party" on record was hosted in the spring of 1917 by Mrs. Julius S. Walsh Jr. of Saint Louis. It was held at high noon and lasted for an hour. Guests sipped Bronx cocktails and Clover Leafs, among other concoctions, served by a white-coated professional drink mixer who presided over a mahogany bar. The event launched the cocktail party as an institution, spawning cocktail dresses and even fashionable cocktail hats.

COCKTAIL TAXONOMY

While the old drink vocabulary of the nineteenth century is now largely arcane cocktail geekery, it nevertheless can be helpful to know your sangaree from your sling, and your flip from your fix. Below are definitions of a few common drink classes.

BUCK: Same as a mule—a combination of liquor, citrus, and ginger beer.

COBBLER: A spirit or fortified wine—or even Champagne—with fruit and sugar over crushed ice. Served with a straw.

COLLINS: A tall iced drink of soda water, lemon or lime juice, sugar, and liquor.

CRUSTA: A cocktail (spirits, sugar, water, bitters) with the addition of lemon juice and a sugared rim—the crust—and lined with a continuous strip of citrus peel in the glass.

DAISY: Oversize sour with a splash of seltzer and syrup often made with either rum or gin, and served over crushed or cracked ice with a straw. At one time, grenadine became the common syrup additive. A daisy made with tequila may have been the origin of the margarita.

FIX: Even drinks writers fret over what exactly makes a fix a fix. Like the daisy (it probably predates the daisy), fixes began life as a sour—liquor, lemon juice, sugar—but began to include syrups such as raspberry or pineapple. A daisy has a splash of soda water, but a fix does not.

FIZZ: Essentially an effervescent sour, a fizz has a base spirit, modifying acidity such as lemon juice, and carbonated water. Similar to a Collins, except the fizz is shaken before the soda water is added and it is served without ice. It can include egg.

FLIP: A drink that involves an egg, along with sugar and a spice of some kind. The name originates from days when hot pokers were used to "flip" a drink, i.e., make it boil and froth. If cream is added, it becomes a nog.

FRAPPÉ: A partially frozen, sometimes fruity drink. Usually a spirit served over crushed ice. From the French word *frapper*, meaning to knock or beat.

HIGHBALL: A tall drink made with a spirit, lemon or lime juice, sugar, and soda. The most common drink nowadays, because it requires only a base spirit and any modifying nonalcoholic mixer. Properly served in a thin cylindrical glass, called a "highball" glass.

JULEP: Originally a julep was a concoction of herbs macerated in sugar. The colonial Virginians enjoyed their medicine with a little booze. Gin and brandy juleps were once popular, although these days a julep is nearly always made with bourbon.

MULE: See Buck.

NOG: A beverage made with beaten eggs, usually with an alcoholic liquor added.

RICKEY: A sugar-less highball cocktail of a base spirit (usually gin) with lime juice and carbonated water, properly served in a highball glass.

SANGAREE: Related to the sangria (derived from the Spanish *sangre*, meaning "blood"); the six sangaree recipes Jerry Thomas recorded involve a base spirit with a little sugar and a dusting of nutmeg. No citrus.

SLING: The first definition of the "cocktail" was "a bittered sling." Slings are a lot like toddies, except they can be cold or hot. They also don't have a spice garnish such as nutmeg. And they're often made with carbonated water or ginger beer Elements: spirit, sugar, water.

SMASH: The smash emerges as distinct from a julep (or is the julep just another smash?) at least as early as the late 1800s. The elements involve a spirit base, sugar, seasonal fruit (in the drink or as garnish) and something herbaceous (often mint, usually muddled).

TODDY: A hot drink of water, sugar, spices, and liquor.

CLOVER CLUB

Acidic, citrus, caramel

Supremely elegant, the Clover Club needs no accoutrements, except for maybe a bowtie and a bowler hat. But if you must nosh: tea sandwiches and sugar cookies.

From the Philadelphia men's club of the same name, this drink appeared in the wood-paneled rooms of the wealthy and powerful before it declined into relative obscurity. Hailing from as early as 1910, the Clover Club has a luxurious mouthfeel and a bracing acidity that makes it an ideal afternoon croquet game accompaniment or poolside sipper. We make this cocktail with dry vermouth, just like the Clover Club bar in New York. Add a spanked mint leaf, and it's called a Clover Leaf.

1½ ounces (45 ml) gin (Plymouth)

½ ounce (15 ml) dry vermouth (Dolin)

½ ounce (15 ml) fresh lemon juice

½ ounce (15 ml) raspberry syrup (see page 242)

¾ ounce (22 ml) egg white

Raspberry, for garnish

Dry shake the ingredients to emulsify the egg. Then, shake with ice and strain into a chilled coupe glass. Garnish with a skewered raspberry resting on the glass.

WIDOW'S KISS

Spice, herbaceous, apple

— • • • • —

**Autumnal and cider-like without any touch
of sweetness, the Widow's Kiss is beautiful and refined. Try it with pâté, or harvest
foods, like butternut squash soup.**

This drink most likely hails from New York's
Holland House, once the most luxurious hotel
in the world. We imagine patrons sipping this
cocktail under its elaborate gold and salmon
ceiling, wondering afterward what hit them—is
the implication that widows are lethal? Apple-y
and minty, this drink may have originally featured
absinthe instead of Benedictine (which became
the stand-in when the green fairy was outlawed
in 1912), and we like it with either—although we
prefer to use a rinse to prevent the drink from
being too sweet. Most recipes also call for yellow
Chartreuse, but we enjoy it equally well with
green, which we more commonly have on hand.
Calvados is an apple brandy from the French
region of Normandy.

2 ounces (60 ml) Calvados

1 ounce (30 ml) yellow or green
  Chartreuse

Benedictine or absinthe, to rinse the glass

Dash of Angostura bitters

Cherry, for garnish

Stir ingredients with ice and strain
into a chilled cocktail glass rinsed with
Benedictine or absinthe.

Note: This drink is also lovely served in a rocks
glass with a single large ice cube. Garnish with
a cherry.

BRONX COCKTAIL

Citrus, orange, juniper

— • • • • —

**Think of this as a refined gin and juice,
fruity but not cloying—a perfect complement to a light lunch, like a cold pasta
salad.**

This fresh and pleasantly acidic cocktail once
rivaled the Martini (page 46) and the Manhattan
(page 41) for popularity. It's a drink with many
progeny, sparking the Satan's Whiskers with
added Grand Marnier or becoming the Income
Tax with the addition of Angostura bitters. It
morphs into a Maurice Cocktail with a dash of
absinthe and is a cousin of the later Monkey
Gland (page 88). It even becomes another
borough-named drink, the Queens Cocktail, if
pineapple is substituted for orange.

2 ounces (60 ml) gin (Plymouth)

½ ounce (15 ml) dry vermouth (Dolin)

½ ounce (15 ml) Italian sweet vermouth
  (Carpano Antica)

1 ounce (30 ml) fresh orange juice

Dash of orange bitters (Regans')

Orange twist, for garnish

Shake ingredients with ice and strain
into a chilled martini glass. To garnish,
twist the peel over the surface of the
cocktail to express the oil. Then, rest
the peel on the side of the glass.

WWI COCKTAILS & THE EUROPEAN INVASION

World War I (1914–1918) and its aftermath brought a wave of internationalism, foreign liquors, and some decidedly French flavor combinations to the glass. Drinks from spots like Harry's Bar in Paris were enjoyed by servicemen and brought home to influence American cocktail creation. Recipes named after artillery (the French 75, page 60) or airplanes (the Aviation, page 65) illustrate how bars were social spaces for conversing about the day's news.

These were the years leading up to Prohibition, and the Anti-Saloon League was loudly trumpeting the evils of alcohol. Despite their caterwauling, "mixed and fancy drinks" continued to flourish, thanks to creative bartenders and thirsty, well-heeled Americans who were willing to dig through their coin purses for 15 to 25 cents for a Martini at the Waldorf.

To encourage lunch-time drinking, bars around the country offered free noon-hour meals, from gumbo in New Orleans to roast beef sandwiches in Chicago, a tradition that sadly disappeared, only to be replaced by late-day snackery—today's "happy hour."

SIDECAR

Citrus, caramel, woodsy

· • • • ·

Dramatic and intense, this is a splendid drink before or with a big meal—we love to serve Sidecars on Easter with maple-glazed ham.

A simplified take on the Brandy Crusta (page 27), this French cocktail from the turn of the century allegedly takes its inspiration from an American army captain who arrived at a Paris bar, chauffeured in a motorcycle's sidecar. The new contraption became hugely popular in America, which may explain why the cocktail gained stateside favor so quickly. This recipe hooked Americans on two glorious French products: high-quality brandy and orange liqueur. While the Sidecar is often served with a sugared rim, we prefer to sugar only half of it.

2 ounces (60 ml) brandy (Pierre Ferrand 1840)

1 ounce (30 ml) Cointreau

¾ ounce (22 ml) fresh lemon juice

Granulated sugar, to rim the glass

Orange peel, for garnish

Prepare a martini glass with a sugared rim (technique, page 264). Shake ingredients with ice and strain into the prepared glass. To garnish, twist the peel over the surface of the cocktail to express the oil. Then, rest the peel on the side of the glass.

FRENCH 75

Citrus, lemon, juniper, brioche

· • • • ·

Let us gush—this cocktail is gorgeous and gloriously fresh. Pair it with crepes, goat cheese, or dainty desserts. It's one of our favorite party drinks.

Named after a French cannon that helped win the war, this knockout was popularized stateside by returning pilots and became a staple of New York's Stork Club, a celebrity hangout run by an ex-bootlegger who knew how to entertain everyone—from starlets like Lucille Ball to mob men like Frank Costello. Elegant and zesty, this is pleasing served straight up in a coupe or served on the rocks in a highball glass with a lemon wheel. We prefer the latter, especially on balmy afternoons. Originally made with Calvados, the gin version we know today didn't evolve until the '20s.

1 ounce (30 ml) gin (Plymouth)

½ ounce (15 ml) fresh lemon juice

½ ounce (15 ml) simple syrup (page 241)

4 ounces (120 ml) Champagne (or crémant)

Lemon peel, for garnish

Shake the gin, lemon juice, and simple syrup together on ice. Strain over ice into a highball glass. Top off with Champagne. To garnish, run the peel around the rim of the glass then drop it into the drink.

CHRYSANTHEMUM

Honey, lemon, herbaceous, mint

• • • •

Herbaceous with a subtle sweetness, this low-proof drink is a poetic aperitif or a brilliant accompaniment to a wide variety of foods—especially anything fried or spicy.

This light yet complex quaffer first appears in Hugo Ensslin's self-published book, *Recipes for Mixed Drinks*, in 1916. While Ensslin's book was a commercial failure, it was enormously influential, containing such recipes as the Aviation (page 65) and the Deshler (page 68). It was, in fact, the last cocktail book by a New York bartender to be published before Prohibition. The Chrysanthemum stands as one of the ultimate low-proof cocktails, with Benedictine providing oomph in conjunction with savory dry vermouth and a faint whisper of absinthe for complexity. The resulting drink is rich while remaining ethereal on the palate.

> 2 ounces (60 ml) dry vermouth (Noilly Prat)
>
> 1 ounce (30 ml) Benedictine
>
> 1 shy teaspoon absinthe
>
> Orange peel, for garnish

Stir ingredients with ice and strain into a chilled coupe glass. To garnish, twist the peel over the surface of the cocktail to express the oil. Then, run the peel around the rim of the glass and drop it into the drink.

STRAITS SLING

Citrus, spice, cherry, juniper

• • • •

Play off the sweet-sour notes and spices here with Chinese food, such as fried rice, or serve it unadorned—it's complex and moody, a sultry sipper.

Cocktail historian Ted Haigh drew us to this drink, which is likely the precursor to the Singapore Sling from the Raffles Hotel in Singapore. We like its cleaner, less syrupy characteristics. Residents originally called Singapore the "straits," and this drink dates back to the years before, or during, World War II. We find the Straits Sling classier than the typical Singapore Sling recipes, which involve grenadine and pineapple, and can be overly sweet. We like to shake and strain this one into a chilled coupe glass—although it can be served on the rocks in a highball with a soda water float. Garnish it with a cocktail umbrella if you have one.

> 2 ounces (60 ml) gin (Plymouth)
>
> ½ ounce (15 ml) Kirschwasser (Clear Creek)
>
> ½ ounce (15 ml) Benedictine
>
> 1 ounce (30 ml) fresh lemon juice
>
> 2 dashes orange bitters (Regans')
>
> 2 dashes Angostura bitters
>
> Quarter of a lemon wheel, for garnish
>
> Cherry, for garnish

Shake ingredients with ice and strain into a chilled coupe glass. Spear the cherry and lemon to garnish.

THE HEMINGWAY BAR

Ernest Hemingway was a notorious cocktail lover, not just an imbiber but also a tastemaker—he liked to put his own twist on classics. He also liked his drinks stiff and without sugar, in line with modern tastes. Part of the popular mystique surrounding "Papa," as he was called, is the struggling American writer in Paris. And there are plenty of cocktails that come from this time period, after World War I and during Prohibition. But there's also the later, twilight Hemingway—think rum daiquiris and mojitos. This is the Caribbean fisherman, when he lived in Key West and Havana, Cuba. Either era supplies the avid cocktailian with exquisite drinks.

To drink like Hemingway, you'll need a liquor cabinet that includes rye whiskey, rum, gin, and absinthe. For a writerly fête, we recommend a range of Hemingway drinks. Leave out your dog-eared copy of *For Whom the Bell Tolls*, and cue up the old Cinemascope version of *The Sun Also Rises*, starring Ava Gardner and Errol Flynn. For more on Hemingway's drink love, check out Philip Greene's *To Have and Have Another: A Hemingway Cocktail Companion*.

Sidecar (page 60)

Jack Rose (page 84)

French 75 (page 60)

Hemingway Daiquiri (page 102)

Death in the Gulf Stream (page 178)

AVIATION

Cherry pit, citrus, violets, juniper

• • • •

Stunningly beautiful and delicate, serve this with cucumber slices topped with herbed goat cheese to impress or to lighten a dark heart. It's a lovely going-away party cocktail.

The bartender's choice for converting vodka drinkers to gin, the Aviation appeared at the beginning of the twentieth century (1916) during America's intense fascination with early aviators Amelia Earhart and Charles Lindbergh. It was rediscovered by cocktail writer Paul Harrington in the late 1990s, and has become wildly famous again throughout the craft cocktail scene. Crème de Violette lends a beautiful sky-blue tinge to this enduring classic that was reimagined with the reappearance of this once popular liqueur on U.S. shores in 2007. We like to serve this with a lemon twist, although some prefer a cherry.

1¾ ounces (52 ml) gin (Plymouth)

¼ ounce (7 ml) maraschino liqueur (Luxardo)

1 to 2 teaspoons Rothman Crème de Violette, to taste

¾ ounce (22 ml) fresh lemon juice

¼ ounce (7 ml) simple syrup (page 241)

Lemon twist, for garnish

Shake ingredients with ice and strain into a chilled coupe glass. To garnish, twist the peel over the surface of the cocktail to express the oil. Then, rest the peel on the side of the glass.

TIPPERARY COCKTAIL

Herbaceous, smoky, bittersweet

• • • •

Powerful and head-clearing, the Tipperary goes down easy on a Friday after work with bar snacks or a hearty bowl of soup.

Think of this as an ideal way to mellow Irish whiskey. Dark and yet bright, it dives toward a Manhattan, then lashes out with a green tail. The original recipe appears in early bar books in different forms, inspired perhaps by the WWI song, "It's a Long Way to Tipperary," which was penned during the same decade. Rather than mixing Chartreuse into the drink, we follow the lead of bartender and writer Gary Regan who gives the glass a Chartreuse wash. A lemon twist or a brandied cherry are common garnishes.

2 ounces (60 ml) Irish whiskey (Bushmills)

1 ounce (30 ml) sweet vermouth (Carpano Antica)

Green Chartreuse, to rinse the glass

Lemon twist, for garnish

Rinse a chilled coupe with Chartreuse. In a mixing glass, stir whiskey and vermouth with ice. Strain into the prepared glass. To garnish, twist the peel over the surface of the cocktail to express the oil. Then, run the peel around the rim of the glass and drop it into the drink.

SEELBACH COCKTAIL

Spice, orange, caramel, woods

⋅ ⋅ ⋅ ⋅

Pair with crudité, nuts, and cheese on Derby Day or around the holidays. It also has a special affinity for pumpernickel bread.

A hoax that a bartender claimed was an original pre-Prohibition cocktail while he was at the Seelbach Hotel in Louisville, this elegant drink is nevertheless right in place as an accurate recreation of ingredients that would have been available to the hotel's bar in 1917. We imagine it sipped by high rollers like Al Capone and F. Scott Fitzgerald (in fact, Daisy married Tom at the Seelbach in *The Great Gatsby*). It combines American whiskey with French elegance to achieve a truly remarkable détente. It is a tall and glamorous sipper served in a champagne flute. Seasoned with two kinds of bitters, it's both uplifting and a little spicy, with hints of star anise and clove.

1 ounce (30 ml) bourbon (Woodford Reserve or the Louisville local favorite, Old Forester)

½ ounce (15 ml) Cointreau

5 dashes of Peychaud's bitters

3 dashes of Angostura bitters

1 to 2 ounces (30 to 60 ml) Champagne (or crémant)

Orange twist, for garnish

Stir the bourbon, Cointreau, and bitters with ice. Strain into a champagne flute. Top off with Champagne, and garnish with an orange twist on the side of the glass.

DUBONNET COCKTAIL

Bitter, aromatic, juniper, dried cherry, lemon

⋅ ⋅ ⋅ ⋅

Pheasant, crown roast, holiday ham—serve this gemlike cocktail with a royal lunch.

While the classic recipe for the Dubonnet, or Zaza Cocktail as it is also called, is equal parts gin and Dubonnet Rouge, the Queen Mother had the right idea with her 2:1 ratio, sporting a lemon wheel under an ice cube. She popularized the drink during WWI by drinking it every day at lunch, and her daughter continued the tradition. This garnet cocktail looks regal and has enough body to conquer a rich lunch while still being refreshing—a versatile daily sipper if there ever was one. Simply smashing.

2 ounces (60 ml) Dubonnet Rouge

1 ounce (30 ml) gin (Beefeater, or the Queen's choice, Gordon's)

Lemon wheel

Drop a lemon wheel into a rocks glass and top it with a single hefty square of ice. Combine Dubonnet and gin in a mixing glass. Stir with ice, then strain into the prepared glass.

THE WONDERS OF DUBONNET

To each nation its particular poison—or in this case, medicine. While the Brits discovered they enjoyed taking their antimalarial quinine with gin (righto, Gin and Tonics!), the French settled on a wine cure (but of course). Dubonnet got its start as a way for the French Foreign Legion to fend off disease in North Africa—and curiously, it became a cause célèbre in England, too, when Her Majesty Queen Elizabeth raised its profile to an upper-class drink. She drank her Dubonnet Cocktail (page 66) every single day, and after you try it you may follow suit. Once you experience its pleasantly bitter, food-friendly charms, we're certain you'll be sipping it often.

Dubonnet is deep burgundy in color, and has a raisin-y aroma with flavors of blackberry, cassis, and quinine. Try it in the Dubonnet Cocktail (page 66), the Napoleon (page 68), the Salomé (page 69), and the Deshler (page 68). The first three of these four drinks combine gin and Dubonnet to great effect, making a royal Dubonnet party a cinch to throw. These are marvelous cocktails to introduce friends to around the holidays. Stock your bar with bottles of Dubonnet, gin, orange curaçao, and dry vermouth—and you can make the first three cocktails on the list. Add whiskey and Peychaud's bitters, and you can make the Deshler, too.

DESHLER

Bitter, aromatic, dried cherry, caramel, bark

· • · • ·

A decadent after-work sipper alongside honey-roasted pecans, or serve with sautéed wild mushrooms or bone marrow.

Named after an American lightweight boxing champion, Dave Deshler, this cousin to the Manhattan needs a high-proof rye like Rittenhouse or Wild Turkey 101 to counter the Dubonnet. Then, since the traditionally-called-for Cointreau renders this drink a bit too sweet, we sub in orange curaçao instead. We couldn't help monkeying with the proportions either, and although tradition calls for both an orange and a lemon twist, we skip the lemon—it's distracting.

> 2 ounces (60 ml) rye whiskey (Rittenhouse)
>
> 1½ ounces (45 ml) Dubonnet Rouge
>
> ¼ ounce (7 ml) orange curaçao (Pierre Ferrand)
>
> 2 dashes Peychaud's bitters
>
> Orange twist, for garnish

Stir ingredients with ice and strain into a chilled coupe glass, or serve it on the rocks. To garnish, twist the peel over the surface of the cocktail to express the oil. Then, run the peel around the rim of the glass and drop it into the drink.

NAPOLEON

Orange, dried cherry, juniper, bitter

· • · • ·

A perfect drink before or after a rich meal. Try it with roast chicken or duck. It pairs well with dishes containing olives or oranges.

This tawny-orange cocktail is quintessentially French, combining a few of our favorite ingredients into luscious notes of apricot-y wonder. The cocktail appears in 1921, thanks to Harry Craddock, one of the most influential mixologists of the 1920s and '30s. When he caught a whiff of Prohibition in the air, he fled the New York bar scene for the Savoy Hotel in London, where he developed a host of canonical cocktails, among them the Napoleon—a brisk but powerful sipper. White-jacketed and witty, Craddock had legions of followers (many expats among them), who elbowed up to the bar to hear him hold forth on the day's news.

> 1½ ounce (45 ml) London Dry gin (Plymouth)
>
> ½ ounce (15 ml) Dubonnet Rouge
>
> ½ ounce (15 ml) orange curaçao (Pierre Ferrand)

Stir with ice and strain into a chilled coupe glass.

SALOMÉ

Herbaceous, bitter, juniper

— • • • —

Play off the herbs in the gin and Dubonnet with a charcuterie board. Pâtés and aged cheeses are first-rate companions.

Also called the Vendôme, after the Vendôme Club in Hollywood—where this drink probably appealed to Tinsel Town royalty like Douglas Fairbanks and Mary Pickford—this cocktail is as seductive as the femme fatale for which it is named. A little dancing, a beheading, you never know what could be in store after a few of these. For a variation called the Appetizer, skip the vermouth. It reinforces the fact that gin and Dubonnet are heaven together.

1 ounce (30 ml) gin (Plymouth)

1 ounce (30 ml) Dubonnet Rouge

1 ounce (30 ml) dry vermouth (Dolin)

Lemon twist, for garnish

Stir with ice and strain into a chilled coupe glass. To garnish, twist the peel over the surface of the cocktail to express the oil. Then, discard the twist.

THE ROARING TWENTIES & PROHIBITION

Prohibition was both a terrible time for alcoholic beverages and a time of renewal. In a classic psychological turn, Prohibition helped spark interest in cocktails by forcing them underground—some say that for every legitimate bar that closed, six speakeasies opened in its place. One big unexpected social impact was that women joined men at the bar. Speakeasies also helped to fuel the Jazz Age, providing spots for musicians to play and the opportunity for social interaction across the economic and racial spectrum.

Popular belief holds that the drinks created during this era are merely a result of the need to cover the harsh flavor of bad booze available from moonshiners; but there was still good liquor being imported by bootleggers, and what comes out of this time period are not just washy hooch-covers, but a number of glamorous cocktails of impeccable subtlety and balance.

It is no coincidence that jazz and the cocktail—two of the greatest American contributions to the world—became codified in this era and endure together in our collective psyche. As *New York Times* writer William Grimes reminds us, "The cocktail shaker was a metronome for a decade in which everything was fast. It matched the speeded-up world of the newsreel and the silent film, the rapid steps of the Charleston, and the frantic arm-waving on the floor of the stock exchange." Huzzah!

COLONY COCKTAIL

Crisp, citrus, cherry pit, juniper

· • • • ·

Where there are vintage evening gowns, there should be Colony Cocktails—and soft shell crab, something for which the Colony Restaurant was famous.

The Colony speakeasy in New York was the hangout of A-list celebrities and society types like the Windsors and the Vanderbilts. Liquor was stored in the building's elevator, which could be quickly dispatched to the basement if the joint was raided. There was even a dry-out hospital with a few beds upstairs to give an added sense of propriety. After Prohibition, the club opened to the public and operated until 1971. Bartender Marco Hattem is thought to have created this signature drink, also called Seventh Heaven, perhaps to appeal to ladies. We adore how the combination of ingredients plays up the nuttiness of the maraschino to bewitching effect.

1½ ounces (45 ml) gin (Plymouth)

2 to 3 teaspoons maraschino liqueur (Luxardo)

¾ ounce (22 ml) fresh grapefruit juice

Grapefruit peel, for garnish

Shake ingredients with ice and strain into chilled coupe glass. To garnish, rest the peel on the edge of the glass.

BLOOD AND SAND

Smoke, cherry, citrus, orange, caramel

· • • • ·

Reminiscent of smoked cherry wood, this drink is a natural companion for ribs or poultry.

Named for the 1922 silent film, *Blood and Sand*, starring Rudolph Valentino, this drink's blood-red color and smoky flavor make it the natural bullfighter's choice. While the ingredients may look off-putting, there's a reason this cocktail is a classic—just be sure to use fresh-squeezed orange juice to achieve proper acidity. The traditional recipe calls for equal parts of all four components, but we like it a bit modernized and double the Scotch. If you can find blood oranges, you can make a Bloody Blood and Sand, which is exceptional. If you love this cocktail, try its cousin, Remember the Maine (page 104).

1½ ounces (45 ml) Scotch (something husky, like Talisker)

¾ ounce (22 ml) cherry heering

¾ ounce (22 ml) sweet vermouth (Carpano Antica)

1 ounce (30 ml) fresh orange juice

Orange peel, for garnish

Shake ingredients with ice and strain into a chilled coupe glass. To garnish, twist the peel over the surface of the cocktail to express the oil. Then, run the peel around the rim of the glass and drop it into the drink.

ADA COLEMAN

During Prohibition, Americans looked to expat bars in foreign cities where imbibers could still thrive and the art of the cocktail endured—spots like London, Paris, and Havana. In London, Ada Coleman presided over the American Bar at the Savoy Hotel. She became rightfully world-famous there, serving an international crew who lapped up her creations and vivacious personality. What's more, Coleman was mentor to Harry Craddock, who worked under her for four years and authored *The Savoy Cocktail Book* (1930), the influential cocktail record of the age.

HANKY PANKY

Herbaceous, mint, juniper, aromatic

⋄ ⋄ ⋄ ⋄ ⋄

Intense and vibrantly colored, this is best nursed amid flickering candles and old jazz records. It's heaven with dark chocolate.

Barman Harry Craddock includes a few of Ada Coleman's drinks in his book, but this is Coley's most famous, created for actor Charles Hawtrey. It is sometimes called the Fernet-Branca Cocktail. Use a juniper-forward gin—such as Tanqueray or Junipero—or the Fernet will overpower it. A drier version ups the gin to two ounces and lowers the vermouth to one ounce. While today we consider "hanky panky" sexual innuendo, Hawtrey and Coley would have understood it to mean "black magic." The orange garnish here is essential to pull all of the flavors together.

> 1½ ounces (45 ml) London Dry gin (Tanqueray or Junipero)
>
> 1½ ounces (45 ml) sweet Italian vermouth (Carpano Antica)
>
> ¼ ounce (7 ml) Fernet-Branca
>
> Orange twist, for garnish

Stir ingredients in a mixing glass with ice, and strain into a cocktail glass. To garnish, twist the peel over the surface of the cocktail to express the oil. Then, drop the peel into the drink.

LEAP YEAR

Plum, dried orange, caramel, citrus

⋄ ⋄ ⋄ ⋄ ⋄

An excellent aperitif with a few almonds and a hunk of sheep's milk cheese such as Petit Basque. Oddly enough, the Leap Year is also a great cocktail alongside eggrolls.

To honor the leap year in 1928, bartender Harry Craddock of London's Savoy Hotel created this special cocktail—an elegant gin drink with a sweet-sour hook. *The Savoy Cocktail Book* (1930) charges this cocktail with a flurry of marriage proposals, as leap-year ladies asked their men to marry them. In a leap year, roles reverse, you know. If you're a martini fan, or an *aspiring* martini fan, this one goes down easy. The addition of Grand Marnier to gin and vermouth adds an aromatic note and a touch of orange flavor. Sublime. Note that the American Bar at the Savoy Hotel in London is still going strong—it's a glorious place to lose one's inhibitions amid art deco decor.

> 2 ounces (60 ml) gin (Plymouth)
>
> ½ ounce (15 ml) sweet vermouth (Vya or Carpano Antica)
>
> ½ ounce (15 ml) Grand Marnier
>
> 1 teaspoon fresh lemon juice
>
> Lemon peel, for garnish

Shake ingredients with ice and strain into chilled coupe glass. To garnish, rest the peel on the side of the glass.

PINK LADY

Citrus, candy apple, juniper

— • • • • —

Try alongside angel food cake and whipped cream or a bag of strawberry licorice twists.

Despite its pink feather boa–like appearance, this cocktail is deceptively nuanced and not the sweet, sticky mess you might imagine it to be. A variant of the Clover Club (page 57) and a sister to the Pink Shimmy (made with ¾ ounces of cream instead of egg white), this version of her ladyship includes an oomph of applejack, which—trust us—will make you light up the dance floor. Frothy and fabulous, this is a superb parlor drink or snappy little nightcap. It's also a marvelous candidate for an edible flower garnish, like candied violets or an orchid.

1½ ounce (45 ml) London Dry gin

1 ounce (30 ml) applejack (Laird's)

¾ ounce (22 ml) fresh lemon juice

¾ ounce (22 ml) egg white

¼ ounce (4 ml) grenadine (page 244)

Cherry or flowers, for garnish

Dry shake ingredients to emulsify, then add ice to the shaker and re-shake. Strain into a chilled coupe glass. Garnish with a cherry in the bottom of the glass or flowers floating on the surface of the drink.

BOBBY BURNS

Herbaceous, smoky, mint, anise

— • • • • —

A stunning umber drink, fine for sipping by a fire after a hearty dinner. Transportive with chocolate chip cookies, fudge, or crème brûlée.

Named after Scottish poet Robert Burns, this cocktail is associated with the speakeasy era, but shows up much earlier. There are two main versions of this drink that have come down through the years, the more common one featuring Benedictine while the other sports absinthe and orange bitters. We actually prefer the recipe by the estimable drinks writer David Embury from *The Fine Art of Mixing Drinks* (1948), in which he replaces Benedictine with Drambuie—the Scotch-based liqueur that is a natural fit here. For a delicious variation called the Preakness Cocktail, substitute bourbon for the Scotch and use Angostura bitters. Serve straight up or on the rocks.

2 ounces (60 ml) Scotch (Famous Grouse or Dewar's)

¾ ounce (22 ml) sweet vermouth (Carpano Antica)

Absinthe or Drambuie, to rinse the glass

Lemon twist, to garnish

Wash a chilled coupe glass with absinthe or Drambuie. Stir Scotch and vermouth with ice and strain into the prepared glass. To garnish, rest a lemon twist on the side of the glass.

ABSINTHE

Absinthe first appeared in Switzerland in the eighteenth century as an anise-flavored spirit containing botanicals, including *Artemisia absinthium*—commonly known as "wormwood." Absinthe can be clear in color, but is often naturally verdant from its herbal ingredients—thus its popular nickname the "green fairy." The spirit gained a raucous reputation through the nineteenth century, with many avant-garde artists, musicians, and writers lauding its supposed hallucinatory properties. It appears in a number of classic, early cocktails.

In 1905, absinthe was banned after a Swiss farmer killed his family, supposedly while under the spirit's spell. During the ensuing backlash, many European countries banned the spirit, with the United States following suit in 1912. As a result, alternatives that did not contain wormwood, such as Herbsaint, were created as a replacement—or bartenders simply switched to Benedictine, another herbal liqueur. Absinthe became legal again in the United States in 2007. Neither wormwood, nor the active ingredient often blamed for absinthe's mythical effects, thujone, cause hallucinations.

We regularly use St. George Absinthe Verte from Alameda, California, or Kübler Absinthe Superieure from Switzerland in our cocktails.

ASTORIA

Crisp, citrus, herbaceous, thyme

· · · ·

The ultimate martini for spicy food, this cocktail should be deployed to a Thai or Indian dinner.

Named for the Astoria Hotel, this drink appears in Albert Crockett's *Old Waldorf-Astoria Bar Book* (1935). William Waldorf Astor built the thirteen-story Waldorf Hotel in 1893 next to his aunt's house—where the Empire State building stands today. He then persuaded his aunt to move, and built the Astor Hotel right next door. An annex connected the two buildings in 1897, and for a time the Waldorf-Astoria was the largest hotel in the world.

The combination of sweet and dry brings balance to this very wet martini, which is why it works so beautifully with spicy dishes.

1 ounce (30 ml) Old Tom gin (Hayman's)

2 ounces (60 ml) dry vermouth (Dolin)

Dash orange bitters (Regans')

Lemon twist, for garnish

Stir ingredients with ice and strain into a chilled martini glass. To garnish, twist the peel over the surface of the cocktail to express the oil. Then, run the peel around the rim of the glass and drop it into the drink.

RATTLESNAKE

Citrus, mint, anise, woodsy, frothy

· · · ·

Herbal notes make for an excellent precursor to a big Italian dinner—a Rattlesnake and spaghetti? Why not?

The Rattlesnake makes its first appearance in *The Savoy Cocktail Book* (1930), and it still rattles its tail in craft cocktail bars, especially around San Francisco. Bartender Harry Craddock wrote that this cocktail "will either cure a rattlesnake bite, or kill rattlesnakes, or make you see them." With a description like that, you'd expect this cocktail to sport fangs, but it is surprisingly smooth, feathery even, thanks to the egg white. Fans of the Whiskey Sour (page 29) should give this a try. Use rye whiskey in place of bourbon, if you want a little more bite (we like to use Old Overholt—a whiskey brand that survived Prohibition).

2 ounces (60 ml) bourbon or rye whiskey (Old Overholt)

½ ounce (15 ml) absinthe

¾ ounce (22 ml) fresh lemon juice

½ ounce (15 ml) simple syrup (page 241)

¾ ounce (22 ml) egg white

2 drops of Angostura bitters, for garnish

Dry shake the ingredients to emulsify the egg, then shake with ice and strain into a chilled coupe glass. Garnish with Angostura "fang marks."

ALGONQUIN

Exotic fruit, herbaceous, caramel, woodsy

· · · ·

Serve with salted peanuts and candied ginger for a summery aperitif.

....

The Algonquin Cocktail, like the hotel in which it was born, is dark, glamorous, and masculine. It's one of several cocktails the bar created to honor itself and the famous figures who lurked there during the 1920s, Dorothy Parker and Harpo Marx among them. Though the "vicious circle" of friends met there regularly during Prohibition over the lunch hour, the Algonquin Hotel was officially a "dry bar," and cocktail expert David Wondrich dashes any notion of these celebrities nursing this particular elixir. They favored the Highball (page 112) and probably did not imbibe at lunch. Dammit, David! We're still fond of drinking this noon-hour cooler on the clock while penning snarky witticisms.

> 1½ ounces (45 ml) rye whiskey (Rittenhouse)
>
> ¾ ounce (22 ml) dry vermouth (Dolin)
>
> ¾ ounce (22 ml) fresh pineapple juice

Shake ingredients with ice and strain into a chilled coupe glass.

CHAMPS-ÉLYSÉES

Crisp, citrus, herbaceous, caramel

· · · ·

This elegant cocktail needs no accompaniment, but if you must eat, pair with escargot.

....

Perhaps the most elegant of all cocktails and named after the most fashionable boulevard in Paris, the Champs-Élysées hilariously appears in *The Savoy Cocktail Book* (1930) as a low-down, get-the-party-started batch recipe. Because why get classy drunk alone? We've scaled it back to a single serving and follow a light, citrus-driven style that renders the drink both invigorating and deliciously boozy without burying the Chartreuse. We also find that with quality brandy we can omit extra sugar from the recipe entirely, as we do here.

> 1½ ounces (45 ml) brandy (Pierre Ferrand Ambre)
>
> ½ ounce (15 ml) green Chartreuse
>
> ½ ounce (15 ml) fresh lemon juice
>
> Dash of Angostura bitters
>
> Lemon twist, for garnish

Shake ingredients with ice and strain into a chilled coupe glass. Garnish with a lemon twist on the rim of the glass.

SCOFFLAW

Citrus, plum, herbaceous, woodsy

—•◦•◦•—

The complex sweetness of this drink can stand up to salty vittles. A sublime palate cleanser when serving cured meats.

....

In 1924, jazz was finally on its way to being regarded as a serious art form. It was also the year Gershwin wrote and performed his iconic American masterpiece, "Rhapsody in Blue." Meanwhile, in Paris, at Harry's Bar, the new hot drink was the Scofflaw. Try slurring the phrase "scoff at the law," and you'll get the pronunciation and the meaning behind this cocktail. During Prohibition, this term was used to describe anyone who drank clandestinely. Use a high-proof rye whiskey for accuracy, put on some '20s jazz, and laugh irreverently as you serve these up behind closed doors.

1½ ounces (45 ml) rye whiskey (Rittenhouse)

1 ounce (30 ml) dry vermouth (Dolin)

¾ ounce (22 ml) fresh lemon juice

¾ ounce (22 ml) grenadine

Lemon twist, for garnish

Shake ingredients with ice and strain into a chilled coupe glass. Garnish with a lemon twist on the edge of the glass.

FIVE SPEAKEASY DRINKS
TO MAKE BEFORE YOU DIE

When drinking went underground, women joined men at the table, and high society often met low in the same drinking establishment. Such varied culture gave rise to a new and dazzling breed of cocktails, often influenced by bartenders abroad who had access to fine spirits. Bartenders developed drinks that were stylish and beautiful in color.

From the world of the speakeasies came enduring cocktails that continue to "speak." We've plucked five that represent the complexity and glamour of the era. Dim the lights, cover your windows, and put on some Prohibition-era jazz. Then invite your friends over to dance the Charleston.

Colony Cocktail (page 71)

Hanky Panky (page 73)

Champs-Élysées (page 77)

Pegu Club (page 87)

Last Word (page 85)

MARY PICKFORD

Exotic citrus, fruity, cherry pit, vanilla, spice

· · · · ·

This makes a first-class Oscar party drink. The touch of sweetness, fruit, and acidity means it plays well with ham or spicier fare like samosas. A knockout with cheesecake.

Named for the famous silent movie actress who was known as the "girl with the curls," this cocktail is attributed to Eddie Woelke, a bartender who fled to Cuba during Prohibition and is often cited as the creator of the El Presidente (page 83). Legend has it that Pickford was shooting a movie in Cuba when this drink was created. Pink, rummy, and tart, it's a little bit tiki but without the crazy garnish.

2 ounces (60 ml) light rum (Flor de Caña 4 Yr)

1 ounce (30 ml) fresh pineapple juice

¼ ounce maraschino liqueur (Luxardo)

¼ ounce grenadine (page 244)

Cherry, for garnish

Shake ingredients with ice and strain into a chilled coupe glass. Garnish with a cherry.

PENDENNIS CLUB

Exotic fruit, citrus, apricot, perfume

· · · · ·

A classy lunchtime sipper, serve it with a chopped salad, turkey club, or even sushi. Break out your pearls and seersucker.

Named after the famous Kentucky social club, this complex drink is thought to have been created by the first published African American bartender, Tom Bullock, author of *The Ideal Bartender* (1917)—although the recipe does not appear in its pages. This cocktail offers a glorious flavor somewhere between grapefruit and guava.

2 ounces (60 ml) Old Tom gin (Hayman's)

1 ounce (30 ml) apricot brandy (Rothman & Winter)

¾ ounce (22 ml) fresh lime juice

3 dashes of Peychaud's bitters

Lime wheel, for garnish

Shake ingredients with ice and strain into a chilled martini glass. Garnish with a lime wheel on the edge of the glass.

APRICOT BRANDY

Apricot brandy was a popular ingredient during Hollywood's Golden Age. One theory for its frequent appearance points to Prohibition moonshiners, who used apricot pits to make spirits. Don't use the sweet, fake-flavored brandy on the bottom shelf; opt for either dry eau-de-vie, like that made by Blume Marillen, or quality liqueurs, such as those made by Rothman & Winter or Marie Brizard. Other apricot brandy cocktails that aficionados may be interested in include the Darb (a martini variation), the Baltimore Bang (a kind of Whiskey Sour), an apricot Manhattan called the Slope, the Zani speakeasy's Zani Zaza, and a gin and dry vermouth–based cocktail called the Claridge.

DOUGLAS FAIRBANKS

Frothy, citrus, ripe apricot, juniper

A luxurious drink, lovely as an aperitif with toasted almonds, or with dessert—try serving it alongside slivers of coconut cake or macaroons.

Named after the star of such silent movies as *Robin Hood* and *The Mark of Zorro*, this swashbuckling silver-screen sipper is velvety and pearlescent, the sort of drink you'd hope for at a winter formal dance. Although this cocktail has virtually disappeared from bar menus (probably because apricot brandy slipped out of favor), it's worth resuscitating. Fairbanks, who was married to actress Mary Pickford, supposedly asked a Cuban bartender to name a drink in his honor. If you host a party for movie buffs, try serving a Douglas Fairbanks and a Mary Pickford (page 80). They pair well with a casual brunch or an elegant party.

1½ ounces (45 ml) gin (Plymouth)

1 ounce (30 ml) apricot brandy (Rothman & Winter)

½ ounce (15 ml) fresh lime juice

¾ ounce (22 ml) egg white

Dry shake ingredients to emulsify the egg white. Then, shake with ice and strain into a chilled coupe glass.

HOTEL NACIONAL

Exotic fruit, citrus, vanilla

• • • •

A sexy beach drink. Conjure a private cove and a starlit table with a feast of grilled fish and jumbo prawns.

A famous celebrity hangout, the Hotel Nacional bar in Havana once served cocktails to the likes of Marlon Brando, Ava Gardner, and, of course, Ernest Hemingway. This recipe, by resident bartender Wil P. Taylor, first appears in print calling for light rum, but Charles H. Baker rightfully makes a switch to gold in his book *The Gentleman's Companion* (1939), complaining that light is too delicate. We split the difference.

> ¾ ounce (22 ml) light rum (Flor de Caña 4 Yr)
>
> ¾ ounce (22 ml) gold rum (Appleton Special)
>
> ¼ ounce (4 ml) apricot liqueur (Rothman & Winter)
>
> ¾ ounce (22 ml) fresh pineapple juice
>
> ½ ounce (15 ml) fresh lime juice
>
> Lime wheel, thinly sliced, for garnish

Shake ingredients with ice and strain into a chilled coupe glass. Float a lime wheel on the surface of the drink.

EL PRESIDENTE

Citrus, herbaceous, vanilla

• • • •

Festive and light, this pale-pink drink deserves elegant finger food, like small crab cakes, lettuce wraps, or pork belly sandwiches.

One of the more popular drinks during Prohibition, this cocktail was named for Cuban president Mario García Menocal. Americans needing respite from a dry country traveled to Cuba and returned with a taste for rum, vermouth, and curaçao. At the suggestion of spirits blogger Matt Robold (RumDood.com), we roll or throw this cocktail (see technique on page 261), which helps blend the flavors without thrashing the drink in a shaker.

> 1½ ounce (45 ml) white rum (Flor de Caña 4 Yr)
>
> ¾ ounce (22 ml) dry vermouth (Dolin)
>
> ¼ ounce (7 ml) orange curaçao (Pierre Ferrand)
>
> ½ teaspoon grenadine (page 244)
>
> Dash of orange bitters (Regans')
>
> Lime wedge, for garnish

In a shaker, roll ingredients back and forth with ice a few times to gently mix. Strain into a chilled cocktail glass. Garnish with a lime wedge on the edge of the glass.

ROSE COCKTAIL

Floral, cherry, raspberry, thyme

· · · · ·

Ethereal! Pair with petit fours or a light salad dotted with edible flowers.

Paris in the 1920s—think Coco Chanel, Josephine Baker, and the Rose Cocktail. Clean, cool, with just a touch of the floral, this clear blush drink is understated and chic. Is it a cocktail, or is it lingerie? Serve it to a starlet who has just stepped out of her bath. Serve it as an offering to a new flame. They'll think you have siphoned the dew off rose petals. If you have a rose petal handy, float it on top.

- 2 ounces (60 ml) dry vermouth (Dolin)
- 1 ounce (30 ml) Kirschwasser (Cedar Creek)
- 1 teaspoon raspberry syrup (page 242)
- Rose petal, for garnish

Shake ingredients over ice and strain into a chilled coupe glass. Garnish with a rose petal on the surface of the drink.

JACK ROSE

Exotic fruit, citrus, apple

· · · · ·

Play off the apple notes with cider-glazed pork chops and roasted root vegetables.

This popular drink of the 1920s and '30s may be named after a New York gangster or a French garden rose; like so many speakeasy drinks, it is layered with more stories than ingredients. Very likely, it gained its name from its rosy color and its base spirit, applejack. It's also famous for being the cocktail that appeared in Hemingway's 1926 novel, *The Sun Also Rises*. Dig out your dog-eared copy and flip to Chapter Six, where you'll find American journalist Jake Barnes ordering up this drink at the Hotel Crillon in Paris as he waits to rendezvous with Lady Brett Ashley. She stands him up, which makes this a very good drink for nursing bruised egos and heartache.

Note: This drink can be made with lime juice, but we prefer lemon.

- 2 ounces (60 ml) Laird's Applejack
- 1 ounce (30 ml) fresh lemon juice
- 2 teaspoons grenadine (page 244)
- Lemon peel, for garnish

Shake ingredients with ice and strain into a chilled coupe glass. To garnish, twist the peel over the surface of the cocktail to express the oil. Then, run the peel around the rim of the glass and drop it into the drink.

BEE'S KNEES

Honey, lemon, citrus, herbaceous

• • • •

Sweet and tart, a perfect drink for the porch. Pair with cucumber-and-mint sandwiches, fried chicken, or steamed asparagus.

This garden party cooler is commonly believed to have appeared during Prohibition, but it may, in fact, be far older. What could be a more natural combination than honey, gin, and lemon? For a modern twist, use honey-based Barr Hill Gin from Vermont and dial back the honey syrup. "Earthy" Plymouth gin works well, too. The key to achieving balance here depends on the intensity and flavor notes of your ingredients, so pick a honey and a gin that can two-step. To read more about gin flavors, see page 272. Variations: For a Honeysuckle, swap rum for gin. Or, top with weiss beer and make a Beers Knees. Add Champagne and you're on your way to a honeyed French 75.

2 ounces (60 ml) Old Tom gin (Hayman's)

³⁄₄ ounce (22 ml) honey syrup (see page 242)

³⁄₄ ounce (22 ml) fresh lemon juice

Lavender sprig, for garnish

Shake ingredients with ice and strain into a chilled coupe glass. Garnish with a sprig of lavender on top of the glass.

LAST WORD

Bracing, citrus, herbaceous, tart

• • • •

A vibrant drink, pale green in color—a seductive quaffer for drinking in the garden after a heavy meal.

The Last Word made its debut in the 1920s at the Detroit Athletic Club, a private association for early automotive executives and industrial leaders, but was reborn by bartender Murray Stenson at Seattle's Zig Zag Café in the mid-2000s. Now it appears on drink lists on both coasts and around Europe. Citrusy and herbaceous, this pale-green potion has been called the signature drink of the Seattle craft cocktail scene. Like the Aviation (page 65) and the Corpse Reviver No. 2 (page 149), it exists in a special class of rediscovered drink recipes that have turned into contemporary cult classics.

1 ounce (30 ml) gin (Tanqueray or St. George Terroir)

³⁄₄ ounce (22 ml) green Chartreuse

¹⁄₂ ounce (15 ml) maraschino liqueur (Luxardo)

³⁄₄ ounce (22 ml) fresh lime juice

¹⁄₄ ounce (7 ml) simple syrup (page 241)

Lime twist, for garnish

Shake ingredients with ice and strain into a chilled coupe. To garnish, rest the lime twist on the edge of the glass.

PEGU CLUB

Citrus, grapefruit, juniper

— • • • • —

Try with an avocado-watercress salad, minty tabbouleh, or a handful of pistachios.

The signature drink of the Pegu Club, an expat hangout in Burma (now Myanmar), this recipe first appears in 1927. Wonderfully grapefruity with a long, sweet finish, this easy sipper spells relaxation and refreshment. Imagine British diplomats in Victorian attire, nursing a few of these in the club's grand courtyard. Lovers of this drink are passionate about it, including legendary bartender Audrey Saunders, who named her Manhattan bar after it. For an interesting variation, see the Pendennis Club (page 80).

2 ounces (60 ml) gin (Plymouth)

1 ounce (30 ml) orange curaçao (Pierre Ferrand)

¾ ounce (22 ml) fresh lime juice

1 to 2 dashes Angostura bitters

Lime wedge, to garnish

Shake ingredients with ice and strain into a chilled coupe glass. To garnish, slice lime along the rind halfway through the wedge, separating the skin from the fruit. Hang it on the rim of the glass.

STORK CLUB COCKTAIL

Citrus, orange, herbaceous

— • • • • —

Thanks to flavors of orange and thyme, the foods of Provence are a natural pairing for this drink—from braised endives to grilled sardines.

New York's Stork Club was one of the most splendid clubs of the age, a place where the Kennedys and Vanderbilts dined, and celebrities frequented the dance floor. Table Fifty, right near the door, was a favorite spot for Marilyn Monroe and Joe DiMaggio. The club's signature drink is credited to head bartender Eddie Whittmer. The original recipe is published in Lucius Beebe's *The Stork Club Bar Book* (1946). This is a slightly boozier version that isn't too sweet.

2 ounces (60 ml) Old Tom gin (Hayman's)

¼ ounce (7 ml) Cointreau

½ ounce (15 ml) orange juice

¼ ounce (7 ml) fresh lime juice

Dash of Angostura bitters

Orange twist, for garnish

Shake ingredients with ice and strain into a chilled coupe. To garnish, rest an orange twist on the rim of the glass.

MONKEY GLAND

Tart, orange, mint

- • - • -

Complex and bright, pair this fresh-tasting gin cocktail with chilled melon soup or a salad topped with goat cheese.

A drink inspired by early experiments in "male enhancement"? Harry McElhone, proprietor of the famed Harry's Bar in Paris, turned this cocktail into a Prohibition-era phenom. The name, like so many cocktails of this time, riffs off front page news, in this case the story of a French surgeon who performed a monkey-to-millionaire gonad transplant. The cocktail made such a splash that the *Washington Post* ran the recipe as a special cable dispatch. Published versions often call for Pastis or Benedictine, but the original calls for absinthe; we like to bow to the eunuch monkeys and do the same.

- 2 ounces (60 ml) gin (Beefeater)
- 1 ounce (30 ml) fresh orange juice
- 1 teaspoon grenadine (page 244)
- Absinthe, to rinse the glass
- Orange twist, for garnish

Rinse a chilled coupe glass with absinthe. Shake remaining ingredients with ice and strain into the prepared glass. Garnish with an orange twist resting on the rim.

BOULEVARDIER ············

Bitter, aromatic, woodsy

- • - • -

Candied nuts and a serious cigar round out this mahogany sipper. A regal drink, dazzling before or after dinner.

This was the drink of Alfred Vanderbilt's nephew, Erskine Gwynne, who was the editor of the Parisian magazine, *The Boulevardier*. It's an update of a drink called the Old Pal, replacing that cocktail's rye whiskey and dry vermouth with bourbon and sweet vermouth. For a modern palate, we like to up the whiskey ratio a bit to let the bourbon shine. Dark and smooth, this is a stunning drink with well-balanced notes of grapefruit, wood, and caramelized sugar.

- 2 ounces (60 ml) bourbon (Buffalo Trace or Four Roses)
- 1 ounce (30 ml) Campari
- 1 ounce (30 ml) sweet vermouth (Carpano Antica)
- Orange twist, for garnish

Stir ingredients with ice and strain into a chilled coupe glass. Garnish with an orange twist.

CAMPARI AND APEROL

Campari and Aperol are boldly colored Italian bitter liqueurs made from infusions of fruit and herbs. But the two are not exactly interchangeable.

Campari, which is bright red, dates back to 1860, when it was originally made with a natural dye from insects. It 1922, it debuted in Harry McElhone's *ABC's of Mixing Cocktails* as a component of the Old Pal, where it is mixed with rye whiskey and dry vermouth. Then it appears again in McElhone's book, *Barflies and Cocktails* (1927), in the Boulevardier (page 88). The most famous Campari drink, the Negroni (page 91), doesn't appear until twenty years later, when it is mentioned by Orson Welles in his correspondence.

It has been said that Campari is the cilantro of the booze world; either people love its bitter charms or hate it. Note that the bitterness can be tamed with the addition of 2 to 4 drops of saline solution in a 1:10 salt to water ratio.

Aperol, which is bright orange, is often called Campari's younger brother, and is flavored with bitter orange and rhubarb. Aperol has more sugar than Campari, half the amount of alcohol, and is smoother and noticeably less bitter. It shines beautifully in the Intro to Aperol (page 165).

NEGRONI

Bitter, grapefruit, herbaceous

• •

Salty snacks, like prosciutto, anchovies, blue cheese, and pecorino, pair well with this big crimson drink.

Once upon a time, the Negroni was built from equal parts gin, Campari, and sweet vermouth. Today, many bartenders back off the vermouth and Campari to let the gin flavor come through a bit. Then, some add a flaming peel. Others top the Negroni with club soda. Some don't use Campari at all, but use Luxardo Aperitivo or some other bitter liqueur. Our favorite version combines modern proportion and some vermouth advice from writer and chef Gabrielle Hamilton of the tiny East Village restaurant, Prune. There the bar serves legions of Negroni lovers who flock to the breezy banquettes on summer evenings to sip this Italian-inspired cocktail over the restaurant's signature bar snack, sardines and Triscuits. Hamilton likes to change up the vermouth, depending on her mood (see vermouth sidebar, page 38), preferring mellow Carpano Antica in winter for its vanilla notes, and Noilly Prat in summer. We also recommend Cocchi Vermouth di Torino and Bluecoat gin together, if you can get your hands on them.

1½ ounces (45 ml) gin (Plymouth or Bluecoat)

1 ounce (30 ml) sweet vermouth (Cocchi Vermouth di Torino or Carpano Antica)

¾ ounce (22 ml) Campari or Luxardo Aperitivo

½ wheel of orange (preferably blood orange), for garnish

Stir ingredients with ice. (Because the Campari will sink to the bottom, make sure to lift the spoon often to integrate the spirits.) Strain into a chilled coupe or rocks glass over ice. Garnish with a wheel of orange on the side of the glass.

BARREL-AGING COCKTAILS

Aging cocktails in a barrel (or in a jar with a barrel stave) mellows and harmonizes flavors to glorious effect. Disparate elements meld into silky unity. After two or three weeks, the wood imparts flavors of light vanilla and caramel.

Explore this process with any spirits-only recipe—please don't try aging fruit juices or eggs. The Manhattan (page 41) and the Negroni (page 91) are ideal choices. Aging transforms them into cocktails of great subtlety and finesse.

Tuthilltown Spirits (tuthilltown.com) is a good resource for small barrels, and for jars with barrel staves. If you don't want to commit to a full barrel, their 375-ml jars will hold four of our Negronis and five Manhattans. Simply stir up the drinks without ice and use a funnel to fill the jars.

We like to begin aging cocktails in October for unveiling around the holidays.

LUCIEN GAUDIN

Herbs, bitter, orange

- • • • -

Play off the orange notes with Moroccan chicken, or try this velvety sipper with duck liver mousse.

A Prohibition drink rediscovered by cocktail writer Ted Haigh, the Lucien Gaudin was named after a gold medal French Olympic fencer who competed in 1924 and 1928. The drink features dry vermouth as well as Cointreau for a long, delectable orange finish. It has a rich but relatively dry character. As a before-dinner aperitif, it won't crush the palate the way a Negroni might.

1 ounce (30 ml) gin (Plymouth)

½ ounce (15 ml) Campari

½ ounce (15 ml) Cointreau

½ ounce (15 ml) dry vermouth (Dolin)

Orange peel, for garnish

Stir ingredients with ice and strain into a chilled coupe. To garnish, twist the peel over the surface of the cocktail to express the oil. Then drop it into the drink.

THE JOURNALIST

Crisp, aromatic, citrus, plum

- • • • -

The magnificent glow of this amber drink should be enjoyed after work with a dish of smoked almonds and a newspaper.

It seems apt that from the hard-drinking world of the newspaper room comes a perfect martini with a little snazz. The gorgeous golden color brings to mind mahogany bars and the halls of power—two of the journalist's favorite haunts. Cool and cutting edge for its era, this is the sort of cocktail that warrants its many ingredients. The Carpano pops; the flavors are well balanced. Some people shake this drink, but we prefer to stir since it's all booze with just a swish of lemon. Long live the press corps!

2 ounces (60 ml) gin (Plymouth)

1 ounce (30 ml) dry vermouth (Dolin)

1 ounce (30 ml) sweet Italian vermouth (Carpano Antica)

1 scant teaspoon orange curaçao (Pierre Ferrand)

1 scant teaspoon lemon juice

Dash of Angostura bitters

Lemon peel, for garnish

Stir ingredients with ice and strain into a chilled martini glass. To garnish, twist the peel over the surface of the cocktail to express the oil. Then rest it on the edge of the glass.

BETWEEN THE SHEETS

Citrus, dried fruit, vanilla

- • - • -

As smooth as silk sheets, this tippler belongs with dessert—or chocolate truffles.

A rum version of a Sidecar (page 60), this cocktail melds brandy and the tropics together for a soft feel that most likely hails from Harry McElhone at Harry's New York Bar in Paris. The bar, which was shipped to Paris from New York, is also the counter where the Monkey Gland (page 88) and the French 75 (page 60) were created. Frequented by artists and musicians, this landmark was home to the piano that George Gershwin used to compose *An American in Paris*. Put on a record, and sip this beauty in bed.

> 1 ounce (30 ml) brandy (Pierre Ferrand Ambre)
>
> 1 ounce (30 ml) light rum (Flor de Caña 4 Yr)
>
> 1 ounce (30 ml) Cointreau
>
> ½ ounce (15 ml) fresh lemon juice
>
> Lemon twist, for garnish

Shake with ice and strain into a chilled coupe glass. Garnish with a twist of lemon on the edge of the glass.

WHITE LADY

Citrus, orange, juniper

- • - • -

With the added egg white, there's enough body to stand up to dishes like lamb with rosemary, but it can also be lovely with fish or Thai food.

A ghostly drink, the first White Lady emerged in 1919 from the mind of master concocter Harry McElhone when he worked at Ciro's Club in London. His original recipe called for crème de menthe (ghastly!), but he came to his senses later and converted this into a Gin Sidecar. It became one of the most beloved elixirs at the Savoy Hotel. Frothy and bright, the drink is like sipping a lemon glacier.

Note: This is sometimes called a Delilah or a Chelsea Sidecar. It's also common practice to add an egg white. We find the recipe superb either way.

> 1½ ounces (45 ml) London Dry gin (Beefeater or Tanqueray)
>
> 1 ounce (30 ml) Cointreau
>
> 1 ounce (30 ml) fresh lemon juice
>
> ¾ ounce (22 ml) egg white
>
> Lemon peel, for garnish

Shake with ice and strain into a chilled martini glass. If you use the egg white, dry shake first to emulsify the ingredients. Garnish with a lemon peel on the edge of the glass.

PLANTER'S PUNCH

Exotic fruit, citrus, vanilla, spice

• •

Serve at a barbecue with grilled meats, or try it with spicy foods like jerk pork or Mexican food.

Early recipes for this lush rum potion were based on this handy rhyme: 1 sour, 2 sweet, 3 strong, 4 weak. Hundreds of versions have appeared over the years, the first being in London's *Fun* magazine (1878), which dubbed this a "West Indian drink!" followed by recipes in the *Kansas City Star* (1903) and the *New York Times* (1908). It got around. In fact, this is the one cocktail that seems to have appeared on every speakeasy's drink list. Later, Don the Beachcomber used it as inspiration for the entire tiki genre (see page 183). Delectable, like a grown-up Orange Julius.

1 ounce (30 ml) dark rum (El Dorado 5 Yr)

1 ounce (30 ml) white rum (Flor de Caña)

½ ounce (15 ml) orange curaçao (Pierre Ferrand)

2 ounces (60 ml) fresh orange juice

2 ounces (60 ml) fresh pineapple juice

¼ ounce (7 ml) fresh lime juice

½ teaspoon grenadine (page 244)

Dash of Angostura bitters

2 ounces (60 ml) soda water

Orange slice, for garnish

Cherry, for garnish

Shake ingredients, minus the soda water, with ice and strain into an ice-filled highball glass. Top with soda. Garnish with an orange slice and a cherry threaded onto a toothpick.

CHICAGO COCKTAIL

Dried fruit, orange, brioche

• • • •

Best sipped with a cigar, but decadent holiday foods are also natural partners.

Appearing in numerous cocktail books going back to the nineteenth century, this masculine drink is all flavor and pizzazz from the City of Big Shoulders. Recipes vary, but they always call for a sugared rim and a splash of bubbly. In its time, this drink—one of the greats of its age—was served as far away as London and Nice.

2 ounces (60 ml) brandy (Pierre Ferrand Ambre)

½ teaspoon Cointreau

1½ ounce (45 ml) Champagne (or crémant)

Dash of Angostura bitters

Granulated sugar, to rim the glass

Rim a coupe glass with sugar (technique, page 264). Stir brandy, Cointreau, and bitters with ice in a mixing glass, and strain into the prepared glass. Top with bubbly.

TWELVE MILES OUT

Spirituous, citrus, tangy

• • • •

A complex cocktail, perfect for kebabs or steak. Drink it to forget a speeding ticket or other infraction.

During early Prohibition, three miles was the limit between the United States and international waters. It wasn't long before enterprising floating bars and casinos lined up to offer their services offshore. The government tried to crack down on this activity, and later extended the limit to twelve miles. A drink was born at each marker, with the Three Miles Out sporting white rum, brandy, lemon juice, and grenadine. But we prefer this take, called the Twelve Miles Out, rediscovered by cocktailian Ted Haigh. Take this to the thirteenth mile with a sugared rim!

1 ounce (30 ml) white rum (Flor de Caña 4 Yr)

½ ounce (15 ml) rye whiskey (Sazerac)

½ ounce (15 ml) brandy (Pierre Ferrand Ambre)

½ ounce (15 ml) grenadine

½ ounce (15 ml) fresh lemon juice

Lemon twist, for garnish

Shake ingredients with ice and strain into a chilled cocktail glass. Garnish with the lemon twist on the edge of the glass.

ARRACK

Arrack is a spirit found across South Asia and Southeast Asia, made variously with coconut sap, sugar cane, rice, or fruit. In the 1700s, it achieved widespread popularity on ships, where a combination of arrack and spices would not spoil on long voyages, as beer did. Arrack is the key spirit in early punches, and many of Jerry Thomas's punch recipes in *The Bon Vivant's Companion* call for it. Batavia (the former name for Jakarta) Arrack forms the basis of Swedish Punsch—a combination of Indonesian "rum" with sugar and spices that became a traditional drink in Sweden from the days of the Swedish East India Company. It became a popular liquor for classic cocktails, but both Batavia Arrack and Swedish Punsch disappeared from American shores following the double-whammy of Prohibition and WWII. Batavia Arrack reappeared in the market in 2007 and Swedish Punsch in 2012.

DIKI-DIKI

Caramel, apple, grapefruit, spice, vanilla

Richly spiced, this drink is amazing with baked acorn squash, lamb or pork chops, and apple pie.

Introduced by bartender Robert Vermeire at the Embassy Club in London in 1922, the Diki-Diki is purportedly named (tongue-in-cheek) after the chief of an island in the Philippines. Beguiling and sophisticated flavors meld into a beautiful orange hue and result in a wonderful aroma. We like to float a very thin cross-section of apple on top, revealing its star-like core.

2 ounces (60 ml) Calvados

1 ounce (30 ml) Kronan Swedish Punsch

1 ounce (30 ml) fresh grapefruit juice

Apple slice, for garnish

Shake ingredients with ice and strain into a chilled cocktail glass. Garnish with apple slice.

HAVANA COCKTAIL

Burnt sugar, citrus, pineapple

• • • •

So good with barbecue, we like to glaze grillables with it.

Crisp and flavored with caramelized pineapple, this clear amber drink is punchy and burnt-sugar sweet. We love the Havana with a dram (four drops) of Bittercube Jamaican No. 2 bitters. *The Savoy Cocktail Book*'s (1930) version is too sweet, so we follow the adaptation that appears in Jeff Masson and Greg Boehm's *The Big Bartender's Book*.

1 ounce (30 ml) Old Tom gin (Hayman's)

1 ounce (30 ml) Kronan Swedish Punsch

½ ounce (15 ml) apricot brandy (Rothman & Winter)

¼ ounce (7 ml) fresh lemon juice

Shake ingredients with ice and strain into a chilled coupe glass.

DOCTOR COCKTAIL

Caramel, clove, lime

• • • •

Smoked meats, lamb burgers, or squash lasagna all pair well with this aromatic drink.

The Doctor may be the ultimate fireside sipper, especially near an outdoor bonfire. The original recipe appeared in a very simplified form back in 1919 as a two-ingredient drink containing Swedish Punsch (see note on page 98) and lime juice, and underwent several iterations by the end of Prohibition. If you've never explored Swedish Punsch, consider this your conversion experience. Rum drinkers, this is a deep Dark 'n' Stormy (page 194), punched up with lime and dialed down with bitters so that it's far from cloying. Layered and luscious.

1½ ounces (45 ml) Kronan Swedish Punsch

¾ ounce (22 ml) dark Jamaican rum (Appleton Estate V/X)

¾ ounce (22 ml) fresh lime juice

3 dashes Angostura bitters

Lime wheel, for garnish

Shake ingredients with ice and strain into a rocks glass with a large ice cube. Garnish with a lime wheel on the edge of the glass.

POST-PROHIBITION '30S:
SWEET & EXOTIC

Following Prohibition, a flood of books hit the market attempting to capitalize on the renewed interest in cocktails, which were now legal. The decade started off with Harry Craddock's *Savoy Cocktail Book* (1930), the most cited and influential tome of the era, which also saw the publication of Albert Crockett's *The Old Waldorf-Astoria Bar Book* (1935). Another must-read from the time period is *The Gentleman's Companion, or, Jigger, Beaker, Flask* (1939) by Charles H. Baker. In it, he recounts anecdotes from his globetrotting escapades with drink.

The '30s trended sweet in flavor—during Prohibition, Americans sought their fix at soda fountains and became addicted to sugary drinks. Tiki first appears in 1934 (which we've separated out for convenience, see page 183). Here, you'll also find the Cuba Libre (page 109), in which America's obsession with soda and cocktails converged. Many former speakeasies continued operation to become some of the most famous clubs through the '40s, '50s, and '60s.

GIBSON

Briny, herbaceous, thyme, juniper

· • · • ·

Pair with anchovies and every briny damn thing, from fresh clams to plump green olives. The gibson is even friendly with a vinegary beet salad and deviled eggs.

While the Gibson may have appeared as early as the 1890s at San Francisco's Bohemian Club, it doesn't show up in print with its signature cocktail onion until the 1920s. There's an onion in both the Onion Cocktail and the L.P.W. Cocktail in Tom Bullock's book, *The Ideal Bartender*, published in 1917—but curiously still not in the Gibson. The gibson was drier than other martinis at the time of its emergence, and went on to become associated with mid-twentieth-century drink culture in books by the likes of Raymond Chandler and John Cheever. Along with the buckeye (which sports a black olive), it takes the martini in a savory direction. Recipes typically call for London Dry gin, but we like to use St. George Terroir (lots of fir, sage, and other botanicals), which mixes with Dolin dry vermouth to elegant effect. Following Hemingway, we use a frozen onion to keep the drink extra cold.

1½ ounces (45 ml) London Dry gin (St. George Terroir)

1 ounce (30 ml) dry vermouth (Dolin)

Frozen cocktail onion, for garnish

Stir gin and vermouth with ice and strain into a chilled martini glass. Garnish with a cocktail onion.

HEMINGWAY DAIQUIRI

Citrus, cherry pit, sour

· • · • ·

An unexpectedly complex little quaffer. Pair with a Cuban sandwich and a page-turner.

Picture Papa Hemingway in his loose white shirt, slugging back this cocktail in a goblet full of shaved ice and you have a snapshot of his life in the '30s at El Floridita, his favorite Cuban bar. Although published versions of this popular recipe added sugar syrup, Hemingway preferred it without. He sometimes drank six to twelve of these in an afternoon, and any extra sweetness would have turned him into a hungover hummingbird the next day. At El Floridita, this drink became known as El Papa Doble, the "double Papa." Hemingway said these cocktails "had no taste of alcohol and felt, as you drank them, the way downhill glacier skiing feels running through powder snow. . . ."

2 ounces (60 ml) white rum (Flor de Caña 4 Yr)

½ ounce (15 ml) maraschino liqueur (Luxardo)

1 ounce (30 ml) fresh lime juice

½ ounce (15 ml) fresh grapefruit juice

Half grapefruit wheel, for garnish

Shake ingredients with ice and strain into a chilled coupe glass. Garnish with a grapefruit wheel on the edge of the glass.

Note: For a blended drink, add ingredients to a blender with ice and whirl until frothy.

HI HO COCKTAIL

Herbaceous, orange, complex

— • • • • —

Try the Hi Ho with a summer lunch of gazpacho and a plate of Brie sandwiches. It would also pair well with a leafy salad, topped with grilled chicken and orange slices.

Named for Hollywood's Hi Ho Club, a celebrity hangout in the 1930s, this is essentially a martini made with white port and a splash of orange bitters. The result is crisp and complex, a glamorous drink with a golden sheen. Be sure to use white port (not red), which is summery with honeyed notes.

2 ounces (60 ml) Old Tom gin (Hayman's)

1½ ounces (45 ml) white port (Niepoort)

4 dashes orange bitters (Regans')

Lemon twist, for garnish

Stir ingredients with ice and strain into a rocks glass with a large ice cube. Garnish with a twist of lemon on the edge of the glass.

COCKTAIL À LA LOUISIANE

Figs, licorice, herbs, spirituous

— • • • • —

A striking digestif, especially after a large seafood dinner or a plate of jambalaya.

A cross between a Manhattan and a Sazerac, this luxe drink was once the signature cocktail of the venerable Restaurant de la Louisiane, a bastion of haute creole cuisine where presidential types signed into a famous guest registry known as the "Golden Book." This drink makes an appearance in the 1937 book *Famous New Orleans Drinks and How to Fix 'Em* and has evolved into a cult classic. It's one of those equal-parts cocktails that turns into a transcendent blend—much tastier than its parts might suggest.

¾ ounce (22 ml) rye whiskey (Wild Turkey 101 or Rittenhouse)

¾ ounce (22 ml) sweet vermouth (Vya or Carpano Antica)

¾ ounce (22 ml) Benedictine

3 dashes Peychaud's bitters

Absinthe, to rinse the glass

Cherry or fresh fig slice, for garnish

Rinse a chilled coupe glass with absinthe. In a mixing glass, add ingredients and stir with ice, then strain into the prepared glass. Drop in a cherry or fig for garnish.

VIEUX CARRÉ

Smooth, complex, herbaceous

— • — • — • —

Pair with pork belly, a BLT, or a thick, well-charred steak.

Wander into the Carousel Bar at the Hotel Monteleone in New Orleans, and you'll find guests sipping this potent drink developed in the '30s by the hotel's head bartender, Walter Bergeron. The French Quarter, or Vieux Carré, gives its name to this cocktail. Locals pronounce it "VOO-kray." The original recipe appears in *Famous New Orleans Drinks and How to Fix 'Em* (1937).

1 ounce (30 ml) rye whiskey (Sazerac)

1 ounce brandy (30 ml) (Pierre Ferrand Ambre)

½ ounce (15 ml) sweet vermouth (Carpano Antica)

¼ teaspoon Benedictine

Dash of Peychaud's bitters

Dash of Angostura bitters

Lemon peel, for garnish

Stir ingredients with ice and strain into a rocks glass with a large cube. To garnish, twist the peel over the surface of the cocktail to express the oil. Then, run the peel around the rim of the glass and drop it into the drink.

REMEMBER THE MAINE ·······

Herbaceous, cherry, mint, caramel

— • — • — • —

With a little cherry sweetness and an absinthe undertow, this may be the ultimate burger or steak cocktail.

Similar to a Manhattan but with more complexity, Charles H. Baker recounts quaffing these during Batista's military coup in Cuba in 1933. The name references the sinking of the USS *Maine* in the Havana harbor in 1898, an event that precipitated the Spanish-American War. We've fallen for this smoky libation that captures the tension of political upheaval.

2 ounces rye whiskey (Rittenhouse or Old Overholt)

¾ ounce (22 ml) sweet vermouth (Carpano Antica)

2 teaspoons cherry heering

Absinthe, to rinse the glass

Cherry, for garnish

Rinse a chilled coupe glass with absinthe. Stir ingredients with ice and strain into the prepared glass. Garnish with the cherry.

QUINTESSENTIAL NEW ORLEANS COCKTAILS

If there's a city that embodies the creativity of the cocktail, surely it's New Orleans. This former pirate town, with its French influence and thriving music scene, has been a source of innovation. In addition to its vibrant drink scene and historic bars, the city is also home to the Museum of the American Cocktail, as well as host to the annual spirit-centric conference, Tales of the Cocktail.

Libations from New Orleans tend toward iconic and eclectic, not to mention bold—like the city itself. We like these six quintessential cocktails because they vary in flavor and texture, from the slushy and head-strong Absinthe Frappé (a plush waker-upper) to the bright and creamy Grasshopper, a cocktail developed by a New Orleans bartender during Prohibition. All of these pair well with spicy food and steamy weather.

Sazerac (page 37)

Ramos Gin Fizz (page 42)

Absinthe Frappé (page 161)

Grasshopper (page 229)

Obituary Cocktail (page 48)

Vieux Carré (page 104)

OLD HICKORY

Aromatic, herbaceous, spice, caramel

—•—•—•—

A cocktail comfortable with New Orleans cuisine and seafood. Try it with oysters!

Appearing in print in 1937, this vermouth double header intrigued us from the menu of Maison Premiere in New York, one of the country's great oyster meccas. Popular belief says that this was a favored drink of Andrew Jackson (nicknamed Old Hickory) when he was stationed in New Orleans in 1815. But that can't be true because dry vermouth wasn't available until much later—the first record of a shipment of French dry vermouth to the United States being Noilly Prat to New Orleans in 1851. So much for historical romance. But no matter, we have a love affair with this drink because of its soft balance of bitter herbs, caramelized sugar, and fresh orange.

1½ ounces (45 ml) sweet vermouth (Carpano Antica)

1 ounce (30 ml) dry vermouth (Dolin)

2 to 3 dashes orange bitters

Dash of Peychaud's bitters

Lemon peel, for garnish

Stir ingredients with ice and strain into a chilled coupe glass. Garnish with lemon peel on the rim of the glass.

BROWN DERBY

Honey, grapefruit, vanilla, spice

—•—•—•—

A very food-friendly drink, especially with salmon or crab cakes. We love it for brunch.

Although associated with the iconic, hat-shaped restaurant in Los Angeles that was the birthplace of the Cobb Salad, this cocktail was actually the signature drink at the nearby Vendôme Club. Sour, floral, and a little sweet, it is an outstanding bourbon cocktail; the original recipe (named the De Rigueur) called for Scotch, which we also find compelling.

2 ounces (60 ml) bourbon (Four Roses)

1 ounce (30 ml) fresh grapefruit juice

½ ounce (15 ml) honey syrup (page 242)

Grapefruit wedge, to garnish

Shake ingredients with ice and strain into a chilled coupe glass. Garnish with the grapefruit wedge on a cocktail pick.

LION'S TAIL

Citrus, spice, prickly, aromatic

—•—•—•—

Hefty spice makes this complex sipper a winning match for fall foods, like squash or anything with apples.

Some people associate this drink with *The Wizard of Oz*, but more likely the name derives from the Britishism "twisting the lion's tail," which means to stir up trouble. This cocktail strangely combines whiskey and lime with allspice dram (also called pimento dram), so we wouldn't be surprised if it harkens from an older age entirely. It looks god awful on paper but give it a try— you'll see, my pretty, and your little dog, too! This is another drink that owes its reappearance to cocktail archaeologist Ted Haigh.

2 ounces (60 ml) bourbon (Buffalo Trace)

½ teaspoon (15 ml) allspice dram (St. Elizabeth)

¾ ounce (22 ml) fresh lime juice

½ ounce (15 ml) simple syrup (page 241)

Lime peel, for garnish

Dash of bitters (Angostura)

Shake ingredients with ice and strain into a chilled coupe. Garnish with lime peel on the rim of the glass.

DAIQUIRI

Astringent, citrus, fresh

—•—•—•—

Simple and quick, the daiquiri makes for a speedy after-work cooler or picnic drink. Pair with chips, shrimp cocktail, or ceviche.

Hailing from Cuba during the Spanish-American War, this inspired concoction—really a family of drinks more than a single cocktail—is purportedly the creation of American miner Jennings Cox. Originally, the drink was built in the glass: sugar, lime juice, and rum—layered and stirred. Later, it developed into a shaken or blended drink, and gained widespread acceptance in the 1940s, when the rationing of other liquors made rum a readily available alternative. Simple and fresh, this is one big citrus burst, not the least bit sweet.

Note: If you substitute grenadine for the simple syrup, you have a Bacardi Cocktail.

2 ounces (60 ml) light rum (Flor de Caña 4 Yr)

1 ounce (30 ml) fresh lime juice

½ ounce (15 ml) simple syrup (page 241)

Lime wheel, for garnish

Shake ingredients with ice and strain into a chilled coupe glass. Alternatively, roll the drink a few times with ice (see page 261) and pour contents straight into a tumbler. Garnish with a lime wheel.

MEXICAN FIRING SQUAD

Tart, pomegranate, lime

• • • •

A stunning deep-purple drink. Try it with fish tacos or fajitas.

Mexico City in the 1930s, and La Cucaracha Bar was the place for cocktails—an arty place with murals depicting Mexican folk dancers and an illustrated menu featuring an iconic cockroach dressed to the nines in tails and spats. The MFS shirks the salt rim of a margarita and sallies forth where few tequila drinks go—into grenadine and bitters. Homemade grenadine (page 244) is key here. This drink will make converts out of people who claim to not like tequila.

2 ounces (60 ml) blanco tequila (Herra-dura)

¾ ounce (22 ml) fresh lime juice

¾ ounce (22 ml) grenadine (page 244)

2 dashes Angostura bitters

Lime wheel, for garnish

6 to 8 pomegranate seeds, for garnish

Shake ingredients with ice and strain into a rocks glass filled with ice. Garnish with a lime wheel on the side of the glass and a few pomegranate seeds sprinkled on top.

CUBA LIBRE

Lime, caramel, vanilla

• • • •

Pizza. Pizza. Pizza. This is a divine complement to a crispy red pie.

Legend has it this drink can be traced back to the early 1900s, when American Rough Riders aided Cuba during the Spanish-American War. A classic mash-up of American culture with the Caribbean, this has become one of the most iconic sippers of our hemisphere. While it is technically a pre-Prohibition drink, it received wide popularity in the 1930s and especially '40s.

2 ounces (60 ml) rum (Appleton V/X)

4 ounces (120 ml) cola (Boylan Cane Cola or Mexican Coke)

2 lime slices, for muddling

Muddle the lime gently in a rocks glass. Top with ice. Add rum and cola.

PICKLEBACK

More of a tradition than a cocktail, the pickleback—literally a shot of liquor with a "back" of pickle juice—was carried to the United States by immigrants who chased harsh booze with salty brine from fermented cabbage and other vegetables. It still thrives in Midwestern states and in Texas—and now in cities where it has appeared at cocktail bars. In Mexico, where the tradition also survives, the pickleback liquor of choice is tequila; in Russia, it's done with vodka. We place it here, associating it with the Great Depression, to honor the hard-working farmers who taught us its charms in the backcountry bars of Iowa and South Dakota. For another farmland drink, see the Haymaker's Punch, or Switchel (page 234).

1 ounce (30 ml) whiskey

1 ounce (30 ml) pickle brine

Down the whiskey, down the brine.

POST-WORLD WAR II ERA:
TO THE BOOZE

During World War II, alcohol made from grain was rationed and used for fuel. The shortage meant that imbibers looked for alternatives to whiskey and gin. They found tequila. Rum, which had been a huge part of the American drinking story early on, but had declined, also returned to fuel a full-blown tiki craze (see page 183). Alongside Polynesian exoticism, there was a push toward dry, booze-forward drinks. The drier the martini, the better. This is the era of James Bond and hard-boiled fiction. By the end of the '50s, Smirnoff launched a campaign to push vodka in the American market and created vodka's killer app, the Moscow Mule (page 122).

During this time of heavy drinking, Americans enjoyed the postwar economic boom with stiff drinks that were heavy on citrus, especially lime. This is the era of the Margarita (page 118), not to mention the Gimlet (page 113)—a creation that employed bottled Rose's lime juice, though most craft cocktailers won't touch the stuff now (we suggest making our lime cordial, page 245). The drinks in this chapter are for when you need a bright wallop-packer in a frosted glass.

HIGHBALL

Ginger, aromatic, caramel

—◆◆◆◆—

This tall, gingery bourbon drink is stunning with Korean barbecue pork.

....

This is the Highball Cocktail, not the group of drinks known as highballs—i.e., a spirit blended with a nonalcoholic mixer. Highballs define simplicity—just pour liquor and add a spritz. For the Highball Cocktail specifically, you can play with a variety of whiskeys and ginger beers to great effect. Try Buffalo Trace & Gosling's, or Wild Turkey Rye Whiskey and Boylan's. Add a little lime to make this drink into a mule or buck. This is a crisp and refreshing sipper any time of year.

2 ounces (60 ml) whiskey (Buffalo Trace)

4 ounces (120 ml) ginger beer (see recipe page 247)

Dash of Angostura bitters

Build over ice in a highball glass.

VESPER

Crisp, juniper, lemon

—◆◆◆◆—

Jolly good with a dish of olives and a double entendre.

....

James Bond liked his drink "large and very strong and very cold and very well made," or so he says in Ian Fleming's *Casino Royale*, published in 1953. The drink is so named because vespers are the traditional sunset evening prayer, known as the "violet hour," aka martini time. The original recipe called for Gordon's gin and vodka, plus half a measure of Kina Lillet. There are some updates in order to achieve this recipe today: Kina Lillet is no longer available, and the closest replacement is Cocchi Americano. The Gordon's gin formula has also changed, so to achieve the original 94-proof taste, use either Tanqueray or Broker's. You'll also want to stir the drink, not shake it like the gigolo Bond.

3 ounces (90 ml) gin (Tanqueray or Broker's)

1 ounce (30 ml) vodka (Stolichnaya)

¼ ounce (7 ml) Cocchi Americano

Lemon twist, for garnish

Stir ingredients with ice and strain into a chilled martini glass. Garnish the lemon twist on the rim of the glass.

GIMLET

Spirituous, lime, juniper

— • • • • —

Heavy lime and juniper are wonderful with lox and cucumber. Gimlets also have an affinity for very spicy South American and Asian food.

It's possible this cocktail is named for a British Naval surgeon, Gimlette, who gave his sailors citrus to prevent scurvy. The drink first appears in 1928, but is associated with hard-boiled types like Raymond Chandler, who liked his Gimlet half lime, half gin—a ratio we follow. It's one of the very few drinks in which it's considered okay to employ Rose's lime juice—but we find the stuff unpalatable, and have developed a lime cordial that achieves both the familiar sweetness and acidity. This is a versatile drink to garnish. We've used lime wheels, a cucumber spear, and even a sprig of rosemary.

- 2 ounces (60 ml) London Dry gin (Beef-eater)
- 2 ounces (60 ml) lime cordial (see recipe page 245)
- 3 to 4 thin lime wheels or cucumber spear, for garnish

Shake ingredients with ice and strain into a rocks glass filled with ice. To garnish, drop the lime wheels into the glass, or add a single spear of cucumber.

LITERARY COCKTAILS

The connection between literature and booze is strong, marked in popular myth by hard-drinking loners who wrestle with their demons while typing. Many famous American authors were inveterate daily drinkers, and some—like Sherwood Anderson, who died when he swallowed a toothpick from his martini—met tragic, alcohol-related ends. Others kept liquor as a constant, fortifying companion—like Carson McCullers, who faced life's struggles with daily rations of sherry and hot tea from a thermos. Here, we pair famous writers with their tipple of choice.

Mark Twain: Mark Twain Cocktail (page 36)

Raymond Chandler: Gimlet (page 113)

Edna St. Vincent Millay: Between the Sheets (page 95)

John Steinbeck: Jack Rose (page 84)

Dorothy Parker: Whiskey Sour (page 29)

William Faulkner: Mint Julep (page 171)

F. Scott Fitzgerald: Gin Rickey (page 161)

Eugene O'Neill: Gibson (page 102)

Tennessee Williams: Ramos Gin Fizz (page 42)

EL DIABLO

Berry, ginger, lime

- -

Ginger beer cuts the heat and helps to digest spicy food. Pair an El Diablo with a burrito, stuffed poblanos, or tacos al pastor.

Trader Vic's *Book of Food and Drink* introduced the "Mexican El Diablo" in 1946, a veritable muscle relaxer that combines tequila, berry liqueur, and the taste of ginger and lime. Fans of the margarita, take heed. Anyone who purports to dislike tequila will be converted. This is one of those easy drinkers that can be dangerous; Trader Vic even says, ". . . go easy on this one because it's tough on your running board." It's lovely with a chili-salt rim.

FOR THE CHILI-SALT RIM

1 teaspoon sea salt

¼ teaspoon ground chili pepper

FOR THE COCKTAIL

2 ounces (60 ml) reposado tequila (Corralejo)

½ ounce (15 ml) crème de cassis

¾ ounce (22 ml) fresh lime juice

3 to 4 ounces (90 to 120 ml) ginger beer (page 247)

Lime wheel, for garnish

To prepare the salt rim, mix salt and ground chili pepper on a saucer. Rub the lip of a rocks glass with lime and dip the rim of the glass into the chili-salt mixture.

To make the cocktail, shake ingredients, except ginger beer, with ice and strain into an ice-filled rocks glass with a salted rim. Top with the ginger beer. Garnish with a lime wheel on the rim of the glass.

TORONTO COCKTAIL

Deeply dry, bitter, woodsy

• • • •

This powerful drink pairs well with salty blue cheese, like Point Reyes Original Blue.

Featuring one of the best uses of Fernet-Branca, this cocktail swings toward a Manhattan by using a digestif in place of vermouth. Simple syrup cuts the bitterness, and the added bitters leverage muscle. Popular in the 1940s, this dark vortex of a drink is a swell choice for closing out the show. A perfect after-dinner drink or nightcap.

2 ounces (60 ml) rye whiskey (Old Overholt)

¼ ounce (7 ml) Fernet-Branca

¼ ounce (7 ml) simple syrup (page 241)

2 dashes Angostura bitters

Orange or tangerine twist, for garnish

Stir ingredients with ice and strain into a chilled coupe glass. Garnish with the orange twist on the rim of the glass.

TEQUILA SUNRISE

Blackberry, lime, sour, aromatic

• • • •

Serve up dry-rubbed pork or spicy shrimp.

Legend has it this is a creation of bartender Gene Sulit when he was at the Arizona Biltmore Hotel in the late 1930s. The more well-known version calls for grenadine and orange juice, but this is the original recipe, and we dare say it's less cloying and far superior in flavor. Be sure to use 100 percent agave tequila for the best taste. For another early tequila drink that is remarkably different, replace the soda water with ginger beer and you have El Diablo (page 115).

1½ ounces (45 ml) blanco tequila (Herradura)

½ ounce (15 ml) fresh lime juice

3 ounces (90 ml) soda water

½ ounce (15 ml) crème de cassis

Lime wheel, for garnish

Shake tequila and lime juice with ice, then strain into a highball glass filled with ice. Add soda water, leaving an inch or so of room at the top of the glass. Top with crème de cassis, and garnish with a lime wheel on the side of the glass.

MARGARITA

Citrus, sour, briny, aromatic

• • • •

Tacos, enchiladas, and other spicy fare are natural complements, but we especially love this crowd-pleaser with light fish dishes.

The origins of the margarita are much disputed. There's mention of a Tequila Daisy (*Margarita* means "daisy" in Spanish) as early as 1936, but no mention of a margarita proper occurs until 1953 in *Esquire* magazine. Cocktail historian Ted Haigh believes it's an Anglo-British invention derived from the Sidecar; he cites the Picador Cocktail, which appears in 1937, a full sixteen years before the drink appears under the name margarita. But it's plausible that thirsty folks simply drifted over the Mexican border during Prohibition and switched from brandy to tequila to achieve this combination. Whatever the history, this drink exploded onto the scene to become one of the most widely known cocktails of all time.

2 ounces (60 ml) blanco tequila (Herradura)

1 ounce (30 ml) Cointreau

1 ounce (30 ml) fresh lime juice

Sea salt, to rim the glass (optional)

Lime wedge, for garnish

Rim a rocks glass with salt (technique, page 264). Then, fill the glass with ice. Shake tequila, Cointreau, and lime juice with ice. Strain into the prepared glass. Garnish with lime.

HURRICANE

Passion fruit, citrus, caramel, vanilla

• • • •

A boisterous party drink. Pair with jambalaya or a big mess of red beans and rice.

During the 1940s, a former New Orleans speakeasy created this drink as an allusion to the password that patrons had used to gain entry during Prohibition: "storm's brewin'." Or so the story goes. It was a saccharine concoction of fruit juices designed to expedite rum drinking at a time when whiskey and Scotch were in short supply. Bartender Pat O'Brien of Mr. O'Brien's Club Tipperary sold the drinks in undulating glassware shaped like hurricane lamps, and—not surprisingly—these became a favorite among sailors.

2 ounces (60 ml) light rum (Flor de Caña 4 Yr)

2 ounces (60 ml) dark rum (Appleton Estate Extra)

2 ounces (60 ml) passion fruit juice

1 ounce (30 ml) fresh orange juice

½ ounce (15 ml) fresh lime juice

1 tablespoon (15 ml) simple syrup (page 241)

1 tablespoon (15 ml) grenadine (page 244)

Orange wedge, for garnish

Cherry, for garnish

Shake ingredients with ice and strain into a hurricane glass—or a highball glass. To garnish, spear the cherry, then the orange wedge on a toothpick, and hang from the side of the glass.

BETSY ROSS

Dark cherry, vanilla, spice

• • • •

A fabulous accompaniment to roast pork loin, thanks to the combination of brandy and port. We like to serve these at Thanksgiving, where they are heavenly with giblet stuffing.

In 1941, a bon vivant named Crosby Gaige published a cocktail companion dedicated to "Hussies and Homebodies," and in it appeared a recipe for the Betsy Ross. Today his illustrated *Cocktail Guide and Ladies Companion* is one of those vintage collectables that goes for hundreds of dollars on eBay, but no one seems to know how Gaige came across this recipe. Moody, spicy, blood-dark—maybe Betsy Ross was a stage name? After all, Gaige produced shows on Broadway when he wasn't hanging out with Dorothy Parker or chairing the American Food & Wine Society or growing onions for the Waldorf-Astoria (a private hobby, he grew over 100 varieties). Wherever the recipe is from, it is a throwback to early cocktails.

2 ounces (60 ml) brandy (Pierre Ferrand Ambre)

½ ounce (15 ml) orange curaçao (Pierre Ferrand)

¾ ounce (22 ml) ruby port (Niepoort)

2 dashes Angostura bitters

Freshly grated nutmeg, for garnish

Stir ingredients with ice and strain into a chilled cocktail glass. Garnish with nutmeg.

AIRMAIL

Citrus, honey, vanilla, brioche

• • • •

This honeyed libation is surprisingly magnificent with Greek fare, such as lamb, spanakopita, and stuffed grape leaves.

Cocktail writer Robert Simonson of the *New York Times* calls this "a sort of fat, swaggering daiquiri made with honey and sparkling wine." Think of it as a strange cross between the Honeysuckle (mentioned on page 85) and the French 75 (page 60). Sometimes we like to up the stakes with rhum agricole and grower Champagne, but good Appleton and American-made bubbly or crémant work beautifully.

2 ounces (60 ml) gold rum (Appleton Estate V/X)

¾ ounce (22 ml) fresh lime juice

¾ ounce (22 ml) honey syrup (page 242)

1½ ounces (45 ml) sparkling wine (crémant)

Shake ingredients, except wine, with ice and strain into a chilled coupe glass. Top with sparkling wine.

ROCK AND RYE

Spice, caramel, woodsy, citrus

— • — —

In winter, keep a jar of Rock and Rye on your counter and serve a shot alongside holiday cookies such as gingerbread men, molasses cookies, or fruitcake. It's also a good mixer.

Back in the old saloon days, you could step into a bar and request a nip from a large murky jar containing a dark potion full of citrus rings and cinnamon sticks. The Rock and Rye, as it was called, combined rock candy and rye whiskey, along with horehound—a bitter herb used as a cough suppressant—and was employed as a bar mixer and home remedy. Mothers spooned it into hot water for sick children, and barmen ladled it into toddies and other concoctions, blurring the lines between medicine and mixology. Even songs pay tribute to it, including a 1934 dance hit "Rock & Rye," first performed by Earl Hines and his orchestra, and later by Benny Goodman. Much loved in the 1800s, it shot back into prominence in the '50s and '60s, alongside martinis and highballs.

Note: Look for horehound tincture at a natural foods store. Rock candy strings are available online or at old-timey candy shops. You can make this in one large 1-quart jar or a pair of pint jars so that you can keep one and gift the other.

MAKES 1 QUART

1 bottle (750 ml) rye whiskey (Rittenhouse)

2 ounces (60 ml) maraschino liqueur (Luxardo)

1 orange, sliced into rings with the top and bottom discarded

1 lemon, sliced into rings with the top and bottom discarded

1 string (6 inches) of rock candy

2 large cinnamon sticks

6 whole cloves

6 star anise

12 drops of horehound tincture (optional)

Fill a 1-quart jar with citrus rings, spices, and rock candy. Add rye whiskey, making sure all the fruit is submerged. Drop in the horehound or add it later to drinks. Store on the counter for at least 2 days before serving.

Serve this neat or on the rocks, or combine with hot water and honey for a soothing "tea." It's excellent in a Hot Toddy (page 216) or an Old Fashioned (page 28).

MOSCOW MULE

Ginger, sweet, citrus

— • • • • —

Try pairing the mule with spicy Thai and Vietnamese cuisine. It's also terrific with grilled fish or roasted root vegetables.

Designed to put vodka into the hands of Americans, the mule sprang into the ring under unusual circumstances. It hit the Cock and Bull Tavern in Los Angeles early in the '40s, served in copper mugs. Why? The bartender had a surplus of ginger beer, his girlfriend worked for a company that fashioned copper kitchenware, and the executives of Smirnoff wanted to make tracks into the American market. (Although vodka existed before Prohibition, most Americans had never heard of it.) The Moscow Mule appeared, icy and stimulating, served in distinctive mugs, and drinkers along the Sunset Strip lapped it up. Try a dash of ground cardamom on top for interest.

2 ounces (60 ml) vodka (Stolichnaya)

½ ounce (15 ml) fresh lime juice

4 to 6 ounces (120 to 180 ml) ginger beer (page 247)

Lime wheel, for garnish

Squeeze half a lime into a chilled rocks glass (or a mug) and then drop it in the glass. Add ice and vodka. Fill the rest of the glass with ginger beer and garnish with a lime wheel on the edge of the glass.

STINGER

Spearmint, dried fruit, caramel

— • • • • —

A postprandial breath-freshener. It's divine with chocolate.

The Stinger's combination of brandy and crème de menthe may appear to be an acquired taste, but as Dale DeGroff notes in *The Craft of the Cocktail*, "In the nineteenth century, many woke up to the brandy-based cocktail and went to bed with the Stinger." Interestingly, this combination of ingredients appears as early as 1892 (when it was called the Judge), but it had a second honeymoon in the late '40s and '50s, when brandy was all the rage. Today gin is also commonly used. Note that this is one of those idiosyncratic drinks that bartenders often shake instead of stir, despite the lack of eggs, fruit juice, or dairy. Shaking gives it a nice froth.

2 ounces (60 ml) brandy (Paul Masson Grande Amber VSOP)

1 ounce (30 ml) white crème de menthe (or Death's Door Wondermint)

Sprig of mint, for garnish

Shake ingredients with ice and strain into a brandy snifter or rocks glass filled with crushed ice. Garnish with mint.

BLACK RUSSIAN

Coffee, caramel, vanilla

• • • •

The drink for a late-night doughnut run! Bittersweet and dessert-y.

Popular in the 1950s and '60s, the Black Russian put a chill on the Cold War with vodka and Kahlua, a rum-based Mexican liqueur with strong notes of vanilla and coffee. Although cocktail historians attribute this drink to a Belgian bartender who supposedly developed it for a lady ambassador, it's worth noting that Kahlua and Smirnoff ran major ad campaigns in *Time* magazine during the midcentury decades, earning both brands a spot in the family liquor cabinet. Kahlua became the go-to cordial after a dinner party, and recipes for Kahlua desserts—from pies to parfaits—made their way into kitchens. As a throwback, the Black Russian still packs a punch and is evocative of an era defined by *American Bandstand* and Marilyn Monroe. In the '60s, a splash of cream added to this drink turned it into a White Russian, an iteration made famous by *The Big Lebowski*.

2 ounces (60 ml) vodka (Stolichnaya)

1 ounce (30 ml) Kahlua

Lemon peel, for garnish

Stir ingredients with ice and strain into an ice-filled rocks glass. Garnish with a lemon peel in the glass.

KANGAROO COCKTAIL

Simple, briny, bright

• • • •

Give your Kangaroo a dish of olives, a plate of oysters, or a heap of king crab legs.

The proper name for a dry vodka martini, the Kangaroo screamed to popularity after the famous Bond scene in 1962's *Dr. No*, when Sean Connery orders it "shaken and not stirred." Before this scene, a martini meant gin, and stirred—the common wisdom being that shaking bruised the gin. But vodka didn't bruise, went the theory, so shaking became the new standard. It felt thoroughly modern at the time, and this cocktail reigned for twenty-five years in Bond-land, until Daniel Craig's 007 returned to the Vesper in *Casino Royale* in 2006.

3½ ounces (105 ml) vodka (Stolichnaya)

Vermouth rinse (Noilly Prat)

Olive or lemon twist, for garnish

Pour a dash of dry vermouth in a chilled martini glass, swirl, and discard. Shake vodka with ice and strain into chilled martini glass. Garnish with an olive or a lemon twist.

THE COCKTAIL DARK AGES:
1960S, '70S & '80S

Baby Boomers didn't do any favors for the American cocktail. The generation born into postwar prosperity elevated convenience over quality and inaugurated vodka drinks served in giant glassware. Think of the Nixon-era cranberry coolers of the New England 1970s and fruity potions that culminated in the infamous Cosmopolitan (page 130). Luckily, by the time the Cosmo went mainstream, thanks to the HBO show *Sex and the City*, the backlash had already begun. Things couldn't get any worse, and the stage for the cocktail's second Golden Age was set.

So why include a chapter about these drinks at all? Despite their questionable place in the cocktail pantheon, a few libations from this era are iconic and present bold flavor profiles unlike any other combinations—like the Rusty Nail (page 127) and the Amaretto Sour (page 127). Others have been reimagined in updated form, making them palatable and maybe even fashionable again, like the Harvey Wallbanger (page 128).

And just in case you find yourself tending bar at a yacht club, we've provided a list of cranberry drinks (page 129) that will likely be requested.

MOVIE NIGHT COCKTAILS

A number of iconic drinks make cameo appearances—or even play starring roles—on the silver screen. Think of how the White Russian is inextricably linked to *The Big Lebowski*. Other drinks appear rather quietly in classic movies—Bette Davis sips a Gibson in *All About Eve*, Audrey Hepburn slings back a Zombie during a party scene in *Breakfast at Tiffany's*.

For an Oscar party or date night, consider bringing a few of these libations to life. Set up your bar, break out the cocktail napkins, and roll out the popcorn.

The Big Lebowski: White Russian (page 123)

Casino Royale: Vesper (page 112)

The Seven Year Itch: Whiskey Sour (page 29)

Breakfast at Tiffany's: Zombie (page 189)

Sex and the City: Cosmopolitan (page 130)

Blood and Sand: Blood and Sand (page 71)

Casablanca: French 75 (page 60)

Some Like It Hot: Manhattan (page 41)

All About Eve: Gibson (page 102)

RUSTY NAIL

Honey, herbaceous, sharp

· · · ·

Like an alcoholic tea, a Rusty Nail makes for unexpectedly fine sipping with scones and clotted cream.

Popular wisdom says that this drink stems from the 1930s, but its provenance is sketchy enough that it may just actually be from the 1960s. It is a drink that started out debonair, with the likes of the Rat Pack enjoying it regularly, but then went straight to suburban rec rooms where it still smolders alongside pool tables and bad carpeting. We like to use a blended Scotch, such as Famous Grouse. Variations abound, the most fun being the Donald Sutherland, which substitutes rye whiskey.

2 ounces (60 ml) Scotch (Famous Grouse)

½ ounce (15 ml) Drambuie

Lemon twist, for garnish

Pour ingredients into a rocks glass over ice, stir, and garnish with a lemon twist in the glass.

AMARETTO SOUR

Frothy, almond, cider, citrus

· · · ·

This updated foofy drink tastes like a Dutch pastry and loves a snickerdoodle.

Bartender Jeffrey Morgenthaler restarted the conversation about Amaretto Sour, adding whiskey, rich simple syrup, and egg white to it—with fresh citrus. It's a smart upgrade using a liqueur that has been around since the sixteenth century. We've always made our version with a dash of Laird's Applejack or Calvados, the apple notes melding with the almond-y Amaretto. Add a dash of bitters to make it a cocktail proper, and to lend a little spice. We've also heard of using maple syrup as the sweetener. If you haven't had one of these in a while, you'll be pleasantly surprised at how tasty this Americana classic can be.

2 ounces (60 ml) Amaretto

1 ounce (30 ml) apple brandy (Laird's Applejack or Calvados)

1 ounce (30 ml) fresh lemon juice

1 teaspoon simple syrup (page 241) or maple syrup

¾ ounce (22 ml) egg white

Half lemon slice and cherry, for garnish

Dry shake ingredients. Then shake with ice and strain into a rocks glass with one large cube of ice. Garnish with the lemon slice wrapped around the cherry and threaded on a cocktail pick.

HARVEY WALLBANGER

Citrus, orange, licorice, mint

• •

Spicy fish dishes and Caribbean cuisine pair well with the sweet notes in this throwback cocktail.

Who was Harvey Wallbanger? Legend has it this drink was named for a surfer who would bump down the hallways at parties when he was drunk, but it's actually an industry-generated cocktail created by Galliano, which supported it in the '70s with an ad campaign featuring a cartoon character named Harvey. Now, the Harvey Wallbanger mostly appears as a novelty cocktail. This recipe is adapted from bartender Don Lee, who updates it by clarifying the orange juice and adding a hint of lemon for a cleaner taste and texture. Essentially a Screwdriver (vodka and orange juice) with a float of Galliano on top, it has a delightful, hard-to-place flavor that is the source of its once-wild popularity.

1½ ounces (45 ml) vodka (Stolichnaya)

½ ounce (15 ml) Galliano

2 ounces (60 ml) fresh orange juice

¼ ounce (7 ml) fresh lemon juice

Dash of Angostura bitters

Half wheel of orange, for garnish

Pinch of coarse sea salt

Strain orange juice and lemon juice through a coffee filter into a mixing glass. Add ice, vodka, Galliano, and Angostura bitters. Stir and strain into a chilled coupe glass. Garnish with an orange wheel on the edge of the glass and a sprinkle of salt.

THE CRANBERRY CONNECTION

Don your preppy shirts and boat shoes, and prepare to set sail with the vodka and cranberry set. In the '60s, Ocean Spray pushed cranberry to the forefront of drink culture, creating a host of rather tacky sippers that are the Yankee Candles of the cocktail world. The most popular of these is the Sea Breeze, but its companions linger on as well, including the Cosmopolitan (page 130). If you find yourself bartending at a country club or serving a room full of Baby Boomers, you may need to know these.

Cape Cod(dder): vodka, cranberry, lime

Sea Breeze: vodka, cranberry, grapefruit juice

Bay Breeze: vodka (try it with rum), cranberry, pineapple

Madras: vodka, cranberry, orange juice

Woo Woo: vodka, cranberry, peach schnapps

Sex on the Beach: vodka, cranberry,
peach schnapps, orange juice

MOJITO

Clean, citrus, mint

• • • •

Serve with plantains, spicy food, or sea-food-based dishes like lobster rolls.

Originally from Cuba, the mojito predates the daiquiri as a working man's drink, probably harkening all the way back to the 1500s. Long before ice and soda water became part of the mix, farmers drank a mixture of mint and rum. The key to a good mojito? Every bartender has her secret—some add a float of dark rum on top, others a little basil. Modern adaptations include pomegranate seeds, strawberries, even green tea. To muddle the mint, gently press the leaves against the glass to release the oils without shredding the leaves.

Note: Although you can use soda water here, we love the intense prickle that mineral water adds to this drink.

- 2 ounces (60 ml) white rum (Flor de Caña 4 Yr)
- ¾ ounce (22 ml) fresh lime juice, plus the rind from half a lime
- ¾ ounce (22 ml) simple syrup (page 241)
- 6 to 8 mint leaves, plus a sprig
- 1 to 2 ounces (30 to 60 ml) of sparkling mineral water

Gently muddle the mint leaves and simple syrup in a rocks glass. Add the lime juice and drop in the spent half a lime. Add rum, and stir. Fill the glass three-quarters full of ice (crushed is lovely), and top with mineral water. Garnish with a mint sprig.

COSMOPOLITAN

Citrus, bright fruit, lime

• • • •

Sporting good acidity, the Cosmo is surprisingly revitalizing with Asian cuisine or spicy foods.

In 1968, Ocean Spray created a drink called the Harpoon. It consisted of vodka, cranberry juice, and lime. The story goes that Dale DeGroff improved upon this recipe—the combo was in the zeitgeist already as the Kamikaze shot (vodka, triple sec, lime)—and served it to Madonna at the Rainbow Room. His version, published in *New York* magazine in 1994, became all the rage and is the version you see here. The sweet pink drink was überpopularized by the show *Sex and the City*. Made correctly, the cocktail is actually quite balanced.

- 1½ ounces (45 ml) citron vodka (Stolichnaya Citros or Absolut Citron)
- ½ ounce (15 ml) Cointreau
- 1 ounce (30 ml) cranberry juice
- ¼ ounce (7 ml) fresh lime juice
- Dash of orange bitters (Regans')
- Lime wheel, for garnish

Shake ingredients with ice and strain into a chilled martini glass. Garnish with a lime wheel on the edge of the glass.

MODERN CLASSICS

Bartender Dale DeGroff is often credited with revitalizing cocktails in the late '80s and early '90s by reintroducing fresh ingredients and classic technique. From behind the bar at New York's Rainbow Room, DeGroff lifted cocktails from the miasma of premade mixes and swampy-tinis, and returned quality and craft back to the glass. His gourmet approach was inspired by his rediscovery of Jerry Thomas's early bartender's guide, *The Bon Vivant's Companion*, from the late nineteenth century.

By the turn of the twenty-first century, a full-blown craft cocktail movement exploded and craft-centric bars appeared featuring ice programs, quality liquor, fresh ingredients, and bartenders with retro mustaches. New York establishments such as Milk & Honey (2000), Employees Only (2004), and Pegu Club (2005) fomented a forward push that then spread across the country. It didn't hurt that a swing dancing and lounge music revival had prepared the way. On the West Coast, Seattle's Vessel opened in '06, along with San Francisco's Bourbon & Branch. In Chicago, the Violet Hour opened in '07. As the movement grew, there was an explosion of creativity. It was the dawn of the cocktail's second Golden Age.

The modern creations in this chapter have been hugely influential and are now considered classics in their own right. In most of these recipes, the specific brands called for are the original selections of the bartender who created the cocktail.

RITZ COCKTAIL
BY DALE DEGROFF

Citrus, honey, caramel, brioche

• • • •

Full of old-school glamour, this is an ideal dinner-party aperitif. Serve it with canapés, shrimp, and a relish tray.

Dale DeGroff, the godfather of the Craft Cocktail Movement, created this modern riff on the brandy drinks of yore while working at Joe Baum's New York restaurant, Aurora, in 1985. Designed as a tribute to the Champagne cocktails once served at the Paris Ritz, it has the telltale signs of a straightforward classic: classy, subtle, and full of sparkle. Most who taste it have no idea that the backbone of this drink is cognac, a French brandy that gained wild popularity in America at the beginning of the nineteenth century.

¾ ounce (22 ml) brandy (Pierre Ferrand Ambre)

½ ounce (15 ml) Cointreau

¼ ounce (7 ml) maraschino liqueur (Luxardo)

¼ ounce (7 ml) fresh lemon juice

2 ounces (60 ml) chilled Champagne (or crémant)

Orange twist, for garnish

Stir the ingredients, except Champagne, with ice and strain into a martini glass. Top with Champagne and garnish with an orange twist on the rim of the glass.

JASMINE
BY PAUL HARRINGTON

Dry, grapefruit, citrus, juniper

• • • •

This cocktail says 11 a.m. in a warm climate— it's the ultimate brunch drink. The bracing acidity cuts through fat, making it a natural match for avocado toast.

Pink drinks usually signify sweetness, and that's where the jasmine smiles her deceptive smile. You expect this cocktail to go down like a candy twist, but instead it tastes like a freshly plucked ruby red grapefruit. The drink was created for a regular named Matt Jasmine at the Townhouse Bar & Grill in Emeryville, California, back in the 1990s. Master bartender Paul Harrington leaned on the Pegu Club (page 87) to create a riff that is layered and bright, a dead ringer for a Prohibition-era sipper. The Jasmine is viewed as a clever bridge with which to lure Cosmo gals and Campari haters across the Golden Gate into the promised land.

1½ ounces (45 ml) gin (Beefeater)

¼ ounce (7 ml) Campari

¼ ounce (7 ml) Cointreau

¾ ounce (22 ml) fresh lemon juice

Lemon twist, garnish

Shake with ice and strain into a chilled coupe glass. Garnish with the lemon twist on the rim of the glass.

GINGIN MULE
BY AUDREY SAUNDERS

Crisp, citrus, herbaceous, tart, ginger

- - - -

Pair with spicy barbecue, jerk chicken or tofu, or blackened fish.

A protégée of Dale DeGroff, Audrey Saunders went on to open Pegu Club, one of New York's first explicitly craft-centric bars. This drink, her recreation of a Gin Buck, was enormously influential because of its emphasis on fresh ingredients like homemade ginger beer. It has also provided an alternative to the vodka-based Moscow Mule. The GinGin Mule is still a staple at Pegu Club, as well as at bars around the world.

1½ ounces (45 ml) London Dry gin (Tanqueray)

¾ ounce (22 ml) fresh lime juice

½ ounce (15 ml) simple syrup (page 241)

1 ounce (30 ml) chilled ginger beer (page 247)

Lime wedge, for garnish

Mint sprig, for garnish, plus 8 to 10 leaves for muddling

Muddle mint leaves with simple syrup and lime juice in a shaker. Add gin, shake with ice, and strain into a rocks glass filled with ice. Top with ginger beer, and garnish with lime and mint sprig.

GIN BLOSSOM
BY JULIE REINER

Citrus, apricot, juniper

- - - -

Try serving with perfumed dishes, like saffron rice, or as an aperitif before an al fresco dinner.

Julie Reiner created this drink to be the house martini at her Brooklyn bar, Clover Club. It's a light, fragrant cocktail that is classic in proportion while pushing the use of eau-de-vie in balance with vermouth. Note that her recipe calls specifically for dry apricot eau-de-vie, not a liqueur such as Rothman & Winter. Once you try it, this easy sipper will become your house martini, too.

1½ ounces (45 ml) gin (Plymouth)

¾ ounce (22 ml) apricot eau-de-vie (Blume Marillen)

¾ ounce (22 ml) sweet white vermouth (Martini Bianco)

2 dashes orange bitters (Regans')

Lemon peel, for garnish

Stir ingredients with ice and strain into a chilled coupe glass. Garnish with lemon peel resting across the top of the glass.

PENICILLIN
BY SAM ROSS

Smoke, ginger, honey, woodsy

— • • • • —

Excellent with smoked trout and crème fraîche or at a harvest dinner.

The most internationally famous drink of the Craft Cocktail Movement, the Penicillin was created at Milk & Honey in New York when Sam Ross was behind the bar. It boasts a base of blended Scotch with an Islay float on top—providing a smokiness that conjoins magically with the honey ginger syrup for a layered effect. The lemon balances the drink, resulting in an eerily gentle cocktail that lingers. Ross is also the creator of the influential Paper Plane cocktail (page 165).

2 ounces (60 ml) Chivas 12 Scotch

¼ ounce (7 ml) Laphroaig 10-year Single Malt

¾ ounce (22 ml) fresh lemon juice

¾ ounce (22 ml) honey ginger syrup (page 242)

Candied ginger, for garnish

Shake ingredients with ice and strain into a rocks glass with a single large ice cube. Garnish with candied ginger—insert two toothpicks, and slip them over the side of the rim.

RED HOOK
BY ENZO ERRICO

Woodsy, bitter, caramel

— • • • • —

This is a sensational after-dinner drink to serve with dark chocolate, especially pot de crème or Black Forest cake.

It is hard to remember a time when bartenders weren't making all sorts of riffs on classics and calling them new names. But there was. And toward the beginning of that phase, this combination by Milk & Honey bartender Enzo Errico reverberated through cocktail-land and inspired new possibilities. A take on the Manhattan, and named after a Brooklyn neighborhood, this mix stands as one of the most influential drinks of the Craft Cocktail Movement. The bitterness of the Punt e Mes is masterfully balanced by the sweetness of the maraschino—although some bartenders drop the maraschino down to ¼ ounce for less pronounced cherry pit flavor.

2 ounces (60 ml) rye whiskey (Old Overholt)

½ ounce (15 ml) Punt e Mes

½ ounce (15 ml) maraschino liqueur (Luxardo)

Cherry, for garnish

Stir with ice and strain into a chilled coupe glass. Garnish with a cherry on the end of a cocktail pick.

FARM-TO-GLASS COCKTAILS

Farmers' market produce and window box herbs make for eye-popping cocktails. We often shop our local markets for seasonal ingredients to get inspired. A sprig of lavender or a little rosemary provides aroma and color. A tuft of mint transforms a muddy, brown drink into a handsome sipper. You can also steep herbs in simple syrup (page 241), if you want to experiment further with integrating flavors.

For a quick way to incorporate fresh herbs into a cocktail, you can spank a leaf to release its oils (see technique, page 264) and then set it on top of a drink. Floating a sage leaf on top of a grapefruit-based drink, like the Paloma (page 153), is one of our favorite tricks.

The following drinks are especially lovely because they incorporate fresh ingredients, including stone fruit and berries, and plenty of spriggy garnish.

BUTTERNUT AND FALERNUM
BY EBEN FREEMAN

Autumnal, spice, rummy

• •

Ideal at Thanksgiving or at a casual fall dinner party with chili and corn bread. It also pairs well with pot pie, smoked meats, and mushroom ravioli.

The concoction that spurred the vegetable-based cocktail trend in 2005, this drink may take a little work to prepare, but it is hugely rewarding. Golden and aromatic, it conjures fall weather, changing leaves, and the onset of the holiday season. We like to serve this when squash is at its peak. To make the butternut squash jus, you'll need a juicer (2 lbs of squash yields about 1 cup of juice). Keep in mind that the jus needs to rest overnight.

FOR THE BUTTERNUT SQUASH JUS

2 lbs (1 kg) butternut squash, cubed with seeds removed

1 tablespoon (15 g) brown sugar

1 tablespoon (15 g) unsalted butter

FOR THE COCKTAIL

2 ounces (60 ml) Matusalem Gran Reserva Rum (or another aged rum, like Flor de Caña 12 Yr)

$^{3}/_{4}$ ounce (22 ml) John D. Taylor's Velvet Falernum

2 ounces (60 ml) butternut squash jus (see below)

Freshly grated nutmeg, for garnish

For the jus, run the squash cubes through a juicer until you have 1 cup of juice. Simmer the juice in a saucepan to reduce it by one-third. Then add brown sugar and stir until dissolved. In a small skillet, heat the butter over medium heat until it melts and turns golden brown. Add it to the squash mixture and stir until incorporated. Cool, then transfer to a jar and refrigerate. Let it sit overnight, then pass the jus through a sieve to remove any butter solids.

To make the cocktail, shake ingredients over ice, and strain into a double rocks glass of ice cubes. Garnish with nutmeg.

JULIET AND ROMEO
BY TOBY MALONEY

Fresh, cucumber, slightly sour

- • • • -

Sushi is an ideal pairing, so are Mediterranean dishes like lamb, hummus, and tabbouleh.

This drink was created at the Violet Hour in Chicago by Toby Maloney, who was attempting to woo a lady. It conjures all the liquid love a drink-maker can pass across the bar to a patron, combining beautiful presentation and sensual aromatics. Whether trying to impress a new flame or get out of the doghouse, this celestial cocktail is a triumphant summation of the art of the drink. It exemplifies how, like great food, cocktails can express emotion.

- 2 ounces (60 ml) gin (Beefeater)
- 3 slices cucumber, for muddling
- Tiny pinch of salt
- Mint sprig, plus one leaf for garnish
- ¾ ounce (22 ml) fresh lime juice
- ¾ ounce (22 ml) simple syrup (page 241)
- 3 drops rose water
- 3 drops Angostura bitters

Muddle the cucumber and salt. Add mint sprig, gin, fresh lime juice, simple syrup, and rose water. Shake vigorously. Strain into a coupe glass. Garnish with mint leaf. Place three drops of Angostura bitters around the leaf.

OAXACA OLD FASHIONED
BY PHILIP WARD

Smoky, spice, balanced

- • • • -

Serve after dinner with dark chocolate. Also an apt pairing for barbacoa and sweet corn.

Smoky mezcal doubles down on tequila for an intense and exciting—and incredibly tasty—riff on a classic. Created when Phil Ward was at Death and Co. in New York, he now operates the tequila and mezcal-centric bar, Mayahuel. A surprisingly versatile sipper, this can be a conversion experience for those who are new to mezcal.

- 1½ ounces (45 ml) reposado tequila (El Tesoro)
- ½ ounce (15 ml) mezcal (Los Amantes Joven)
- 1 teaspoon agave nectar or simple syrup (page 241)
- Dash of Bittermens Xocolatl Mole bitters (or Angostura)
- Orange peel, for garnish

Stir ingredients with ice and strain into an ice-filled rocks glass. To garnish, flame the peel by expressing the oil over the drink and using a lighter to ignite it (technique, page 264).

BENTON'S OLD FASHIONED
BY DON LEE

Smoky, caramel, maple

- -

Life-changing with doughnuts or French toast. It's also terrific with fried chicken.

A famous drink from the modern-day speakeasy in New York, PDT (Please Don't Tell), fat-infusions and fat washes became the rage after this bacon-infused bourbon cocktail appeared in 2007. The infusion is simple, and can be used in a number of applications—bacon Manhattans or even bacon-y juleps. Keep in mind that the bacon-infused bourbon needs a good six hours to infuse and chill, so it's best to make it a day ahead.

FOR THE BACON-INFUSED BOURBON

1½ ounces (45 ml) bacon fat (preferably Benton's, or a thick-cut bacon)

1 bottle (750 ml) bourbon (Four Roses)

FOR THE COCKTAIL

2 ounces (60 ml) bacon-infused bourbon

¼ ounce (7 ml) grade B maple syrup

2 dashes Angostura bitters

Orange peel, for garnish

To make the bacon-infused bourbon, warm bacon fat in a small saucepan over low heat. Stir it for 3 to 5 minutes, or until it melts. Combine the molten fat and bourbon in a large non-reactive container and stir. Cover and infuse for 6 hours or overnight, then place the container in the freezer for 2 hours. Scrape off the fat solids, then strain the bourbon through a fine mesh sieve or cheesecloth. Pour it into a clean bottle and refrigerate.

For the cocktail, stir ingredients with ice in a mixing glass. Strain into a rocks glass filled with ice. To garnish, twist the peel over the surface of the cocktail to express the oil. Then, run the peel around the rim of the glass and drop it into the drink.

THE LAST TANGO IN MODENA
BY MATTHEW BIANCANIELLO

Floral, caramel, strawberry

Serve this as an aperitif with baked ricotta, carpaccio, or prosciutto-wrapped breadsticks.

There are few better places to experience field-to-glass cocktails than at the Library Bar in L.A.'s Roosevelt Hotel, known for bartenders who shop the farmers' market for fresh ingredients. The bar's small, intimate counter is covered in cups and glasses brimming with the earth's bounty waiting to be used in imaginative creations. When Matthew Biancaniello was bartending there, he created this original, which plays off the classic Italian pairing of fresh strawberries drizzled with aged balsamic. Note that this drink requires an ISI whip (a kitchen tool used to whip cream) in order to create the St. Germain foam.

FOR THE ST. GERMAIN FOAM

1 cup (240 ml) St. Germain

1 cup (240 ml) egg whites

1 ounce (30 ml) fresh lime juice

FOR THE COCKTAIL

2 ounces (60 ml) gin (Hendrick's)

1 ounce (30 ml) 25-year aged balsamic vinegar

3 to 4 medium strawberries, plus half a strawberry for garnish

St. Germain foam

To make the St. Germain foam, add ingredients into an ISI whip. Charge it twice with nitrous oxide (N_2O) and shake well.

For the cocktail, muddle the strawberries with balsamic vinegar in a shaker. Add gin and shake with ice. Strain over ice into a rocks glass. Top with St. Germain foam. Garnish.

TRINIDAD SOUR
BY GIUSEPPE GONZALEZ

Clove, apple, citrus, tart

◆ ◆ ◆ ◆

Serve with steak, barbecue, or winter stew. It also pairs well with fall desserts, like pumpkin pie.

While this cocktail reads like an extreme sport, thanks to the full ounce of bitters, it is, in fact, a balanced must-try that tastes like a holiday fantasy. Angostura takes the lead here, calmed and sweetened by orgeat and fresh citrus, then deepened by the tastes of rye and caramel that round out the drink. More than just a novelty, this cocktail pushes the boundary of the possible and explores the unexpected.

$\frac{1}{2}$ ounce (15 ml) rye whiskey (Rittenhouse)

1 ounce (30 ml) orgeat (page 244)

1 ounce (30 ml) Angostura bitters

$\frac{3}{4}$ ounce (22 ml) fresh lemon juice

Shake with ice and strain into a chilled coupe glass.

GIN BASIL SMASH ············
BY JÖERG MEYER

Brisk, herbaceous, basil, juniper

◆ ◆ ◆ ◆

A perfect accent for an outdoor supper during tomato season. In winter, it revives the palate as an aperitif.

This drink demonstrates so ably how fresh ingredients can be incorporated into everyday drinking cocktails. Head to your kitchen garden or snag a big bunch of basil at the farmers' market, and you're mere steps from a living drink that will make your head dizzy. This drink smashes basil, but you can smash anything—tarragon, thyme, cilantro, or kefir lime leaves. Let this drink inspire you. We like to host a garden party with an assortment of fresh herbs and gins, and let friends muddle their way through an array of flavors.

2 ounces (60 ml) gin (Beefeater)

1 ounce (30 ml) fresh lemon juice

$\frac{2}{3}$ ounce (20 ml) simple syrup (page 241)

Small bunch basil leaves (about 10)

Basil sprig, for garnish

Muddle basil leaves with lemon juice and simple syrup. Add ice and gin and shake. Double-strain into a chilled cocktail glass with ice. Garnish with a basil sprig.

BARBACOA
BY JULIAN COX

Spice, citrus, ginger, smoke

Sip this by the grill as you're turning shrimp skewers and grilled pineapple, or batch it for a party. We like to serve it with guacamole and chips.

Hitting all the flavor notes—sweet, sour, bitter, salty, umami—the Barbacoa was created at the Restaurant Rivera in Los Angeles, and it puts some unusual ingredients to work in a smoky, savory masterpiece. It even includes a strip of beef jerky as an accent (vegetarians can use vegan jerky—we like Stonewall's Jerquee). Impressively garnished and loaded with lime wheels, this is one of those party drinks that people never forget.

Note: This drink originally calls for a quarter ounce of agave syrup and a quarter ounce of ginger syrup, which we replace with a honey ginger syrup. Chipotle purée is available in cans at most grocery stores.

FOR THE CHIPOTLE PURÉE

1 can (7 ounces) chipotle peppers, in adobe sauce

FOR THE COCKTAIL

2 ounces (60 ml) mezcal or blanco tequila

½ ounce (15 ml) fresh lemon juice

½ ounce (15 ml) honey ginger syrup (see page 242)

1 teaspoon chipotle purée

4 lime wheels, thinly sliced

1 thin strip red bell pepper, for garnish

1 strip of beef jerky, for garnish

To make the chipotle purée, pour peppers and adobe sauce in a blender or food processor and pulse until smooth. Refrigerate any unused portion.

For the cocktail, combine lemon juice, syrup, chipotle purée, and lime wheels in a mixing glass. Muddle, then add ice and spirit. Stir. Pour the mixture into a chilled rocks glass. Slip in the red pepper strip and beef jerky as garnish.

ART OF CHOKE
BY KYLE DAVIDSON

Bitter, floral, herbaceous, vegetal

• • • •

A complex refresher, like a boozy iced tea. Try it with barbecue fare or with fancy appetizers involving smoked fish or caviar.

Cynar is an Italian amaro made with artichokes that has a wonderful vegetal, leathery, and very bitter taste to it—in a good way. It can be used to create the delightful Cynar Flip (2½ ounces Cynar and a whole egg), and makes for a mean Cynar Julep. This brilliantly named cocktail by Kyle Davidson from his days at the Violet Hour in Chicago, is a kind of Cynar Daiquiri that needs to be tasted to be believed. It's unexpectedly refreshing and vibrant, one of our favorite drinks to serve as a nightcap.

1 ounce (30 ml) white rum (Flor de Caña 4 Yr)

1 ounce (30 ml) Cynar

¼ ounce (7 ml) green Chartreuse

⅛ ounce (3.5 ml) fresh lime juice

⅛ ounce (3.5 ml) rich Demerara syrup (see page 242)

2 small mint sprigs, divided

Gently muddle the mint leaves from one sprig in the bottom of a mixing glass. Add the ingredients. Stir with ice and strain over fresh ice into a chilled rocks glass. Garnish with the second mint sprig.

FRENCH MAID
BY JIM MEEHAN

Fresh, ginger, mint, spice

• • • •

A wild drink that pairs well with spicy chicken thighs, black beans and rice, or squash curry.

Jim Meehan created this elegant quaffer while at New York's PDT, a speakeasy hidden behind a hot dog stand. It's something like a mix between Audrey Saunder's gingery GinGin Mule (page 133) and a drink by Sam Ross called the Kentucky Maid, which combines bourbon and cucumber. For cocktail geeks, it's the equivalent of a jackalope. This particular Maid is a perfect excuse to whip up a batch of homemade ginger beer and slay the unruly mint taking over your garden.

1½ ounces (45 ml) Hine VSOP cognac

¼ ounce (7 ml) John D. Taylor's Velvet Falernum

1 ounce (30 ml) ginger beer (page 247)

¾ ounce (22 ml) fresh lime juice

¾ ounce (22 ml) simple syrup (page 241)

4 cucumber wheels, divided

6 to 8 mint leaves, plus mint sprig, for garnish

In a shaker, muddle simple syrup, 3 cucumber wheels, and the mint leaves. Add everything else and shake with ice, then strain into a chilled highball filled with ice. Garnish with a mint sprig threaded through the center of a cucumber wheel.

PART THREE
SEASONAL & OCCASIONAL

HAIR OF THE DOG

Drinking cocktails before noon has been an American practice since at least the 1800s, when bitters were taken in the morning as a restorative. The term "hair of the dog" dates back almost that long, too, and refers to a folk belief that a bite from a rabid dog could be cured by pressing its fur into the wound. While we don't recommend a stiff drink every a.m., we do love a brunch tipple, especially for a festive occasion—a holiday, a birthday, or a beach weekend with friends.

In this chapter, you'll find traditional hair-of-the-dog mood lifters, like the Morning Glory (page 149) and the Fog Cutter (page 157), along with some new inventions like the Mezcalada (page 160) that are suitable for bedazzling house guests. The marmalade-tinged Breakfast Martini (page 151) is particularly genius—quick, easy, and alluring first thing in the morning with a side of buttered toast. During tomato season, serve a round of Red Snappers (page 158)—the original Bloody Mary—on the patio. Bright and reviving, the Snapper is full of fresh-squeezed ripe tomatoes and lemons—intoxicating, even before you add gin.

MORNING GLORY

Caramel, maple syrup, orange, herbs

• • • • •

Order this up alongside a spinach omelet. Pancakes and bacon pair brilliantly, too.

....

An aromatic cocktail that blends rye whiskey and brandy to magical effect, the Morning Glory wakes up the senses with absinthe and lemon. We daresay this 1800s-era libation hits all the notes from gruff to gay, and is a smooth yet sufficiently startling quaffer for breakfast. Top of the mornin' to ye!

1 ounce (30 ml) rye whiskey (Ritten-house)

1 ounce (30 ml) brandy (Pierre Ferrand Ambre)

1 teaspoon orange curaçao (Pierre Ferrand)

½ teaspoon simple syrup (page 241)

2 dashes Angostura bitters

1 ounce (30 ml) soda water

Absinthe, to rinse the glass

Lemon peel, for garnish

Rinse a chilled rocks glass with absinthe. Stir ingredients, except soda, and strain into the prepared glass over a single large cube of ice. Add a dash of soda. To garnish, twist the peel over the surface of the cocktail to express the oil and drop it into the drink.

CORPSE REVIVER NO. 2

Tart, mint, citrus

• • • • •

Pair a reviver with a couple of aspirin and a breakfast sandwich.

....

Corpse Revivers are a whole class of drinks designed to be imbibed in the morning to help drinkers shake off a particularly numbing hangover. The original recipe calls for Lillet, an aperitif from France. Sadly, the formula for Lillet changed in 1987, when the company made their aperitif sweeter and removed the cinchona bark—containing bitter quinine—to make its product more palatable to modern tastes. The unfortunate result was that this reformulation threw off the balance of a number of classics, including this one. Hence the excitement when Cocchi Americano, an Italian aperitif that tastes similar to the original formulation of Lillet, became available in 2006.

1 ounce (30 ml) gin (Plymouth)

¾ ounce (22 ml) Cointreau

¾ ounce (22 ml) Cocchi Americano

¾ ounce (22 ml) fresh lemon juice

Absinthe, to rinse the glass

Rinse a chilled coupe glass with absinthe. Shake ingredients with ice and strain into the prepared glass.

BREAKFAST MARTINI

Bright, citrus, clean

· · · ◆ · ◆ · ◆ · ·

There's no better way to serve this than with buttered toast, preferably as part of breakfast in bed.

You have gin? You have marmalade? You have a cocktail. This famous combination, created by the "maestro" Salvatore Calabrese, uses a classic breakfast staple to ingenious effect. While *The Savoy Cocktail Book* (1930) also has a Marmalade Cocktail, Calabrese maintains that he was inspired by his English wife Sally's morning toast and jam. He snatched the jar when she was eating at the bar, and the rest is history. This drink has since been an inspiration to bartenders and home enthusiasts everywhere, who also discover astonishing ingredients and inspiration from trips to the fridge.

> 2 ounces (60 ml) gin (Plymouth, Barr Hill, or Tanqueray)
>
> ½ ounce (15 ml) fresh lemon juice
>
> ½ ounce (15 ml) Cointreau
>
> 1½ teaspoons orange marmalade
>
> Orange twist, for garnish

Shake ingredients and strain into a chilled martini glass. Garnish with the orange twist on the rim of the glass.

ITALIAN GREYHOUND

Citrus, grapefruit, bitter, juniper

· · · ◆ · ◆ · ◆ · ·

Strong flavors, like lox and "everything" bagels, pair well here. So does a breakfast salad topped with lardons.

A riff off the standard Greyhound—made with vodka and grapefruit juice—this drink deserves to be packed into a thermos and taken to the dog park. The Italian Greyhound cocktail is angular and sleek, thanks to a bitter kick and a graceful switch from vodka to gin. Many versions call for Campari, but we think Aperol, which is less boozy and less bitter, hits the sweet spot. Note that replacing gin with tequila in a 2-1-2 ratio (in the same order as the recipe below) yields another of our favorite morning Aperol cures— the Two-One-Two by bartenders Aisha Sharpe and Willy Shine.

> 1½ ounces (45 ml) gin (Plymouth)
>
> ½ ounce (15 ml) Aperol
>
> 1½ ounces (45 ml) fresh pink grapefruit juice
>
> Rosemary sprig, for garnish (optional)

Shake ingredients and strain into a chilled coupe glass. Garnish with a sprig of rosemary resting across the top of the glass.

BUCK'S FIZZ

Orange, brioche, faint juniper

— • • • • —

An easy drink to fix for a crowd, serve these Fizzes with a big skillet of scrambled eggs, English muffins, and fruit salad.

Where the F is my Mimosa?! We've given it over for the Buck's Fizz, the Mimosa's sexier cousin from across the pond. Before you call us traitors, hear us out—the Buck's Fizz has about the same amount of alcohol but is less sweet. Unlike a true Mimosa, it does not have triple sec and sports a higher ratio of Champagne to O.J. Popular in the 1920s at London's Buck's Club, bartender Pat McGarry created this bright concoction, to which we add a bit of gin. Oops!

3 ounces (90 ml) Champagne (or crémant)

2 ounces (60 ml) fresh orange juice

Splash of gin

Orange slice, for garnish

In a flute glass, add orange juice and top with Champagne. Add gin and garnish with the orange slice on the rim of the glass.

SOUTHSIDE

Citrus, mint, bright

— • • • • —

Serve this with crab cakes at a summery brunch. The cleansing citrus notes cut through heavy foods, like eggs Benedict.

This spectacular gin drink is similar to a French 75 (page 60)—if a French 75 forgot to pick up Champagne at the store and brought home a mint bouquet instead. Smart. For a variation, add muddled cucumber and switch to lime juice, and you've got an Eastside. The history of this particular recipe is nebulous—some say it was named after Chicago's notorious Southside gang, while others date it back to the 21 Club in New York. Either way, this is a gloriously reviving drink, almost puckery but not quite.

2 ounces (60 ml) gin (Junipero)

1 ounce (30 ml) fresh lemon juice

½ ounce (15 ml) simple syrup (page 241)

6 to 8 mint leaves

Lime wheel, for garnish

Shake ingredients with ice and strain into an ice-filled highball glass. Garnish with a lime wheel on the rim of the glass, and serve with a straw.

PALOMA

Effervescent, grapefruit, salt

• • • •

Serve a batch of these bracingly fresh drinks poolside, with guacamole and chips.

The origin of the Paloma (which means "dove") goes back to legendary bartender Don Javier Delgado Corona, who has been serving up La Paloma at his family's bar in the dusty town of Tequila for decades. Though some recipes call for blanco (silver) tequila, we love the deep, smooth flavor of reposado here—the woodsy notes wrap around the acidity of the fruit juices to create a cocktail that is tart but polished.

> 2 ounces (60 ml) reposado tequila (Corralejo)
>
> 3 ounces (90 ml) fresh grapefruit juice
>
> ½ ounce (15 ml) fresh lime juice
>
> 2 teaspoons simple syrup (page 241)
>
> 2 to 3 ounces (60 to 90 ml) club soda
>
> Sea salt, to rim the glass
>
> Lime wheel or sage leaf, for garnish

Salt the rim of a chilled rocks glass (technique, page 264), then fill it with ice. Shake tequila, fresh grapefruit juice, lime juice, and simple syrup with ice. Strain into the prepared glass. Top with soda. Garnish with a lime wheel on the rim, or spank a sage leaf and float it on top.

STOUT FLIP

Frothy, coffee, chocolate, vanilla

• • • •

Make a flip and fry up some sausage and pancakes. It's also a decadent partner for mac 'n' cheese.

Here, the flip—once a favorite of American colonists—gets reborn with dark beer for a frothy cocktail that tamps down a hangover with egg and blackstrap rum. Try playing around with coffee stouts and oatmeal stouts for other ethereal wakeup calls.

> 3 ounces (60 ml) milk stout (Left Hand Brewing)
>
> 1 ounce (30 ml) black rum (Hamilton Jamaican Pot Still Black Rum or Cruzan Blackstrap)
>
> ½ ounce (15 ml) simple syrup (page 241)
>
> 1 fresh small whole egg
>
> 2 dashes Angostura bitters
>
> Freshly grated nutmeg, for garnish

Dry shake ingredients to emulsify, then shake with ice. Strain into a chilled wine glass and garnish with nutmeg.

COCTAILS FOR OYSTERS

Citrus-forward cocktails pair well with seafood, and so do drinks made with sparkling white wine. If you know something about the flavor profile of your bivalves, you can aim for an ideal pairing.

West Coast oysters tend to have a vegetal profile—think steamed spinach—which makes a cucumber cooler, like a Pimm's Cup, or a gin martini like the Marguerite, easy choices. The salty profile of East Coast oysters calls for citrus and a touch of sweetness, like a Southside or a Gimlet.

If you're unsure about the flavor profile of your oysters, lean on something with a Champagne base, like a St. Germain Cocktail. A Red Snapper, made with gin and freshly squeezed tomatoes, is glorious with a cold tray of oysters and light mignonette sauce. Drinks that pair particularly well with oysters:

Old Hickory (page 107)

Marguerite (page 47)

Bijou (page 51)

Pimm's Cup (page 171)

Southside (page 152)

Red Snapper (page 158)

St. Germain Cocktail (page 209)

Gimlet (page 113)

MILK PUNCH

Creamy, caramel, vanilla

· · · · ·

This fortifying cocktail goes with waffles, sticky buns, or a breakfast burger—let it stand in for your milk shake.

Originating as early as the 1600s, milk punches are now associated with New Orleans, where they're enjoyed at brunch or during holidays. We love their relaxing, fortifying character on warm afternoons, especially if we're craving ice cream but prefer something light. Traditionally, brandy is used, although we also like it with bourbon. Over the past few years, milk punches have become something of a phenomenon, with bars going beyond the classic recipe and clarifying the drinks into clear, textural revelations. Below is a recipe for a standard, non-time-consuming version. Trying letting the booze and milk sit mixed overnight to mellow and meld flavors.

2 ounces (60 ml) brandy or bourbon
  (Buffalo Trace)

½ cup (120 ml) whole milk

1 teaspoon powdered sugar

¼ teaspoon vanilla extract

Freshly grated nutmeg or a single star
  anise float, for garnish

Shake ingredients with ice and strain into a chilled rocks glass or a wine glass filled with ice. Garnish with grated nutmeg or star anise.

FOG CUTTER

Rummy, almond, citrus, plum

· · · · ·

A big, complex morning-after drink. Pair it with ham and eggs, and grilled grapefruit halves or pineapple.

Say you wake up feeling spongy and need to cut through the clouds, the Fog Cutter will certainly help you take hold of the throttle—or so the story goes. This Trader Vic classic combines rum, gin, and brandy with fresh citrus and a sherry float. It's beautiful to look at and balanced in taste—not too sweet. Skip the mimosa and make one of these when you need a staycation. Beware, this monster might send you right back into a fog!

2 ounces (60 ml) light rum (Flor de Caña
  4 Yr)

1 ounce (30 ml) brandy (Paul Masson
  Grande Amber VS)

½ ounce (15 ml) London Dry gin

2 ounces (60 ml) fresh lemon juice

1 ounce (30 ml) fresh orange juice

¾ ounce (22 ml) orgeat (see page 244)

½ ounce (15 ml) dry sherry, to float

Orange wheel, for garnish

Cherry, for garnish

Shake ingredients, except sherry, with ice and strain into an ice-filled highball glass. Float the sherry on top using the back of a bar spoon. Garnish with the orange slice and cherry.

RED SNAPPER

Crisp, tomato, herbs, tamarind

- ● -

Pair a Snapper with poached eggs and toast, or a caviar brunch.

Freshly squeezed tomato juice is the backbone for this stunning, garden-fresh version of a Bloody Mary. It's the exact opposite of a kitchen-sink brunch drink. Use a juicer to express the tomato water or push chopped tomatoes through a sieve using the back of large spoon. Don't fuss about it! It's worth it. You'll never buy canned 'mater juice again. Amazingly, this recipe can be traced back to 1930s Paris. The Red Snapper is clarity, simplicity, and purity. Use ripe—even very ripe—tomatoes for the best results.

FOR THE SALT RIM

1 teaspoon celery salt

½ teaspoon black pepper

Dash of cayenne pepper

FOR THE COCKTAIL

3 ounces (90 ml) gin (Plymouth)

6 ounces (175 ml) fresh tomato juice
(about three medium ripe tomatoes)

1 ounce (30 ml) fresh lemon juice

6 drops hot sauce (Tabasco)

Dash of Worcestershire sauce

Dash of Angostura bitters

Green olive, for garnish

Lemon wheel, for garnish

Prepare a glass with a salt rim (technique, page 264). Shake ingredients with ice, and strain into the ice-filled glass. To garnish, spear olive and lemon with a cocktail pick.

MEZCALADA

Smoke, heat, lime, salt

- -

Intensely flavored and light on alcohol, this is a perfect cocktail to accompany morning huevos rancheros or chilaquiles.

A takeoff on the Michelada—a Mexican beer, lime, and hot sauce drink sold at roadside stands and bars below the border—the Mezcalada is its smokier, brunch-ready cousin. An easy-to-make party concoction, this drink can be batched in advance and stored in the fridge—just add the beer before serving.

FOR CHIPOTLE PURÉE

1 can (7 ounces) chipotle peppers, in adobe sauce

FOR THE COCKTAIL

4 ounces (120 ml) Mexican beer (Tecate or Corona)

½ ounce (15 ml) mezcal (Del Maguey)

½ ounce (1 tablespoon or 15 ml) chipotle pepper purée

1½ ounces (45 ml) Clamato Picante

¾ ounce (2 ml) fresh lime juice

Smoked sea salt, to rim the glass

To make the chipotle purée, pour peppers and adobe sauce in a blender or food processer and pulse until smooth.

For the cocktail, rim a chilled rocks glass with salt (technique, page 264). Dry shake chipotle purée, mezcal, Clamato, and lime juice. Pour over ice and top with beer. Give the mix a quick stir, and serve.

ABSINTHE FRAPPÉ

Intense, herbaceous, spirituous

••••

Think of this as a boozy licorice slushy—rousing after a big lunch, terrific after a salty muffuletta crammed full of cured meats.

Before the American ban on absinthe in 1912, drinking an Absinthe Frappé in the morning was fashionable. Today, the ban on absinthe has been lifted, and a little wormwood for breakfast is no longer taboo, especially in New Orleans at bars like the Old Absinthe House. Frappé comes from the French word *frapper*, meaning to knock or beat, referring to the crushed ice used to make this hot weather livener.

1½ ounces (45 ml) absinthe

½ ounce (15 ml) Anis del Mono, or French anisette (optional)

½ ounce (15 ml) simple syrup (page 241)

Mint sprig, for garnish

Shake and strain over a small rocks glass heaped with crushed or shaved ice. Garnish with mint, and serve with a straw.

GIN RICKEY

Effervescent, juniper, lime

••••

Simply exhilarating paired with a Caesar salad or a plate of cucumbers, sliced and salted.

A Rickey is a sugar-free cocktail made with spirits, lime, and seltzer water. It purportedly got its start in a Washington D.C. bar called Shoomaker's, where a charismatic lobbyist by the name of "Colonel" Joe Rickey took a shine to this simple combination. He encouraged others to try it, and launched a fad that reached the local press. The *Washington Post* ran his claim that seltzer and lime cooled the blood, whereas sugar "heated" it. The colonel preferred his Rickey with whiskey, but gin became much more popular. It's our go-to highball a clean, quick fix after a long day at work.

2 ounces (60 ml) London Dry gin (Beefeater)

½ ounce (15 ml) lime juice

2 to 3 ounces (60 to 90 ml) seltzer or mineral water

Lime wheel, for garnish

Pour lime juice into an ice-filled highball glass. Add gin and top with sparkling water. Stir briefly and garnish with a lime wheel on the rim of the glass.

A COCKTAIL FOR ALL SEASONS

SPRING

Lean on Fizzes and Sours for light and enlivening drinks that feature green herbs or slivers of spring produce. A sprig of mint or dill tucked along the edge of a glass can be reviving on a gray day. This is a perfect time to make a Strawberry Shrub (page 248) with fresh berries from the market and to incorporate the first cucumbers into a Pimm's Cup (page 171). Floral flavors from bottles of St. Germaine or crème de Violette are reminiscent of the first wildflowers along forest paths. We suggest:

Gin Fizz (page 42)

Aviation (page 65)

St. Germain Cocktail (page 209)

Chartreuse Swizzle (page 198)

The Last Tango in Modena (page 141)

Juniper and Tonic (page 233)

Moral Suasion (page 34)

SUMMER

Break out the highball glasses for tall coolers featuring melon, berries, or stone fruit. This is barbecue weather, so consider incorporating coconut milk and layered tiki drinks into your repertoire, especially for evening affairs. Or, expand your tequila selection to include smoky mezcal. This is a great season to explore rum and rhum agricole, or to pick up a bottle of cachaça. In the afternoons, low-proof cocktails (page 231) can be less dehydrating for those who enjoy imbibing in the sun. The sharply herbaceous flavor of absinthe revives after a day on the beach, as does homemade ginger beer (page 247). We suggest:

Gin Basil Smash (page 142)

Absinthe Frappé (page 161)

Highland Cooler (page 174)

Mezcalada (page 160)

Red Snapper (page 158)

Sky Juice (page 201)

FALL

Move to warming flavors and umber colors in the fall. Try a cocktail featuring dark beer or hard cider, and play off notes of apple, pear, or pumpkin. Use this season to experiment with applejack and Calvados, two apple-based spirits that appear in numerous recipes, adding musky fruit tones. As the days shorten, serve hot drinks and heavier flavors with cocktails that feature sherry or an amaro made with bitter herbs; this is a good time to break out a bottle of Fernet-Branca or Cynar. We suggest:

Doctor Cocktail (page 100)   Roasted Apple Toddy (page 216)

Butternut and Falernum (page 138)   Lion's Tail (page 108)

Claret Cup (page 211)

WINTER

Spirituous drinks, like Manhattans and Old Fashioneds, are especially welcome during the cold months—they're dark and warming, yet festive. It's a good time to work your way through some of the finer vermouths on the market, such as Carpano Antica or Vya, and to experiment with boozy infusions, like bacon-infused bourbon, for gifting or for serving at a holiday party. Creamy nogs and Milk Punch (page 157) can be used in place of dessert after a heavy meal. They're ideal pairings for gingerbread, candied fruit, nuts, and spice cookies. We suggest:

Benton's Old Fashioned (page 140)   Brandy Alexander (page 223)

Penicillin (page 135)   Blood and Sand (page 71)

Sazerac (page 37)   Tom and Jerry (page 219)

Grasshopper (page 229)

REFRESHING EVERYDAY & PARTY STARTERS

The cocktails in this chapter include the Gin and Tonic, the Mint Julep, and the Pimm's Cup—cocktails so agreeable you can relax with them daily. We've also compiled some of our favorite party drinks, many of them modern classics. We love to dazzle guests with tastes they've never encountered in a drink before and with cocktails that are stunning in color. Intro to Aperol (page 165), for example, is the famous bitters cocktail created by bartender Audrey Saunders—it looks like a ruby sunset in a rocks glass, and it goes down as easy as fresh-squeezed pink grapefruit juice. The deep-purple Bramble (page 178) brings a room full of chatter to a hush, especially when it's presented over shaved ice with fresh blackberries speared on cocktail forks.

The Flutterby Lassi (page 176) is our favorite palate cleanser, especially between courses during a spicy meal. It combines yogurt, cucumber, and absinthe to create a silk sari of a drink that practically floats inside a chilled coupe. Fresh and unexpected, it's a cocktail that raises eyebrows and causes people to recline across couches, content and bemused.

INTRO TO APEROL

Citrus, herbaceous, orange

• • • •

Gorgeously colored, this is a vibrant pool-side drink. Serve with prawns, avocado, and a spinach salad.

Bartender Audrey Saunders invented the recipe to introduce squeamish Americans to the wonders of bitter cocktails. One of the best party drinks ever invented, it's a universal crowd pleaser that features Aperol (page 90), a glowing aperitif made in part from crushed orange peels. Buoyed by gin and lemon, Aperol's slightly bitter finish becomes polished and palatable, even for those who frown at the thought of bitter flavors.

2 ounces (60 ml) Aperol

1 ounce (30 ml) London Dry gin (Beefeater)

¾ ounce (22 ml) fresh lemon juice

¼ ounce (7 ml) simple syrup (page 241)

Dash of Angostura bitters

Orange peel, for garnish

Shake ingredients with ice and strain into a chilled coupe glass. Garnish with an orange peel perched on the rim of the glass.

PAPER PLANE

Woodsy, bitter, bright

• • • •

Serve as a starter with bacon-wrapped dates and hard cheese, like pecorino or manchego.

Created by Sam Ross at Milk & Honey in New York, this complex sipper has spawned a multitude of variations: Paper Airplane, Paper Jetplane, Balsa Airplane, and more. In addition to how easy this modern classic is to adapt, it is a surprise for drinkers who think they don't like brown spirits. While the combination looks rich and heavy on the page, it transforms into a light drink in the glass.

¾ ounce (22 ml) bourbon (Elijah Craig)

¾ ounce (22 ml) amaro (Nonino Quintessentia)

¾ ounce (22 ml) Aperol

¾ ounce (22 ml) fresh lemon juice

Lemon peel, for garnish

Shake ingredients with ice and strain into a chilled coupe glass. Garnish with the lemon peel on the rim of the glass.

GIN AND TONIC

Fresh, bitter, medicinal, juniper

· · · · ·

Smoky and spicy flavors meld well with the G&T's snappy flavor profile. Think smoked salmon, almonds, or oysters.

Anywhere there are Brits, someone will ask, "Fancy a Gin and Tonic?" Originally, tonic made with quinine was used to prevent malaria among colonials stationed in India and Africa. But the drink that was born as a way to make taking medicine palatable morphed into a national passion. Today there are all sorts of quality tonics on the market, spawned by the emergence of multitudinous craft gins. For one of our favorite craft G&T combinations, we use the very botanical Junipero gin, which pairs beautifully with Fentimans tonic.

2 ounces (60 ml) gin (Junipero or Blue Coat)

3 ounces (90 ml) tonic water, or 1 ounce (30 ml) tonic syrup (page 251) and 2 to 3 ounces seltzer

Lime wedge, for garnish

Fill a rocks glass with ice. Add gin and tonic water. Stir briefly. Garnish with a lime wedge in the glass.

TOM COLLINS/ JOHN COLLINS

Effervescent, lemon, juniper

· · · · ·

The sweet-sour notes of this drink meld well with a chicken salad sandwich or cold pasta salad. It loves common herbs like basil, rosemary, or thyme. Try it with pesto.

The Collins is often confused with a Gin Fizz (served without ice in a short glass) or a Gin Rickey (usually made with lime instead of lemon, and no sugar). The tall Collins glass, which rose to preeminence in New York during the 1850s, was a way to harness fizziness and dazzle drinkers with something fresh and new when bottled soda waters first appeared on the market. This drink should always be served in a tall glass with a straw, and should properly be made using Old Tom gin, which is a sweeter style that originated before London Dry. Also, try the John Collins, which employs genever, gin's malty precursor.

2 ounces (60 ml) Old Tom gin or Bols Genever

1 ounce (30 ml) fresh lemon juice

$1/2$ ounce (15 ml) simple syrup (page 241)

3 to 4 ounces (90 to 120 ml) soda water

Lemon wheel, for garnish

Shake ingredients, except soda water, with ice and strain into a highball—or Collins—glass filled with ice. Top with soda water and garnish with a lemon wheel on the rim of the glass. Serve with a straw.

BUILD YOUR OWN
GIN AND TONIC BAR

The humble G&T has entered the craft age, thanks to a wave of artisan gins and small-batch tonics, including Fever-Tree and Jack Rudy's tonic syrup. In Spain, the drink has evolved into an art form called "Gintonic." Bartenders in the Basque region are known for wheeling out a cart with a variety of options so customers can create their own blends. It is common to pair wild garnishes—liquorice, pink peppercorns, star anise—to specific botanicals in the spirit.

If you're a G&T fan, why not experiment? Pick up a couple of new bottles, or ask to sample a flight of gins in a bar—you'll taste (and smell) a huge difference between brands and styles. Some gins have strong herbal notes, like thyme or sage, while others are citrus-forward or slightly sweet—depending on the formula.

Host a tasting party at which guests can sample multiple combinations. In addition to limes, set out a variety of garnishes that can be used to accentuate particular flavor notes. These can be muddled in the bottom of the glass or served on the rim: cucumber wheels, grapefruit slivers, strawberries, and sprigs of fresh thyme, dill, and sage.

Our tasting notes in the back of this book can help you choose some new gins (page 273). We also have a recipe for homemade tonic (page 251).

MINT JULEP

Enlivening, mint, woodsy

• • • •

Pair a julep with fried oysters, a burger, or a club sandwich. The mint brings refreshment to a salty, heavy lunch.

Today, juleps are associated with bourbon, mint, and the Kentucky Derby, but the word *julep* dates back to the 1400s and the Persian word *gul-ab*, meaning "rosewater." The drink developed in the Southern United States, where it originally included peach brandy, and became famous throughout the world. The proper making of a julep is hotly contested—some call for muddling the mint with sugar, others prefer a minted syrup, while strict Bourbonites call for no mint at all except as a garnish. Use crushed ice—or shaved—and plenty of mint. If you're making just one, muddle by all means. But if you're serving a crowd, make a mint syrup (page 243) to batch multiple drinks quickly.

Note: For a novel variation, slip a slice of bourbon soaked peach into the bottom of the glass before adding ice.

2 ounces (60 ml) bourbon (Four Roses)

½ ounce (15 ml) simple syrup (page 241)

6 mint leaves, plus sprig for garnish

Muddle mint and simple syrup in a rocks glass or silver julep cup. Top with crushed or shaved ice. Pour the bourbon over the top, and stir until the cup frosts. Garnish with a sprig of mint and serve with a straw.

PIMM'S CUP

Fruity, herbaceous, vegetal

• • • •

A Pimm's cup is smashing with fresh oysters and with seafood, especially lobster rolls.

Springy and fresh, the Pimm's Cup may be the original garden cocktail with its floating coins of cucumber. Lemon and ginger join at the hip with a special spirit, Pimm's No. 1, a tea-colored liqueur that was invented by the owner of a British oyster bar. It has been sold commercially since 1859, when it was first promoted by bicycle hawkers. Today, it's still enjoyed across London, and drinking a tall Pimm's Cup on the lawn of the Tate Modern with the River Thames in view is a must for any summer traveler. Variations on this recipe include soda water and Prosecco, but we like the classic combination of Pimm's and ginger beer, preferably homemade.

2 ounces (60 ml) Pimm's No. 1

½ ounce (15 ml) fresh lemon juice

5 ounces (148 ml) ginger beer (page 247)

4 mint leaves

1 strawberry, sliced

Cucumber slices, for garnish

Gently muddle mint and strawberry with lemon juice in a rocks glass. Add Pimm's, ice, and top with ginger beer. Stir and garnish with cucumber slices in the glass.

COCKTAILS FOR A CHEESE BOARD

The key to pairing cocktails with a few hunks of cheese is to select harmonizing or contrasting flavors. Herbaceous notes in gin are fantastic for underscoring hints of wild pasture in hard, salty sheep's milk cheeses, like rough-hewn Italian pecorino.

Plummy notes in vermouth, port, or sherry drinks temper salty notes in blues, like Stilton or Roquefort. Whiskey or Scotch-based drinks purr around earthy cheeses, like clothbound Cheddars, and smoked cheeses.

Champagnes are fabulous with luxe cheeses, like triple crèmes— hence, the classic pairing of Champagne with Brie.

For a casual mixer or an after-dinner cheese board, serve a combination of clothbound cheddar, pecorino, and Stilton with assorted nuts, honey, dried fruit, flatbreads, and any of the following cocktails.

GIN: Gibson (page 102), Martinez (page 46),
Colony Cocktail (page 71)

SHERRY OR VERMOUTH: Dubonnet Cocktail (page 66),
Bamboo (page 51)

SCOTCH: Highland Cooler (page 52), Rob Roy (page 174)

CHAMPAGNE: French 75 (page 60),
Champagne Cocktail (page 205)

JERSEY COCKTAIL

Apple, spice, lemon

— • • • —

Pork chops and baked squash are an ideal pairing here. For lunch, try a burger.

New Jersey was once known as the land of apple orchards, and it's still home to Laird & Company—the country's oldest maker of applejack. This cider-centric drink appears in print in 1887 but is probably older. Today, cider is experiencing a renaissance, and it's worth trying new varieties with this recipe to see how they perform. Think of this drink as a summery mulled cider, though it works year-round. Along similar lines, we also love the Jersey Sour: cider, lemon juice, shaken and topped with berries.

4 ounces (120 ml) hard cider

2 dashes Angostura bitters

½ teaspoon simple syrup (page 241)

Lemon twist and 3 thin apple slices, for garnish

Fill a rocks glass with ice and add the bitters and simple syrup. Top with hard cider and stir. To garnish, fan the apple slices along the side of the glass and add a lemon twist.

HIGHLAND COOLER

Woodsy, citrus, richly aromatic

— • • • —

Picnic perfect—try alongside cured salmon, grilled meats, or apples and cheese.

Serious Scotch drinkers and men of the kilt should avert their eyes here—we mean no offense by "sullying" Scotch with ginger and lemon. But think of it this way: on a forest picnic, you might crave a peaty refresher, and say you have a hip flask with a bit of Scotch sloshing about? Why not break off a branch for a stirring rod, spread out your tartan blanket, and serve yourself one of these for a change? A scrap of moss makes a very nice coaster.

1 ounce (30 ml) blended Scotch (Dewar's or Famous Grouse)

1 teaspoon powdered sugar

1 ounce (30 ml) fresh lemon juice

2 dashes Angostura bitters

4 ounces (120 ml) ginger beer (page 247)

Lemon wheel, for garnish

Add ingredients to a highball glass filled with ice and stir. Garnish with a lemon wheel in the glass.

SHANDYGAFF

Ginger, yeast, spice

— • • • • —

A Shandygaff loves bar snacks, like soft pretzels or fries, or a meaty sandwich.

Who doesn't want a Shandygaff based on the name alone? If you're a ginger-aholic or a low-proof lover, embrace this easy sipper. The combination of beer and ginger dates back to at least the 1800s, so it's surprising that the Shandygaff hasn't held more sway as an American classic. Proportions should be adjusted depending on the flavor profile of the beer and ginger you choose, but in general, this is an equal-parts affair. In fall and winter, we like to move toward darker beers and dash in a few drops of Angostura bitters.

½ pint (240 ml) hefeweizen or pilsner

½ pint (240 ml) ginger beer (page 247)

Combine ingredients in a pint glass. Stir briefly, then serve.

LAMBIC SANGRIA

Sparkling, peach, berry, mint

— • • • • —

In summer, serve this on the back porch with fried chicken and biscuits.

Most sangria calls for wine, sugar, fruit juice, and something effervescent, but lambic—a Belgian fruit-based beer—is a quick sangria hack. You get delicate sweetness, plenty of effervescence, and you don't need to load up on extra sugar. This recipe calls for peach lambic, which is widely available, but you can also explore other lambic varieties, including framboise (raspberry) or kriek (cherry) and experiment with different spirits. Adapted from a recipe that we love from The Kitchn, this sangria is especially winning during peach season. Because lambic is sold in large bottles, this creation is designed to fill a pitcher.

SERVES 6

1 bottle (750 ml) peach lambic, chilled

¼ cup (177 ml) rye whiskey (Four Roses)

¾ cup (94 g) chopped peaches

¾ cup (94 g) chopped strawberries

8 to 10 fresh mint leaves

1½ cups (355 ml) club soda, chilled

Combine fruit, mint, and rye whiskey in a large pitcher and let steep for 30 minutes. Add lambic and club soda. Stir briefly, and serve in ice-filled tumblers or wine glasses.

KENTUCKY BUCK

Ginger, citrus, clove

— • • • • —

This buck goes especially well with Carolina-pulled pork and vinegary slaw.

A buck, also called a mule, is any drink containing liquor, citrus, and ginger beer or ginger ale. It's an easy pleaser at parties and a way to show off your own fermented ginger beer, which is a snap to make and takes just a couple of days to prep in advance (page 247). Back in the late 1800s, the buck gained popularity (thanks to a singer of "light opera" named Mamie Taylor who loved it) and it fizzed its way on through Prohibition. We love this bourbon-based update, created by Erick Castro at San Francisco's Bourbon & Branch, because it's a summer drink that tastes good all the way through fall, thanks to the Angostura.

2 ounces (60 ml) rye whiskey (Rittenhouse)

¾ ounce (22 ml) fresh lemon juice

1 strawberry, halved

½ ounce (15 ml) simple syrup (page 241)

2 to 3 ounces (60 to 90 ml) chilled ginger beer (page 247)

2 dashes Angostura bitters, for garnish

Lemon wheel, for garnish

Muddle lemon juice and half a strawberry in a mixing glass. Add ice, bourbon, and simple syrup. Shake with ice and strain into a rocks glass. Top with ginger beer. Garnish with bitters, a lemon wheel, and half a strawberry.

FLUTTERBY LASSI ············

Creamy, mint, citrus, cucumber

— • • • • —

A brilliant pairing for tandoori chicken or other spicy dishes from the subcontinent.

This unexpected libation originally calls for Butterfly Boston absinthe, but other absinthes will do—or even Pastis. A spin-off of the yogurt drink so popular in India, Bangladesh, and Pakistan, the Flutterby Lassi is a breezy blend of cucumber and dill. Muddling the two together releases flavor notes that uplift the absinthe's mintiness and soften its intensity. Sip this as a digestif while listening to sitar music, and float away in a restorative meditation. This recipe is adapted from Gymkhana restaurant in London.

1 ounce (30 ml) absinthe (Butterfly Boston)

½ ounce (15 ml) fresh lime juice

½ ounce (15 ml) simple syrup (page 241)

2 ounces (60 ml) yogurt

3 small dill sprigs, separated

2 slices of English cucumber, peeled

Cucumber peel, to garnish

In a shaker, muddle 2 sprigs of dill and the cucumber. Add the remaining ingredients with ice and shake, then double-strain. To garnish, roll a long cucumber peel into a scroll and stick with a sprig of dill.

DEATH IN THE GULF STREAM

Glacial, citrus, spice

◆·◆·◆

Superb on a dock at sunset, alongside grilled or pan-fried fish.

The effect of this Hemingway favorite is like diving into polar waters. Bright and astringent, it resets the brain and makes you almost sputter. According to the instructions of Charles H. Baker: "Take a tall thin water tumbler and fill it with finely cracked ice. Lace this broken debris with four purple splashes of Angostura, add the juice and crushed peel of 1 green lime, and fill the glass almost full with Holland gin. . . . No sugar, no fancying." If you prefer a truly bracing experience, leave the sugar out. Hemingway would have, but most bartenders today add a teaspoon of sweetness to bring the genever and lime together.

2 ounces (60 ml) genever (Bols)

1 sugar cube (or 1 teaspoon sugar)

4 dashes Angostura bitters

Half a large lime, cut into wedges for muddling

In a rocks glass, top the sugar cube with bitters. Let this sit for 2 minutes to dissolve. Add the lime wedges and muddle. Then add ice and genever and stir briefly.

BRAMBLE

Blackberry, citrus, aromatic

◆·◆·◆

Jammy and acidic, this deserves to be served with a wedge of whiffy Taleggio cheese and a plate of spicy charcuterie.

Dick Bradsell is credited with the creation of this drink, which spread like wildfire from Fred's Club in London through all of Britain but is still a relative rarity in the United States. It's a conundrum, because the concoction has all the attributes of a runaway hit—it's pretty, easy to drink, delicious, and glamorous. There are other historic drinks with similar ingredients, like the Parisian and the Arnaud, but they're just not as good. It's the lemon juice—it brings freshness and acidity. Note that this drink calls for blackberry liqueur (crème de mûres), but you can use black currant (crème de cassis). It's lovely to muddle fresh blackberries in the bottom of the glass, if you have extra, and to serve this over shaved ice.

1½ ounces (45 ml) gin (Plymouth)

¾ ounces (22 ml) crème de mûres or crème de cassis

¾ ounce (22 ml) fresh lemon juice

½ ounce (15 ml) simple syrup (page 241)

3 blackberries, for garnish

Lemon twist, for garnish

Shake ingredients with ice and strain into a rocks glass filled with crushed (or shaved) ice. Garnish with a skewer of blackberries, and slip in the lemon twist.

PUNCH

Long before cocktails, there were punches. The word is ancient—from the Hindi word *panch*, meaning "five elements"—and was picked up by the English from India during the 1600s. A properly made punch includes alcohol, sugar, lemon, water, and tea or spices.

Since their heyday as a communal rite, punches have gotten something of an undeserved bad reputation, thanks to the potent mystery bowls that are popular at college parties. David Wondrich's book, *Punch!* (2010), has helped restore these concoctions to their proper dignity. To this end, a number of punch houses have emerged to return punches to their original social function and esteem, among them: New York's Dead Rabbit, Chicago's Punch House, Boston's Drink, Pasadena's Punch, and London's Punch Room at the Edition Hotel, just to name a few.

Because the art of punch-making is its own special branch of the cocktail world, we include only a few recipes here. They're easy-to-make holdovers from the punch era that can be executed in a relative jiffy. Think of them as punch "light," if you please—not requiring too-expensive ingredients, whale blubber, or tricky flaming techniques.

BOURBON SWEET TEA

Citrus, floral, woodsy

• •

Serve with southern snacks, like pimento cheese sand-wiches and fried chicken. This easy, make-ahead punch fits well into a festive summer picnic. It's also an exciting little pick-me-up to serve on a camping trip.

Like a true punch, the recipe calls for a combination of sweet and sour ingredients, along with black tea. Many versions of this southern classic call for juice concentrates, but use fresh fruit. A proper punch starts with muddling citrus peels in sugar and letting them sit for about an hour to draw out the oils in the skin, creating what's called *oleo saccharum* (for more details, see page 261). While this step will lift your sweet tea flavor into the heavens, it can be left out—just omit the extra peel.

SERVES 6 TO 8

1 cup (240 ml) bourbon (Buffalo Trace)

Peel of half a lemon

½ cup (100 g) Demerara sugar

3 black tea bags

3 cups (710 ml) boiling water

1 lemon, sliced into wedges

1 lime, sliced into wedges

1 orange, sliced into wedges

Mint sprigs, for garnish

Muddle lemon peel in the sugar in a bowl and let sit for 1 hour on the counter. In a large pitcher, steep tea bags in 3 cups of boiling water for 5 minutes. Remove the tea bags, let cool briefly, and stir in the sugar mixture. Remove peel. Once the mixture cools to room temperature, add the bourbon and the citrus wedges. Chill and serve over ice with mint to garnish.

PHILADELPHIA FISH HOUSE PUNCH

Rummy, tart, citrus

• •

Break out grandmother's punch bowl, or pack this historic punch in a thermos and take it fishing—in the spirit of our American forefathers.

It would be remiss not to include perhaps the most famous of American punches, a creation which stems from an early gentlemen's fishing club that declared its own statehood on an island in Philadelphia's Schuylkill River. According to legend, George Washington enjoyed a few rounds of Fish House Punch on one of his visits (a fishing weekend?) and was unable to write in his diary for three days. Blissfully stiff, this potion should be prepared the night before a party to meld the flavors of citrus, brandy, and rum.

SERVES 12 TO 15

1 bottle (750 ml) dark rum (El Dorado 5 Yr)

1½ cups (355 ml) brandy (Pierre Ferrand Ambre)

2 ounces (30 ml) peach brandy or liqueur (Mathilde)

Peel of 3 lemons

¾ cups (150 g) Demerara sugar

3 cups (710 ml) hot water

1½ cups (355 ml) lemon juice (6 to 8 lemons)

8 x 8-inch (20 cm) ice block

Freeze ice in a mold or bowl. In a large pitcher or jar, muddle lemon peels in sugar and let the mixture sit for 1 hour on the counter. Remove lemon peels and stir in hot water (not boiling) until the sugar dissolves. Cool, then add rum, brandy, lemon juice, and peach brandy. Cover and store in the refrigerator for 4 hours, or overnight. Serve in a punch bowl with ice block.

ST. CECILIA PUNCH

Tart, rummy, effervescent

• •

Turn on the Southern charm with a smorgasbord of crab cakes, fried chicken, potato salad, greens, beans, pecan sandies, and this punch.

Brothers Matt and Ted Lee, authors of the extraordinary *The Lee Bros. Southern Cookbook*, created a modern update on the St. Cecilia punch—a beverage associated with an exclusive ladies club in Charleston, South Carolina, that dates back to 1767. Sweetened with fresh pineapple and peaches, this ornamental drink deserves an ice block and a vintage bowl. It makes a stunning centerpiece on a holiday sideboard and is ideal for a Sunday gathering, a shower, or a reunion. If you don't have access to ripe peaches, use frozen organic ones. We've adapted this recipe using simple syrup; you can also substitute our minted syrup (page 243) or honey ginger syrup (page 242).

SERVES 10 TO 12

3 cups (710 ml) brandy (Paul Masson Grande Amber VS)

¾ ounce (22 ml) dark rum (El Dorado 5 Yr)

2 teaspoons grated fresh ginger

2 lemons, thinly sliced

3 ripe peaches, thinly sliced

3 cups (710 ml) brewed strong black tea (preferably a Breakfast Blend)

1 small pineapple, peeled, cored, and sliced into thin half-moons

2 ounces (60 ml) simple syrup (page 241)

1 bottle (750 ml) of dry Champagne (or crémant)

1 quart (950 ml) seltzer water

1 round block of ice

Place the ginger in a tea strainer, or wrap it in cheesecloth or a coffee filter. Place it in a 2-quart mason jar or pitcher, along with the lemons and peaches. Add brandy, rum, and tea. Cover and refrigerate for at least 2 hours.

To make the punch, discard the ginger and place the peach mixture in a 6-quart punch bowl. Add Champagne and seltzer, along with ice.

TIKI, TROPICAL & BEYOND

Tropical and tiki drinks have a bad reputation for being too sweet, too kitschy, and too difficult to make with their combination of hard-to-find juices and esoteric liqueurs. But constructed of quality ingredients, and in proper proportion, they are among the most thrillingly delicious and culinary of all cocktails. Your extra effort will be rewarded.

Entrepreneurs Victor J. Bergeron (of Trader Vic fame) and Don the Beachcomber (born Ernest Raymond Beaumont Gantt) revolutionized cocktails, layering rums with tropical fruit juices and setting them in a Polynesian wonderland that brought happy hour to the beachfront. Down went the cocktail glass of the speakeasy sin dens, and up came the shapely hurricane of outdoor paradise.

Today there's a tiki revival underway, with tropical drinks getting their proper due, thanks to writers like Jeff Berry (*Beach Bum Barry's Grog Log*), and bars like Chicago's Three Dots and a Dash or San Francisco's Smuggler's Cove.

More of a rum-induced, scantily-clad dream than a riff on a specific place, tiki's Polynesian romance is caught up in the story of the Caribbean—hence the Navy Grogs and island drinks. We add to these a few food-friendly, must-know classics from the tropics and beyond that belong in your repertoire, including the Caipirinha (page 203) from Brazil and the Pisco Sour (page 199), so beloved in Peru and Chile.

NAVY GROG

Fiery, citrus, caramel, vanilla

— • • • • —

This is a drink born for ribs and game, or beans and rice served with grilled pineapple.

Trader Vic championed this popular tiki drink on his restaurant menus, substituting Pimento Dram (an allspice liqueur, such as St. Elizabeth) for the honey syrup, which adds flavors of nutmeg and clove—a nice touch, especially if you're celebrating Christmas in July. Navy Grog dates back to the 1700s as a drink for sailors, where rum was combined with lemon, spices, and honey or molasses to prevent scurvy. During the height of tiki fever, this drink was sometimes served with a special ice cone—you can still find Navy Grog ice-cone makers in kitchen stores and online.

1 ounce (30 ml) light rum (Flor de Caña 4 Yr)

1 ounce (30 ml) dark rum (Appleton Estate Extra)

1 ounce (30 ml) Demerara rum (El Dorado 5 Yr)

¾ ounce (22 ml) fresh lime juice

¾ ounce (22 ml) fresh grapefruit juice

¾ ounce (22 ml) honey syrup (page 242)

1 ounce (30 ml) club soda

Mint sprig, for garnish

Shake ingredients, except soda, with ice and strain into a rocks glass filled with ice. Top with club soda and garnish with the sprig of mint.

BUMBO

Robust, coconut, spice

— • • • • —

This makes a fun Halloween party starter. Serve with Caribbean-spiced wings or fried plantains.

Arrgh! This be the drink of pirates. Similar to Navy Grog, but traditionally made without citrus, Bumbo was the preferred drink of swashbucklers. Surprisingly, the concoction was also commonly used to bribe voters during elections, employed even by George Washington in his campaign for the Virginia House of Burgess. While the classic recipe adds a little water to overproof rum, we like to add coconut water to aged rum for fuller flavor.

2 ounces (60 ml) aged rum (Flor de Caña 12 Year)

2 ounces (60 ml) coconut water

½ teaspoon molasses

Freshly grated nutmeg, for garnish

Dash of cinnamon, for garnish

Lime wedge, for garnish

Shake ingredients with ice, and strain into a rocks glass with a large ice cube. Garnish with the lime wedge.

MAI TAI

Citrus, vanilla, spice, pineapple, mint

– • • • –

One of our favorite party drinks. Serve with glazed pork or chicken skewers.

....

A signature drink at Trader Vic restaurants, this 1940s invention is sadly often served as a sticky umbrella drink designed to deliver more kick than class. The original formula, however, called for high-shelf liquor, including a 17-year Jamaican rum, along with orgeat and orange curaçao, for subtlety. "Trader Vic" Bergeron shook the drink and strained it over shaved ice—no blender at all—and when he served his first edition to a couple from Tahiti, the wife reputedly exclaimed, "Mai Tai!"—*out of this world!* And so the grande dame of tiki drinks was born. Made with high-quality ingredients, this cocktail is a stunner.

   1 ounce (30 ml) dark rum (Appleton
     Estate Extra)

   1 ounce (30 ml) amber rum (Clement VSOP)

   ½ ounce (15 ml) orange curaçao (Pierre
     Ferrand)

   1 ounce (30 ml) fresh lime juice

   ¼ ounce (7 ml) orgeat (page 244)

   Mint sprig, for garnish

   Lime wheel, for garnish

Shake ingredients with ice and strain into a rocks glass filled with ice. Garnish with lime and mint.

MISSIONARY'S DOWNFALL

Peach-pineapple, honey, mint

– • • • –

Put on some R&B, and roast a chicken. This is a two-person drink that likes spice and slow beats.

....

Considered a Don the Beachcomber masterpiece, the Downfall is an example of his garden-to-glass ethos, prefiguring that sensibility by a good seventy years. It's easy to see why this minty pineapple slush became a sensation in tiki bars around the country. Like the best cocktails from this era, the taste of alcohol completely disappears into an herbaceous embrace. Whatever you do, don't pick out a bottom-shelf peach brandy. We use Mathilde Pêche—properly a liqueur, not brandy—but It works well.

MAKES 2 (OR 1 LARGE DRINK)

   2 ounces (60 ml) light rum (Flor de Caña
     4 Yr)

   1 ounce (30 ml) peach brandy (Mathilde
     Pêche)

   2 ounces (60 ml) honey syrup (see page
     242)

   1 ounce (30 ml) fresh lime juice

   ½ cup (65 g) diced fresh pineapple

   ¼ cup (5 g) loosely packed mint leaves,
     plus a few leaves to garnish

Combine all ingredients in a blender with ice. Pour into a pair of chilled cocktail glasses and garnish with a sprig of mint.

ORGEAT

Orgeat (pronounced OR-zsat in English, or, OR-zsa in French) is a nonalcoholic almond-based syrup that tastes like marzipan. It appears as a frequent ingredient in tiki drinks, most famously in the Mai Tai (page 185), but also in early drinks such as the Japanese Cocktail (page 33). It lends thick texture along with a touch of *je ne sais quoi*, thanks to the addition of orange flower water. This is one of the great mixers in the entire cocktailian toolbox—you've never had a Mai Tai until you've had one with high-quality orgeat. Most commercial versions contain stabilizers or high-fructose corn syrup, so we supply an easy-to-make recipe on page 244.

FALERNUM

Falernum is a key tiki ingredient with a fuzzy past. It's a sweetened lime and spice syrup that most likely hails from the island of Barbados. It's old enough that Charles Dickens mentioned it in his travel writings, and it's sold as both a liqueur (John D. Taylor's Velvet Falernum) and a nonalcoholic version (such as Fee Brothers). Recipes for falernum vary (see ours on page 246), but its flavor profile typically contains almonds, ginger, allspice, and cloves.

TEST PILOT

Intricate, fresh, vanilla, spice, orange

- • • • -

Mussels in coconut broth or squash curry pair well, thanks to the spice combination here—think licorice and clove.

Pernod in a Tiki drink? That was just one of the ingredients that Don the Beachcomber loved to layer into his signature potions, which—at their best—managed to be both exotic and intellectually interesting. His flair for spice-opulent concoctions that delivered waves of flavor took mixology in a new direction. In appearance, tiki drinks were as flamboyant as Don was in person (he loved hats and bone necklaces)—demanding a bar full of garnishes.

1½ ounces (45 ml) dark rum
(Appleton Estate Extra)

¾ ounce (22 ml) light rum
(Flor de Caña 4 Yr)

3 teaspoons Cointreau

½ ounce (15 ml) falernum

⅛ teaspoon Pernod

½ ounce (15 ml) fresh lime juice

Dash of Angostura bitters

Cherry and pineapple wedge, to garnish

Shake ingredients with ice and serve in a rocks glass over crushed ice. Garnish with the cherry and pineapple wedge on a cocktail pick.

THREE DOTS & A DASH

Spirituous, allspice, citrus, pineapple

- • • • -

A sensational drink with luau fare, like roast pork and salads served in carved-out melons.

A cult Don Beachcomber concoction, the original recipe for this cocktail was designed to celebrate the end of World War II. Don garnished the drink with a skewer driven through three cherries and a strip of pineapple, forming three dots and a dash—Morse Code for the "V" in Victory. Complexly spiced, this can be served on the rocks or as a blended drink.

1½ ounces (45 ml) amber rum
(Clement VSOP)

1 ounce (30 ml) Demerara rum
(El Dorado 5 Yr)

¼ ounce (7 ml) Pimento Dram
(St. Elizabeth Allspice)

¼ ounce (7 ml) falernum

½ ounce (15 ml) fresh lime juice

½ ounce (15 ml) fresh orange juice

½ ounce (15 ml) honey syrup
(see page 242)

2 dashes Angostura bitters

3 cherries, to garnish

Pineapple stick, to garnish

Put ingredients into a blender with ice. Blend at high speed for 5 to 10 seconds. Pour into a highball glass and garnish with a skewer of three cherries and a pineapple stick.

RUM RUNNER

Fruity, citrus, spice, festive

• • • •

The rum practically disappears in this sunset-orange cooler, a terrific poolside drink. Try it alongside spicy pork tacos.

The Rum Runner is said to be a Florida creation, concocted at the Holiday Isle Tiki Bar Hotel and named for the rum runners of the Prohibition era who transported illegal hooch by boat between Florida and the Bahamas. Like many blender benders from the '50s, the drink calls for a bevy of liqueurs—legend has it one of the bar's patrons came up with a way to use up extra bottles of blackberry brandy and crème de banane. Amazingly, it all works together to create a glorious cocktail that is easy to keep drinking all night long. Rather than blending, we prefer to serve it in a rocks glass with a tangerine wheel to set off the vibrant color.

1½ (45 ml) ounces gold rum (Appleton Special)

½ ounce (15 ml) crème de mûres or crème de cassis

½ ounce (15 ml) crème de banane (Lejay-Lagoute, or the widely distributed Bols version)

½ ounce (15 ml) falernum

4 ounces (120 ml) fresh tangerine juice

Tangerine slice, for garnish

Shake ingredients with ice and strain into an ice-filled rocks glass or a curvy hurricane. Garnish with the tangerine slice on the rim of the glass.

PAINKILLER

Nutmeg, coconut, orange

• • • •

An easy accompaniment to coconut shrimp, conch fritters, and plantain chips.

Pusser's rum trademarked the Painkiller, and you can use Pusser's Navy Rum, but other rum options work well, too. This is an easygoing tropical classic that goes down fast, and does what its name suggests. Word is, it hails from a bar in the British Virgin Islands called the Soggy Dollar—and is shaken rather than blended because there was no electricity on Jost Van Dyke.

Note: This calls for a can of Coco Lopez coconut cream, which is coconut milk sweetened with sugar cane syrup—a tropical drink staple.

2½ ounces (75 ml) dark rum (Pusser's Navy Rum)

4 ounces (120) fresh pineapple juice

1 ounce (30 ml) fresh orange juice

1 ounce (30 ml) coconut cream (Lopez)

Freshly grated nutmeg, for garnish

Shake ingredients with ice and pour unstrained into a highball or hurricane glass. Garnish with nutmeg.

ZOMBIE

Fiery, aromatic, rummy, adventurous

- • -

The Zombie's wickedness needs only itself, or steak tartare.

This drink is a testament to Don the Beachcomber's canny business sense. You see, Don had a problem: all his fruity drinks were catnip to the ladies, and they fluttered to his bar like hungry fruit bats. But there wasn't much to attract the guys, many of whom found the offerings too feminine. Enter the Zombie, Don's killer app for getting machismo into the scene. In a bit of marketing genius, he limited customers to two of these skull-punchers apiece. That did it. The surfin' rubes sucked 'em down in droves. Recipes vary wildly. Tiki authority Jeff (Beach Bum) Berry has spent untold hours uncovering the original mix, the secret of which is a cinnamon-grapefruit juice. It's recreated here using cinnamon syrup, which you can find in a store or make yourself.

1½ (45 ml) ounces aged Jamaican rum (Appleton Estate Extra)

1½ (45 ml) ounces gold rum (Flor de Caña Gold 4 Yr)

1 ounce (30 ml) 151-proof Demerara rum (Hamilton Demerara 151 or Lemon Hart 151)

½ ounce (15 ml) falernum

⅛ teaspoon Pernod

¾ ounce (22 ml) fresh lime juice

2 teaspoons fresh white grapefruit juice

1 teaspoon cinnamon syrup (page 243)

1 teaspoon grenadine (page 244)

1 dash Angostura bitters

1 mint sprig, for garnish

Pour ingredients into the blender with ice. Blend and serve in a chilled hurricane or a highball glass. Garnish with the sprig of mint.

TIKI TAKEOUT (FUN PAIRINGS FOR LAZY DINNERS)

Even if you're too frazzled to cook, you can enliven a takeout supper with a cocktail made of fresh juices and served in a festive glass. With their heady mix of spices and their layers of flavor, tiki drinks are outstanding with tangy, salty, or spicy foods. They can lift lo mein to new heights and provide a cooling backdrop for blazin' hot wings.

In general, cocktails that contain citrus and rum are dazzling with Jamaican, Thai, or Indian food—they complement coconut milk and cut through rich sauces. Drinks made with Angostura bitters taste terrific alongside Chinese takeout, like fried rice or anything with plum sauce or five-spice powder.

A Queen's Park Swizzle and pad thai? Fantastic. The Three Dots and a Dash is one of our favorite revivers alongside tacos or burritos. For really spicy food, we love the taste-bud comforting Mai Tai. You may never order empanadas again without fixing a Painkiller once you try them together. The Dark 'n' Stormy cries out for pizza, and the Scorpion Bowl is a winner with wings or fried chicken. Here are a few cocktails to get you started on a tiki takeout binge.

Queen's Park Swizzle (page 198)

Three Dots and a Dash (page 187)

Mai Tai (page 185)

Painkiller (page 188)

Dark 'n' Stormy (page 194)

Scorpion Bowl (page 192)

Test Pilot (page 187)

SCORPION BOWL

Spirituous, orange, racy, effervescent

— • • • • —

Pair with wings, fried chicken, calamari, or bacon-wrapped anything.

Presentation is half of the Scorpion's charm and reputation. Served in a ceramic volcano bowl with dry ice, an orchid, and a float of high-proof rum aflame, it certainly has a wow factor. But the drink itself is a delicious bombshell of booze and bubbles. It was traditionally served with a flaming 151 rum float, which adds flavor and punch, but we like to replace it with Champagne and serve it for brunch in a pair of rocks glasses, festooned with pineapple and mint.

2 ounces (60 ml) light rum (Flor de Caña 4 Yr)

½ ounce (15 ml) brandy (Pierre Ferrand Ambre)

¾ ounce (22 ml) fresh lemon juice

1½ ounces (45 ml) fresh orange juice

½ ounce (15 ml) orgeat (page 244)

1 ounce (30 ml) Champagne (optional)

Pineapple wedge, for garnish

Muddle the pineapple wedge in a shaker, add the remaining ingredients (except Champagne), and shake with ice. Strain into an ice-filled rocks glass. Top with bubbly and garnish with a pineapple wedge on the rim of the glass.

JUNGLE BIRD · · · · · · · · · · · · · ·

Bitter, spice, pineapple

— • • • • —

A bittersweet charmer, pair with barbecue or chocolate. It's also superb with Mexican mole.

This '70s drink from the Aviary bar in Kuala Lumpur, Malaysia, is a bartender favorite. It's easy to see why, as it presents a fine balance of sweet and fruity. It brings a bitter note into the tiki kingdom, thanks to the addition of Campari. If you use a fresh pineapple, snip off a few of the long leaves and tuck them down into the glass to look like feathers.

1½ ounces (45 ml) black rum (Hamilton Pot Still Black Rum or Cruzan Black-strap)

¾ ounce (22 ml) Campari

1 ounce (30 ml) fresh pineapple juice

½ ounce (15 ml) fresh lime juice

½ ounce (15 ml) simple syrup (page 241)

Pineapple wedge and leaves, for garnish

Shake ingredients with ice and strain into a rocks glass filled with ice. Garnish with the pineapple wedge on the edge of the glass and slide in a pair of leaves.

CORN 'N' OIL

Molasses, clove, vanilla, lime

— • • • —

This drink smells like pure vanilla and tastes like a psychedelic Cuba Libre—it's exquisite with barbecue. We love to serve this spicy sipper around the holidays.

From Barbados, this gold dark elixir was spirited into the American craft cocktail scene thanks to Seattle bartender Murray Stenson of the Zig Zag Café. Imbibers turned it into a cult classic so that it shot around the country, appearing on drink menus everywhere. In Barbados, a Corn 'n' Oil allegedly uses aged local rum, falernum, lime, and bitters. Stenson chose blackstrap rum with heavy molasses flavor from the Caribbean, which achieves the effect of making this drink look like it's made from crude oil. Tradition suggests a rum from Barbados, which allows the spice notes to shine through. You can build this drink in the glass or shake and strain. We prefer the latter.

2 ounces (60 ml) black rum (Hamilton Jamaican Pot Still Black Rum or Cruzan Blackstrap)

½ ounce (15 ml) falernum

½ ounce (15 ml) fresh lime juice

2 to 3 dashes Angostura bitters

Lime wheel, for garnish

Shake and strain into a rocks glass over a single large cube of ice. Garnish with a lime wheel on the edge of the glass.

DARK 'N' STORMY · · · · · · · · · · ·

Rummy, ginger, lime

— • • • —

Pair this easy fixer with a hot day and a pulled pork sandwich. It's great served poolside, beachside, or within view of a harbor.

When you pour ginger ale over a glass of black dark rum, the two liquids merge like a storm front rolling across a dusky sky. This is a drink that British sailors drank by the boatload in Bermuda between 1860 and 1920. The Navy manufactured rum on the island, and local ginger beer was plentiful, hence this quick invigorator served with a squeeze of lime. Today, the Dark 'n' Stormy is considered Bermuda's national drink; it's trademarked by Gosling's, the island's oldest rum company.

2 ounces (60 ml) dark rum (Gosling's Black Seal or Cruzan Blackstrap)

4 ounces (120 ml) ginger beer (page 247)

Lime wheel, for garnish

Candied ginger, for garnish

Fill a rocks glass with ice. Add rum and ginger beer and stir. Garnish with a lime wheel and candied ginger on a cocktail pick.

PIÑA COLADA

Velvety, pineapple, coconut, clove

• • • •

This quintessential beachside sipper pairs well with toasted almonds, shrimp, or grilled fish and fried plantains.

The Caribe Hilton in San Juan, Puerto Rico, is famously chronicled in Hunter S. Thompson's *The Rum Diaries*, where the bar claims to have developed this cunning pleasure-giver, now the island's signature drink. Others backdate it to 1820 and a Robin Hood character named El Pirata Confresi, who buoyed his men with this beverage and thus prevented scurvy. Use real pineapple—not frozen mixers—and try combining both dark and light rum here, for more complexity. Sometimes we trick this out with a frozen banana and a handful of chia seeds to build a "super food colada" we call the Super Collider.

1½ ounces (45 ml) light rum
   (Flor de Caña 4 Yr)

1 ounce (30 ml) dark rum
   (El Dorado 5 Yr)

2 ounces (60 ml) coconut milk

1 cup (125 g) frozen pineapple wedges

2 dashes Angostura bitters

4 ice cubes

Pineapple wedge, for garnish

In a blender, blend ingredients with ice for 15 seconds. Pour into a chilled hurricane or highball. Garnish with a pineapple wedge on the rim of the glass. Serve with a straw.

'TI PUNCH

Earth, lime, citrus

• • • •

This needs a humid afternoon or evening, and little else. It's one of the best easy-to-fix drinks in this book.

In Martinique, 'Ti Punch—short for "petit punch" and pronounced *tee pauncchhh*—is the ultimate kickback drink, a little glass of punch served in a juice glass. Locals enjoy this as an aperitif, using their local white rhum (blanc). Preparing the drink is ritualistic, much like offering a guest a cup of tea, except that it's made fresh for each person and always built in the glass. Using real cane syrup ("sirop de canne") is considered essential, but if you can't find it, you can improvise with a drop of honey added to simple syrup.

Note: In Martinique, bartenders pare off a disk of rind (about the size of a quarter) from one side of the fruit, working from top to bottom. It looks like a hefty hank of peel.

2 ounces (60 ml) rhum agricole
   (Niesson Blanc or Plantation)

¼ ounce (7 ml) cane syrup (see headnote)

2 to 3 inches (5 to 8 cm) of lime peel,
   thickly cut to include pith and fruit
   (see headnote)

In a small juice glass, pour the rhum agricole and the cane syrup. Stir. Squeeze the lime so that you get the essential oils from the peel, along with some of the juice, then drop it into the glass. Add one or two ice cubes, no more.

WHAT'S A SWIZZLE?

The original swizzle stick was a multi-prong branch cut from an allspice bush. It was first used in Bermuda, and the idea was to whisk a drink into a froth—long before the hand-held blender. Watching someone swizzle a drink in the islands was an experience. The drink inspired a popular phrase, "Swizzle in, swagger out!" To swizzle a drink, simply hold a bar spoon or swizzle stick between your palms and roll it back and forth until the glass fogs and your drink froths. At Cane & Table in New Orleans, bartenders swizzle drinks with a power drill—because why not?

QUEEN'S PARK SWIZZLE

Rummy, lime, mint, spice

— • • • —

A great porch drink—serve with a BLT or a spinach salad.

In Trinidad, the late Queen's Park Hotel was once a bastion of luxuriant splendor, a place where princes brought their brides and the who's who lounged on verandas overlooking a glorious park. Enjoying a swizzle over a cricket match was a quick way to cool one's brow. This easy crowd-pleaser and cousin to the Mojito (page 130) went on to become a Trader Vic favorite.

2 ounces (60 ml) Demerara rum
  (El Dorado 5 Yr)

½ ounce (15 ml) fresh lime juice

½ ounce (15 ml) simple syrup (page 241)

6 to 8 mint leaves, plus mint sprig for
  garnish

3 dashes Angostura bitters, for garnish

In a rocks or highball glass, gently muddle the mint leaves with simple syrup. Add rum, lime, juice, and fill the glass about one-thirds full of crushed ice. Swizzle with a swizzle stick or bar spoon. Top with crushed ice. Dash bitters over the top, and garnish with mint. Serve with a straw.

CHARTREUSE SWIZZLE

Herbaceous, citrus, pineapple, spice

— • • • —

A festive green drink that makes a terrific aperitif while you're grilling fish. It has a lot going on, so keep pairings simple: a plate of cucumber slices, a bowl of grilled pineapple.

A modern take on the swizzle that swaps out the rum and drops in an herbaceous wallop of Chartreuse, this has become the swizzle of San Francisco, thanks to bartender Marcovaldo Dionysos. Pale green in color, it's often served with a wild tuft of mint and a smattering of freshly grated nutmeg on top. Introduce this at your next pool party—you can pass around a swizzle stick and take turns making this drink. Chartreuse and falernum, both used here, are spice-based spirits that appear in a number of historic cocktails.

1¼ ounces (37 ml) green Chartreuse

½ ounce (15 ml) falernum

1 ounce (30 ml) fresh pineapple juice

¾ ounce (22 ml) fresh lime juice

Freshly grated nutmeg, for garnish

Mint sprig, for garnish

Combine ingredients in a highball glass with crushed ice and swizzle until the drink froths and the glass turns frosty. Add more crushed ice. Garnish with nutmeg and the mint sprig.

SAOCO

Coconut, sweet-salty, lime

· · · ·

A clean-tasting refresher that's a little bit sporty, thanks to the sea salt. Drink this after a workout or a day in the sun, alongside tortilla chips and mango salsa.

Imagine a Cuban margarita, a cooler that pulls coconut water into alignment with lime and rum, creating an electrolyte-rich cocktail that tastes, oh, just a little bit like a very glamorous adult sports drink. Pronounced (Sa-OH-ko), we like to add a pinch of salt—to bring down the acid and take the edge off the sweetness. You can buy fresh coconuts (a coconut yields about 4 ounces of water) or use bottled—but make sure it is 100 percent pure, and not from concentrate.

1½ ounces (45 ml) light rum (Flor de Caña)

2½ ounces (75 ml) coconut water

2 teaspoons fresh lime juice

2 teaspoons sugar

Pinch of sea salt

Lime wheel, for garnish

Combine rum, coconut water, lime juice, and sugar in a shaker glass. Stir until sugar dissolves. Add ice and shake. Strain over a rocks glass filled with a single large ice cube. Add a sprinkle of sea salt. Garnish with a lime wheel on the edge of the glass.

PISCO SOUR

Frothy, sweet-sour, floral, spice

· · · ·

A compelling cocktail for a steamy evening. Serve with empanadas or grilled hanger steak topped with chimichurri sauce.

Both Chile and Peru call Pisco their national booze; Peru even has a holiday based around it. Books written on the subject of Pisco point to different bartenders who may have created this cocktail, most likely in the 1920s at an esteemed hotel bar, though an earlier recipe appears in a Peruvian cookbook as early as 1903. Beloved as a hangover cure—thanks to the egg white and the vitamin C boost from the citrus juice—the Pisco Sour can also be made with lemon, rather than lime.

2 ounces (60 ml) Pisco

1 ounce (30 ml) fresh lime juice

½ ounce (15 ml) simple syrup (page 241)

¾ ounce (22 ml) egg white

3 drops orange flower water

3 drops Angostura bitters

Dry shake ingredients to emulsify. Then shake again with ice and strain into a chilled coupe glass. Float a few drops of Angostura bitters on top of the drink.

SKY JUICE

Milky, herbaceous, coconut

- - - • -

Serve with Thai takeout or grilled shrimp tossed onto rollicking salads full of mango, red bell pepper, and toasted cashews.

Get out your sunglasses, and call your gin-loving friends. This cooler is all spices and coconut—a drink that goes down easy with grilled fish, jerk chicken, or anything with heat. In his book, *The Barbecue Bible* (1998), grill god Steven Raichlen claims this is *the* drink to sip while you're cooking over hot coals. He's right. It's awesomely tropical and creamy but also herbaceous, thanks to the gin. We love to play that up with a sprig of Thai basil as a garnish.

2 ounces (60 ml) London Dry gin (Tanqueray)

2 ounces (60 ml) evaporated milk

4 ounces (120 ml) coconut water

2½ teaspoons sugar

Dash of cinnamon

Freshly grated nutmeg, for garnish

Sprig of Thai basil, for garnish

Lime wedge, for garnish

Shake ingredients with ice and strain into an ice-filled rocks glass. Garnish with basil, nutmeg, and lime wedge. Serve with a straw.

Note: We like to use fresh coconuts for this drink. A coconut will yield about a ½ cup (4 ounces or 120 ml) of coconut water.

RUMCHATA (DRUNKEN HORCHATA)

Rice, cinnamon, vanilla

- - - • -

Prepare a pitcher of Rumchata for a Mexican dinner party or a hot summer day.

Horchata, a beverage made in roadside stands throughout Mexico and also beloved in Spain, is simple to make and just requires soaking rice and cinnamon overnight, then blending and straining it the next morning. Our horchata recipe (page 250) is delicious straight or spiked, which makes it a terrific party drink that can be batched and served to both kids and adults.

1 ounce (30 ml) dark rum (El Dorado 5 Yr)

4 ounces (120 ml) horchata (page 250)

Dash of cinnamon, for garnish

Fill a chilled rocks or highball glass with ice. Add rum and horchata. Stir. Garnish with cinnamon on top of the drink.

CACHAÇA

Pronounced "kah-SHAH-sah," the national spirit of Brazil has only recently been recognized in the United States as something other than "Brazilian Rum." Made from fermented fresh sugarcane juice, this spirit is referred to by many names, including *abre-coração* (heart-opener) and *bafo-de-tigre* (tiger breath), if that gives you any clue to its powers. In Brazil, *cachaçarias* stock numerous bottles from more than 5,000 distilleries around the country. Most cachaça today is industrially produced, though artisan brands are beginning to appear stateside.

Tasting through even a few of them reveals a range of flavors, from rough and grassy un-aged versions (clear) to barrel-aged cachaça (gold) that can be extremely smooth, even smoky. A sniff of this spirit will reveal what, in rum land, is referred to as "hogo," a slightly funky aroma that is strangely alluring.

CAIPIRINHA

Bright, lime, musky

— • • • —

Steak and grilled meats pair well—as does anything with a little char, even seared tuna.

In Brazil, this limey drink (pronounced kye-peer-EEN-ya) is ubiquitous, from dance halls to beaches to backyard parties. Its name derives from the word *caipira*, or "bush cutter," and dates back to the turn of the century, when this drink was essentially a folk remedy (it contained garlic). Today, it's a breezy alternative to a margarita. Make sure to muddle the limes well so that you get some bitter aromatics from the peel to counterbalance the sugar. Some people build this drink in the glass, but we prefer to give it a shake.

> 2 ounces (60 ml) cachaça
>
> 2 teaspoons sugar
>
> 2 small Key limes quartered or 1 whole lime cut into eight wedges
>
> Lime wheel, for garnish

Muddle the lime and sugar in a shaker, then add cachaça. Shake and strain into a rocks glass filled with ice. Garnish with a lime wheel on the rim of the glass.

CASHEW BATIDA

Nutty, funky, sweet

— • • • —

Like a deluxe protein shake, this drink is thick and creamy. Serve it on a hot night after dancing.

If you like salted caramels, you will probably love a Cashew Batida. In Brazil, *batida de cajú* can be made from cashew milk or cashews ground with a mortar and pestle. Here, we use cashew butter for the sake of ease, but if you have a strong blender you can simply toss in a quarter cup of raw cashews. Because this drink is dessert-like, we often serve it in shot glasses at the end of a big summer dinner bash. We like to sprinkle a few crystals of gray salt on top before they leave the kitchen. If you can't find gray salt, just use plain sea salt.

> 2 ounces (60 ml) cachaça
>
> 2 teaspoons cashew nut butter
>
> ½ ounce (15 ml) sweetened condensed milk
>
> Pinch of gray salt
>
> 1 cashew, for garnish

Combine ingredients in a blender with ice. Blend well. Pour into a chilled rocks glass or wine glass, topped with a whole cashew. Serve with a straw or spoon.

CHAMPAGNE & WINE COCKTAILS

Drinks made with Champagne or white wine make for splendid aperitifs—they're fizzy and festive, the first thing to offer when a guest comes through the door. They're also often low-proof, making them perfect for an afternoon croquet party, a shower, or drinks on the porch before dinner. The Europeans are especially adept at turning an aperitif into an afternoon ritual—a shot of pop 'n' sparkle at 4 p.m. brightens moods and pairs well with salty nibbles. Try an Aperol Spritz (page 209) or a Bicyclette (page 211) with a plate of open-faced sandwiches.

For brunch, try a Bellini (page 206) with French toast, or serve a round of smoky-looking Stratospheres (page 207) at a holiday gathering—whole cloves and a splash of violet liqueur harmonize in subtle ways, adding a wisp of old Hollywood.

True Champagne can be spendy so we often substitute crémant—bubbly made in the same method but outside of the Champagne region. American sparklers such as Gruet also make fine mixers.

CHAMPAGNE COCKTAIL

Brioche, caramel, citrus

• •

This striking drink adds to a festive occasion, like a wedding, graduation, or a shower. It's also a decadent companion with soft cheese or sushi.

Dropping a sugar cube into Champagne is done for effect here, to create a beautiful plume of bubbles within the glass. A few drops of bitters and a lemon twist turn this into an aromatic sipper—lovely in summer or winter. The proper bubbly here is, of course, true French Brut Champagne. However, we've used American fizz, or crémant—sparkling wine produced outside the Champagne region—to great effect. For an interesting twist, try a float of Grand Marnier. We like the rough-hewn look of Demerara sugar cubes, but you can also use plain white.

4 ounces (120 ml) sparkling wine

1 Demerara sugar cube

Dash of Angostura bitters

Lemon twist, for garnish

Drop a sugar cube in a champagne flute. Lightly moisten the cube with a dash of Angostura bitters. Fill the glass with sparkly, and garnish with a lemon twist on the edge of the glass.

THE KNABENSHUE: A VARIATION

For a curious variation on the Champagne Cocktail, try the Knabenshue, named after the first American dirigible pilot. Born in Toledo, Ohio, he wowed the world in 1905, when he sailed over New York, from Central Park to the Times Building and back. To make a Knabenshue, use the basic recipe for a Champagne Cocktail, but grab a mug instead of a champagne flute, and add a lump of ice to it. Instead of a lemon twist, add a sprig of mint for garnish. The result is buoyant.

BELLINI

Effervescent, peach, brioche

- • -

A summer brunch or a warm afternoon during peach season calls for a Bellini. Serve with small bites, like crostini, nuts, and olive oil crackers.

Interpretations of Venice's signature cocktail abound—some call for peach pulp, others for strained juice. The original drink from Harry's Bar clearly made use of two regional specialties that are crucial: white peaches (not yellow) and Prosecco (not Champagne). In summer, few things are lovelier than this pale-pink cooler, preferably served along a canal to long-legged women in stilettos. Legend has it that this drink was inspired by the renaissance garb of a saint depicted in a painting by Giovanni Bellini, making this ethereal concoction ideal for the Venice Biennale, where it is always served. Because the white peaches we find in the United States aren't quite sweet enough, we add a dash of peach liqueur.

3 ounces (90 ml) Prosecco

¼ ounce (7 ml) peach liqueur (Mathilde)

1 ounce of cold, fresh white peach juice (see note)

Pour peach juice and liqueur into a chilled champagne flute, then add bubbles. Gently stir to blend.

Note: To make fresh peach juice, use a juicer, or purée 2 peeled ripe white peaches in a blender, then layer a fine mesh strainer with a double layer of cheesecloth and let it drain over a bowl. Chill before using.

KIR/KIR ROYALE

Aromatic, currant, citrus

⋆ ⋆ ⋆ ⋆

What's better than a Kir Royale and a red velvet cupcake?

Blush-colored and fresh, this combination of crème de cassis and white wine (or Champagne, for a Kir Royale) is a glamorous sipper. It originated in Burgundy, France, where the mayor of Dijon, Felix Kir, began mixing the local black currant liqueur with the local white wine, Aligoté. Cassis adds a touch of sweetness and drama. The Kir Royale, made with Champagne, was developed later. It's pricier and a shade more festive. Both versions make a lovely brunch drink or aperitif.

½ ounce (15 ml) crème de cassis

4 ounces (120 ml) dry white wine (or Champagne, for a Royale)

Lemon twist, for garnish

Pour the crème de cassis in a wine glass or champagne flute. Add wine or bubbles and garnish with a lemon twist on the rim of the glass.

STRATOSPHERE COCKTAIL

Violets, clove, brioche, citrus

⋆ ⋆ ⋆ ⋆

Pair with caviar, a plate of cold smoked trout, or play off the purple color with a bright beet salad.

Also known as the "thinking woman's Kir Royale," this intriguing dusty-pink drink adapted from *The Stork Club Bar Book* is served with two floating cloves and a twist of lemon. The result is a complex, hard-to-pin-down taste that makes for a good conversation starter. The original recipe calls for Crème Yvette, a liqueur from 1890 that was made from violets, berries, and spices—it fell out of favor for a century but has recently been reintroduced by the Cooper Spirits Company in Philadelphia, the makers of St. Germain. Some bartenders substitute crème de Violette, which is more floral. We love the foxy gait of the classic. The clove garnish may seem superfluous at first, but it accentuates the spice notes in the liqueur as you get deeper into the drink.

¼ ounce (7 ml) Crème Yvette (or crème de Violette)

4 ounces (120 ml) Brut Champagne

2 whole cloves

Lemon twist, for garnish

Measure Crème Yvette into a champagne flute, then top off with Champagne and drop in two cloves. Garnish with a lemon twist on the side of the glass.

COCKTAILING FOR COUPLES: SIX ROMANTIC DRINKS

Like cooking for someone, making a gorgeous cocktail is a seductive art. If you're looking to woo a hunk or honey, let these visually stunning elixirs set the mood. Draw a bath and serve an opulent Rose Cocktail. Plan a proposal around a Leap Year or Juliet and Romeo—both have good stories. Or, if you need to redeem yourself: a bar of chocolate and a Between the Sheets.

Champagne cocktails bring shimmer and luxury to celebratory events like birthdays and anniversaries. For a spectacular toast, choose the deep purple bubbles of a Kir Royale, or go all out with the Soyer au Champagne.

Rose Cocktail (page 84)

Juliet and Romeo (page 139)

Between the Sheets (page 95)

Leap Year (page 73)

Kir Royale (page 207)

Soyer au Champagne (page 225)

APEROL SPRITZ

Bitter orange, effervescent, citrus

· · · · ·

Serve this aperitif the way the northern Italians do, with a trio of bowls filled with peanuts, big green olives, and potato chips or olive oil crackers.

In northeastern Italy, at around four o'clock, the light in the piazzas begins to shift from stone gray to gold as waiters emerge with trays of these neon-orange cocktails in bulbous wine glasses. Against the heaviness of so many marble facades, these drinks have the effect of floating lanterns—delighting the eye. Aperol, a bittersweet aperitif containing orange and rhubarb, forms the backbone of this rejuvenating sparkler. The taste, especially after a hot day of trotting around, is magnificently refreshing. Slightly bitter, sweetly citric, and bright as a sunlit rose window, it humanizes the weary traveler.

1 ounce (30 ml) Aperol

3 ounces (90 ml) Prosecco

Splash of soda water (about ½ ounce, or 15 ml)

Half an orange slice, for garnish

Fill a wine glass (or a highball glass, if you prefer) half-full of ice. Add Aperol, then Prosecco. Top off with a splash of sparkling water. Stir, then drop in an orange slice.

ST. GERMAIN COCKTAIL

Floral, effervescent, citrus

· · · · ·

Pair this elegant Champagne drink with light fare, like tea sandwiches, sushi, or a fruit salad.

The St. Germain cocktail is a modern classic that appeared when elderflower liqueur hit the market in 2007. It immediately became widespread in cocktail bars throughout the country, and incited renewed interest in liqueurs generally. Elderflower now appears in a number of cocktails as a sweet and floral alternative to simple syrup, giving lift to otherwise bitter or blasé drinks.

1½ ounces (45 ml) St. Germain

2 ounces (60 ml) Champagne (or crémant)

Club soda, to top off

Lemon twist, for garnish

Pour St. Germain and Champagne in a wine glass or highball glass with ice and stir. Top with soda and garnish with a lemon twist in the glass.

CLARET CUP

Wine, orange, plum, effervescent

Pair with a spread of charcuterie, pâté, and clothbound Cheddar.

The precursor to the Pimm's Cup (page 171), the old Claret Cup employs a wine base to make a drink that is light and redolent of additions such as borage, cucumber, or strawberries. There are multiple recipes, but we like a simple one that modifies wine with just a bit of sherry (or even vermouth, in a pinch). Claret was what the English used to call wines from Bordeaux. Really, any red jammy wine will do—Cabernets or even Syrah, although a decent Côtes du Rhône or a Beaujolais is what we use most often. Don't overthink it—use whatever fruit you've got in the fridge and see what you prefer. In fall, it's lovely to grate a little nutmeg and cinnamon on top.

3 ounces (90 ml) red wine

½ ounce (15 ml) sherry (preferably Amontillado) or sweet vermouth

½ ounce (15 ml) orange curaçao (or triple sec if you like it sweeter)

½ ounce (15 ml) fresh lemon juice

2 ounces (60 ml) soda water

Cucumber slices, for garnish

Orange slices, for garnish

Stir ingredients, except soda, with ice and strain into an ice-filled highball glass. Top with soda and garnish with cucumber and orange slices in the glass.

BICYCLETTE, OR BICICLETTA

Bitter, grapefruit, floral

Serve with rosemary crackers and antipasti.

Sometimes simplicity is the ticket, and the waifish, breezy Bicyclette appears with all the charm of a European aperitif—ready to infuse a quick dash of glam into your day. Popular in both France as La Bicyclette and Italy as La Bicicletta, it's usually served in the afternoon at cafés. However, it is also a perfect final drink of the night, a relatively low-alcohol quaffer that says, "I'm done." The sweetness of the white wine is balanced perfectly by the bitter Campari. Traditional recipes calls for equal parts, but we dial it back to about 3 to 1. Any light white wine will do.

3 ounces (90 ml) dry white wine

1½ ounces (45 ml) Campari

Lemon twist, for garnish

Pour ingredients over ice in a highball or wine glass and stir. Garnish with a lemon twist in the glass.

AMERICANA

Brioche, citrus, caramel, vanilla, peach

·–·–·–·

A natural match for a big game dinner.

This drink is not to be confused with an Americano, and there is quite a bit of debate as to its proper manufacture. But we cling to it because, like the Seelbach (page 66), it marries bourbon and Champagne. Good old France and the U.S. of A. in a glass together. Like a Champagne Cocktail gone native.

3½ ounces (104 ml) Champagne (or crémant)

½ ounce (15 ml) bourbon (Buffalo Trace)

1 Demerara sugar cube

3 dashes Angostura bitters

Dash of orange bitters (Regans')

Slice of peach, for garnish

Drop a sugar cube into a champagne flute, and season it with the bitters. Add bourbon, and top with Champagne. Garnish with the slice of peach skewered and resting on top of the flute.

NEW YORK SOUR ··········

Tart, caramel, spice, berry

·–·–·–·

Play off the taste of bourbon and fruit with pork loin or pot roast and a side of mashed sweet potatoes.

This drink was purportedly created in Chicago around the 1870s and was first called the Continental Sour, or the Southern Whiskey Sour, before becoming the New York Sour. It was once known as a "claret snap," claret being the name for Bordeaux-style red wine, and the "snap" referring to floating it on the drink. It's a pretty cocktail, garnet in color, that coaxes flavors from the whiskey and wine so that they enhance each other.

2 ounces (60 ml) rye whiskey or bourbon

1 ounce (30 ml) fresh lemon juice

½ ounce (15 ml) simple syrup (page 241)

½ ounce (15 ml) red wine, to float

Lemon wheel, for garnish

Cherry, for garnish

Shake whiskey, lemon juice, and simple syrup with ice and strain into a rocks glass over ice. Float wine on top. For the garnish, use a bamboo skewer or toothpick to thread a lemon wheel around a cherry.

COLD-WEATHER WARMERS

Hot drinks are coziness in a glass. Whether it's a foggy morning or frosty evening, they restore and rejuvenate. There's something about steam coming off the top of a mug that leads to contemplation and conviviality.

In this chapter, you'll find drinks involving fire, spice, and even baked apples slipped into the bottom of mugs. Pair these with pie, a plate of cookies, doughnuts, or a homemade crisp. The Smoking Bishop (page 221) is easy to prepare for a party and will fill your house with the aroma of toasted orange and spice. A Tom and Jerry (page 219) is also delightful for gatherings—a boozy whipped creamlike drink that's worth the effort. Hot Vietnamese Coffee (page 218) is a delightful twist on after-dinner coffee.

Consider serving these warmers in place of dessert or as an excuse to climb up onto the roof with a thermos and a blanket to stargaze.

HOT (SPICED) BUTTERED RUM

Rummy, cardamom, nutmeg

**A ravishing drink to serve with mincemeat or apple pie—
or buttered toast.**

Spiced butter lifts this drink from the prosaic to the paradisiacal. And it's easy to make: simply mix sugar and spices into good quality, room-temperature butter. We like to use cardamom and fresh orange zest, along with a pinch of nutmeg and cinnamon. The butter will melt and rise like a foamy cloud to the top of the mug when the water is added.

FOR THE SPICED BUTTER

¼ cup (57 g) butter (½ stick), room temperature

¼ cup (43 g) dark brown sugar

1 teaspoon ground cardamom

½ teaspoon orange zest

¼ teaspoon cinnamon

Pinch of freshly grated nutmeg

FOR THE COCKTAIL

1½ ounces (45 ml) rum (El Dorado 5 Yr)

1 to 2 teaspoons spiced butter (recipe above)

¾ cup (177 ml) boiling water

Cinnamon stick, for garnish

Orange wheel, for garnish

For the spiced butter: combine butter, sugar, and spices in a small bowl and mash until well combined. (A fork works well.) Chill until ready to use.

For the cocktail: add rum and butter to a warm mug. Top with boiling water and stir. Serve with a cinnamon stick and half an orange wheel, if desired.

HOT TODDY

Honey, clove, citrus

· • · • ·

Use this restorative to warm the belly and stave off winter chills, alongside a plate of oatmeal cookies.

When you're feeling a cold coming on or when you've just spent an hour digging your car out of the snow, few things are more reviving than a hot toddy. Some people add black tea, but most go straight for booze, honey, and lemon. Either way, the combination soothes a scratchy throat and warms the gullet. Most recipes call for bourbon or whiskey, but you can also use rum or brandy. The key to a well-made toddy is serving it blazing hot, so make sure to warm the glass.

2 ounces (60 ml) brandy or bourbon

2 tablespoons (30 ml) honey

1 ounce (30 ml) fresh lemon juice

6 ounces (177 ml) hot water or black tea

1 thick-cut lemon wheel, for garnish

3 cloves, for garnish

Add brandy, honey, and lemon juice to a warmed mug or pint glass. Top with water or tea. Stir. Drop in a lemon wheel pierced with 3 cloves. Serve.

ROASTED APPLE TODDY

Brown sugar, apple, cinnamon

· • · • ·

Pair with spice cake, or with popcorn and chestnuts around a fire.

A hot toddy with half a baked apple in it? Yes, please. Inspired by early bartender Jerry Thomas, this recipe should be in the repertoire of anyone who enjoys fall camping. Just double-wrap the apples in foil, put them on the coals of your bonfire, and remove them when they're soft. But the oven will also do.

2 ounces (60 ml) apple brandy (Laird's)

½ small apple, cored

½ tablespoon (7 g) butter

1 tablespoon (15 g) brown sugar

¼ teaspoon cinnamon

Freshly grated nutmeg, for garnish

Boiling water

Preheat the oven to 350°F. Place the apple faceup in a small baking dish and top with butter, sugar, and cinnamon. Cover with foil and bake for 20 to 30 minutes, or until fork tender.

To prepare the toddy, drop the apple half into a glass coffee mug (make sure to scoop up any drippings, and add that, too), then top with brandy and boiling water. Grate nutmeg over the top. Serve with a spoon.

HOLIDAY COCKTAILS

For a holiday open house, consider offering both a hot drink and a cool, frothy drink that are easy to prepare in advance. You can keep one warming on the stove and serve the other from a pitcher in the fridge. For a holiday dinner, serve a round of Trinidad Sours or Seelbach cocktails before the meal—both are festive and pair well with cheese and charcuterie.

If you want to impress guests with something adventurous, prepare a round of Stout Flips—think dark beer and nutmeg—or a Smoking Bishop, which involves roasting a whole orange and floating it in fortified wine. Serve either with cookies and popcorn, and break out a game. Don't forget to send guests home with recipe cards.

Eggnog (page 229)

Roasted Apple Hot Toddy (page 216)

Trinidad Sour (page 142)

Seelbach Cocktail (page 66)

Smoking Bishop (page 221)

Stout Flip (page 153)

Atholl Brose (page 230)

Burning Branch (page 237)

HOT VIETNAMESE COFFEE

Bittersweet, nutty, caramel

◆ ◆ ◆ ◆

Pair with flan, bread pudding, or ladyfingers.

Spiked Vietnamese coffee is a unique brunch perk or a lovely dessert drink. The caramel flavors from the brandy and condensed milk meld harmoniously to give this favorite coffee drink an extra boozy lift. Expensive brandy—i.e. cognac—isn't necessary here, as it's mostly buried, so we like to use any decent American brandy instead. Traditional Vietnamese coffee—a strong blend of coffee sweetened with condensed milk—is usually served cold, which is an option here as well if you prefer a boozy iced coffee. Don't skip the salt, which prevents this drink from being cloying.

1½ ounces (45 ml) brandy (Paul Masson Grande Amber VS)

4 ounces (120 ml) strong hot coffee

1½ tablespoons (22 ml) sweetened condensed milk

Pinch of sea salt

In a small, warm coffee cup, add sweetened condensed milk and stir in coffee. Top with brandy and a pinch of salt. Give another quick stir, and serve.

IRISH COFFEE

Bittersweet, caramel, spice

◆ ◆ ◆ ◆

Serve a round of Irish coffees with cookies, spice cake, or pumpkin pie.

A cockle-warmer from County Limerick, this hot drink was first served in the 1940s to a group of sea plane passengers who arrived bone cold into Foynes' Port. Bartender Joe Sheridan dosed their coffee with whiskey, and when one of the party asked "Is this Colombian coffee?" he responded, "No, this is Irish coffee." By the '50s, nearly all of San Francisco was sipping spiked coffee through cloudy cream. Brown sugar rounds out the sweetness of the booze here, and real cream is essential. We like to add a dash of Angostura to the cream after it's been whipped.

FOR THE ANGOSTURA WHIPPED CREAM

¼ cup (60 ml) heavy cream

Dash Angostura bitters

FOR EACH COFFEE

1½ ounces (45 ml) Irish whiskey (Powers)

4 ounces (120 ml) hot coffee

2 teaspoons brown sugar, to taste

2 tablespoons (30 ml) real whipped cream

Freshly grated nutmeg, for garnish

Whip cream in a small cold mixing bowl until light and fluffy. Dash in the Angostura and stir briefly.

In a warm mug, add whiskey, coffee, and brown sugar. Stir. Top with freshly whipped cream and grated nutmeg.

TOM AND JERRY

Custard, vanilla, spice

- • - •

Serve this drink in mugs at a tree-trimming party, along with candied orange peel and gingerbread.

Think of eggnog crossed with a mug of white hot chocolate, and you can begin to imagine the taste of this winter warmer from the 1800s, once served up at the Planters' House Hotel in Saint Louis by legendary bartender Jerry Thomas. (He claimed that he named the drink after his pet pair of white mice, although references to the recipe appear much earlier.) In Midwestern states like Wisconsin, Tom and Jerry "batter" is still sold in freezer sections at grocery stores, but there is no substitute for homemade. Some use whiskey for this drink, but we like to make this with brandy or—better yet—with a split shot of brandy and Jamaican rum. The key to this cocktail is to stir the batter into the booze before adding hot milk so that the eggs don't curdle.

SERVES 4

FOR THE BATTER

3 large eggs, separated

3 tablespoons (24 g) confectioner's sugar

1 teaspoon vanilla

½ teaspoon ground cinnamon

½ teaspoon ground allspice

¼ teaspoon ground cloves

½ teaspoon freshly ground nutmeg, plus extra for garnish

FOR THE COCKTAIL

4 ounces (120 ml) brandy (Paul Masson Grande Amber VS), divided

4 ounces (120 ml) gold rum (Appleton Special), divided

3 cups (710 ml) hot milk, divided

To make the batter, beat egg whites in a bowl until it forms a stiff froth. In a separate bowl, beat yolks until thin as water, then add sugar, vanilla, and spices. Fold the whites into the yolk mixture.

To make the hot drink, heat milk on the stove in a saucepan and bring to a near simmer. Then, divide the brandy and rum between four warm mugs—1 shot of each spirit into each mug. Stir in 2 heaping scoops of batter to the booze in each mug. Then, stir in hot milk (a small whisk works well). Garnish with extra nutmeg.

SMOKING BISHOP

Cherry, orange, clove, aromatic

• - •

Break out the molasses cookies and board games.

This fragrant Victorian punch starts with roasted citrus fruit and includes both red wine and port for a rich, warming drink. Famously mentioned in *A Christmas Carol*—it's Scrooge's conversion drink—this is a perfect libation for after the theater or for a Dickens-themed dinner. Plus, roasting the fruit will make your house smell incredible. Note that this drink needs twenty-four hours to steep, and it's best to use unwaxed, organic fruit.

1 bottle (750 ml) medium bodied red wine

1 bottle (750 ml) ruby port

4 oranges

1 ruby red grapefruit

35 cloves

½ cup (100 g) sugar

Preheat the oven to 350°F. Wash the citrus, and place them whole on a cookie sheet lined with parchment paper. Roast the fruit until it begins to brown, about 1 hour. Cool the fruit until it's just warm enough to touch, then use a paring knife to make 7 incisions in each fruit so that you can insert a total of 35 cloves.

Stack the fruit in a pitcher, jar, or small stock pot. Add sugar, then wine. Some of the fruit may be exposed. Cover and let sit in a warm place for 24 hours (the oven works well).

After the fruit is done soaking, remove it with tongs and place it on a plate. Cut the oranges and grapefruit in half, then squeeze the juice through a sieve into the wine. Transfer the wine mixture to a stockpot on the stove. Add the port. Heat, but do not boil. Serve in warm mugs or goblets.

DESSERT COCKTAILS

Many of these drinks involve cream or ice cream, turning them into boozy milk shakes that can be served on hot afternoons or after a meal. Some, like the Brandy Alexander (page 223), recall old supper clubs around Chicago or in Wisconsin (birthplace of the blender), where mobsters brought their ladies for a steak and a scenic drive. A creamy drink satisfied her sweet tooth after dinner, while he chuffed on a cigar.

Other recipes, like the sorbet-based Sgroppino (page 223), can be served between courses or as a poolside sipper. Try serving a round of Grasshoppers (page 229) midafternoon during the holidays. It's minty and thick—hefty enough to hold everyone over until supper. The Guinness Punch (page 226) is traditionally served after Sunday dinner, but can be heavenly at brunch or as a party starter. Soyer au Champagne (page 225) defines decadence; try it after a luxe meal.

SGROPPINO

Bright, lemon, effervescent

- • - • - •

A cooling sorbet-studded drink that is glamorous and soothing.

After a big meal in Italy's Veneto or Friuli regions, this drink is sent out as a chaser to cleanse the palate and aid digestion. The word *Sgroppino*, loosely translated, means "stomach un-knotter." After a nightlong Feast of the Seven Fishes, nothing is more gratifying. Though some recipes call for blending this drink, the sorbet melts quickly enough, and you really don't need to dirty one more appliance during a dinner party, do you?

1 ounce (30 ml) vodka

3 ounces (90 ml) Prosecco

1 scoop lemon sorbet (approximately ⅓ cup)

Lemon slice, for garnish

Pour vodka and Prosecco into a champagne flute. Drop in a scoop of lemon sorbet and garnish with the lemon slice on the rim of the glass.

BRANDY ALEXANDER

Delicate, creamy, spice

- • - • - •

Drink a Brandy Alexander after dinner with biscotti.

The Brandy Alexander is a plush, noggy drink topped with nutmeg, making it a splendid afternooner on a winter weekend. Serve it forth in snifters or cocktail glasses, and cue up any number of films that feature it, including *Days of Wine and Roses* or *Sgt. Bilko*. An earlier version of this drink, simply called an Alexander, was made with gin in the 1920s. The latter is downright Christmas-y with its combination of nutmeg and juniper.

Note: Supper clubs in the '50s and '60s served the Brandy Alexander as an ice cream drink after dinner. Just swap out the half-and-half for a couple scoops of vanilla ice cream, and blend.

1 ounces (30 ml) brandy (Paul Masson Grande Amber VS)

1 ounce (30 ml) dark crème de cacao

2 ounces (60 ml) half-and-half (or a scoop of vanilla ice cream)

Freshly grated nutmeg, for garnish

Shake ingredients with ice and strain into a chilled cocktail glass or brandy snifter. Garnish with nutmeg.

SOYER AU CHAMPAGNE

Creamy, effervescent, dark fruit

• •

Serve this elegant brandy drink after a big meal or a romantic dinner.

Translating to mean "Silk with Champagne," this drink combines ice cream and Champagne to create a textural composition once known as a "Plush." The recipe dates back to the 1800s, when a blend of spirits and milk topped with nutmeg came into fashion. Here, instead of blending the ingredients, we shake the spirits and pour them over a scoop of ice cream, then top it with Champagne. Prepare this tableside for the entertainment of your guests. This cocktail doesn't go with dessert, this *is* dessert!

½ ounce (15 ml) brandy (Pierre Ferrand Ambre)

½ ounce (15 ml) orange curaçao (Pierre Ferrand)

½ ounce (15 ml) maraschino liqueur (Luxardo)

1 scoop vanilla ice cream or gelato

2 ounces (60 ml) Champagne, to top off

Freshly grated nutmeg, for garnish (optional)

Shake brandy, curaçao, and maraschino with ice and strain into a chilled cocktail glass over a scoop of ice cream. Top with Champagne and garnish with nutmeg, if desired.

GUINNESS PUNCH

Malty, creamy, coffee, chocolate

• •

Blend and serve this milky punch after a spicy Jamaican affair.

In Jamaica, Guinness Punch is traditionally consumed after Sunday dinner. Guinness has a bottling plant on the island, where Guinness Foreign Extra Stout (a spikier drink than its Irish cousin) is brewed—likely the inspiration behind this cooling concoction. Locals have devised a clever way to lighten this heavy brew with milk and ice, rounding out the flavor of roasted barley with cinnamon and nutmeg. Add a couple dashes of Angostura bitters if you like a little more spice.

SERVES 4

12 ounces (355 ml) Guinness or other stout

1 cup (240 ml) whole milk

½ cup (120 ml) sweetened condensed milk

1 teaspoon vanilla

1 cup (240 ml) ice

Freshly grated nutmeg, for garnish

Cinnamon, for garnish

In a blender, combine stout, milk, condensed milk, and vanilla with ice and pulse for 10 to 15 seconds, or until well combined. Serve in chilled rocks glasses, garnished with cinnamon and nutmeg.

BITTER COCKTAILS WE'RE SWEET ON

Bitterness as a flavor in cocktails has exploded in popularity. It can be achieved by using bitters—tinctures of herbs, spices, and botanicals that get their puckery bite from natural ingredients like gentian root, cassia bark, wormwood, or dandelion—or from amaro or bitter liqueurs like Campari and Aperol.

Since many of the herbs used in these blends are believed to aid digestion, bitters-forward cocktails can be soothing after a rich meal. Their flavors are also a good way to offset the sweetness of a dessert tray. We love to serve a round of Torontos with chocolate cake or a Jungle Bird with carrot cake.

Negroni (page 91)

Paper Plane (page 165)

Toronto (page 117)

Americano (page 33)

Boulevardier (page 88)

Jungle Bird (page 192)

GRASSHOPPER

Milky, mint, chocolate

- • • • -

For a throw-back dessert, serve this shake with a few Thin Mints.

A popular after-dinner drink in the 1960s, this vintage classic actually dates back to Prohibition, when it was submitted to a New York cocktail competition by New Orleans bartender Philibert Guichet of Tujaque's. It won second place, but it didn't become a phenom until much later, when an advertising campaign aimed at lady shoppers pushed its green glow. Although Grasshopper recipes abound, we love bartender Jeffrey Morgenthaler's update: he adds a splash of Fernet-Branca and a pinch of sea salt to cut the sweetness.

1½ ounces (45 ml) green crème de menthe (Marie Brizard or Death's Door Wondermint)

1½ ounces (15 ml) white crème de cacao

1 teaspoon Fernet-Branca

1 scoop vanilla ice cream

⅛ teaspoon sea salt

1 cup ice cubes

Mint sprig, for garnish

Combine ingredients in blender. Serve in a chilled rocks or cocktail glass. Garnish with the mint sprig.

EGGNOG

Creamy, plum, spice

- • • • -

Comfort in a glass, serve this nog around the holidays with a dish of nuts.

Derived from a medieval concoction called "posset," eggnog was a popular drink amid early colonists. The most famous modern version is by food writer Craig Claiborne, who ran his family's recipe in the *New York Times* in 1958. It generated a fervor for a nog so thick and fluffy it was practically a mousse—spooned rather than sipped. For a cocktailer's version, we offer this adaptation by German bartender Stephan Hinz.

1½ ounces (45 ml) brandy or rum

1 ounce (30 ml) Pedro Ximénez sherry

1 egg yolk

½ ounce (15 ml) half-and-half

2 teaspoons powdered sugar

¼ teaspoon vanilla

Freshly grated nutmeg, for garnish

Dry shake brandy, sherry, egg, half-and-half, powdered sugar, and vanilla. Then shake with ice and strain into a chilled coupe. Garnish with nutmeg.

ATHOLL BROSE

Creamy, malty, oaty

•-

A perfect brunch libation with doughnuts, or the ultimate nightcap with gingersnaps.

A traditional Scottish concoction from the first Earl of Atholl in the 1400s, this broth (or, "Brose") is made from extracting the "liquor" from soaked oatmeal, then adding cream, Scotch, and honey. On a cold morning, this drunken oatmeal cures the blues and restores the soul to good standing. Like a milk shake and a cookie in one, this is one of the most unexpectedly delicious drinks in this book. You can serve it up, or serve it down on an ice cube. Try adding a dash of nutmeg.

FOR THE OATMEAL LIQUOR

½ cup (50 g) rolled oats (not instant or steel cut)

1½ (355 ml) cups water

FOR THE COCKTAIL

2 ounces (60 ml) Scotch (a blend, like Dewar's or Famous Grouse works well)

2 ounces (60 ml) oatmeal liquor

1 ounce (30 ml) half-and-half

1 tablespoon (15 ml) honey

For oatmeal liquor, steep oatmeal in room-temperature water overnight in a covered jar or a measuring cup draped with a dish towel. In the morning, strain the oatmeal through a mesh strainer lined with cheesecloth—you will need to give it a squeeze to extract the liquid. Collect this "liquor" in a bowl or jar, and discard the oats.

For the drink, add all of the ingredients to a shaker and dry shake. Then, add ice to the shaker. Shake and strain into a chilled rocks glass or brandy snifter filled with ice.

NO-PROOF & LOW-PROOF COCKTAILS

Not every cocktail has to pack a wallop. In fact, nonalcoholic or "no-impact" cocktails are part of a growing trend as bars cater to designated drivers, health-conscious consumers, and non-drinkers.

If you're hosting a party, offer a few of these mocktails as alternatives to soda. Prepare a couple of herbed simple syrups (page 239) and set out some soda water and garnishes. Or, pack these drinks on picnics, take them to work for a luncheon, or serve them as sophisticated sippers for a young adult shindig or an alcohol-free mixer.

Mocktails have come a long way since the Shirley Temple—although that classic is much improved with homemade grenadine (page 244). Check out the herbaceous Juniper and Tonic (page 233) or the blackberry-studded Virgin Bramble (page 235)—both use juniper syrup in place of gin. Hankering for the taste of smoky Scotch? Explore the Burning Branch (page 237).

Best of all, these drinks are easily adjusted, depending on your taste. Play around with different herbs from your garden, vary the berries, and garnish with wild abandon. Little details, like tufts of mint or pineapple spears, help these drinks morph from simple refreshers into head-turning peacocks.

LOW-PROOF COCKTAILS

If you want drinks that pair exceptionally well with food and are easy on the liver, you're looking for these seven low-alcohol cocktails. The Shandygaff is the lightest of the bunch, a simple combination of beer and ginger beer. You'll also find two Champagne-based cocktails, the Aperol Spritz and the Knabenshue. Festive and effervescent, these are appealing any time of day. At parties, we always make at least one of these drinks available.

For a dark elixir that is easy to nurse all night, check out the Fancy Vermouth Cocktail—a vintage recipe that highlights the wonderful Italian vermouth, Carpano Antica. Give the Sherry Flip a try, too—it's frothy and dramatic, with a deep purple sheen.

HORSE'S NECK

Ginger, citrus, bitter peel

・→・◆・←・

A simple refresher—pair with spicy Asian foods.

One of the earliest nonalcoholic drinks to appear in print (1895), the Horse's Neck is named for its garnish, a cutting of lemon peel that hangs down the side of a glass. This drink is simply ginger and lemon. Still, it's a snappy way to showcase homemade or high-quality ginger beer and your lemon-peeling skills. Add brandy or bourbon for a Horse's Neck with a Kick.

4 to 5 ounces (120 to 150 ml) ginger beer (page 247)

Spiral peel of half a lemon, for garnish

Dash of Angostura bitters (optional)

Fill a highball glass with ice. Add ginger beer and bitters. Garnish with the long lemon peel draped down the side of the glass.

JUNIPER AND TONIC

Fresh, bitter, herbaceous, lime

・→・◆・←・

Serve this effervescent libation with seafood, barbecue, or a plate of cheese and charcuterie.

Mixing a homemade herbal syrup with some quality tonic water can make an inspired drink that shimmers with the same aromatics used to flavor gin. It's easy and quick. Nurse them on muggy afternoons when you want a garden-y beverage without the sluggish after-effects of an actual Gin and Tonic (page 167). In addition to a squeeze of lime, this drink is lovely served with a sprig of mint or rosemary, or a spanked sage leaf.

½ ounce (15 ml) juniper syrup (page 243)

3 to 4 ounces (90 to 120 ml) tonic (Fentimans)

Lime wedge or herbs, for garnish

Fill a rocks or highball glass with ice. Add syrup and tonic, then stir briefly. Garnish with lime wedge in the glass.

LITTLE PINK PEARL

Floral, citrus, almond

・・・・・

Perfect for serving at a bridal or baby shower or a sweet sixteen party. The tartness pairs with everything from white cake to grilled meats.

The Little Pink Pearl is one of the all-time great mocktails. Loosely based on the Pink Pearl, a drink that features vodka and grapefruit juice, this nonalcoholic version is similarly glamorous and pearlescent. You can purchase orgeat, an almond syrup that is popular in tiki drinks, but it's a cinch to make from scratch (page 244). It's the key to this drink's opaque sheen and silky texture.

> 1 ounce (30 ml) fresh lime juice
>
> 2 ounces (60 ml) fresh pink grapefruit juice
>
> ½ ounce (15 ml) orgeat (page 244)
>
> Grapefruit quarter wheel, for garnish

Shake ingredients with ice and strain into a chilled coupe glass. Garnish with grapefruit quarter on the edge of the glass.

SWITCHEL, OR HAYMAKER'S PUNCH

Ginger, sour, spice, citrus

・・・・・

Pack a jar of Switchel on a picnic. Its kick of vinegar and molasses makes it an excellent companion to pulled pork.

This drink has its origins in the Caribbean before spreading to the American colonies, where it became associated with harvest time. Jars of it were carried into the field to slake the thirst of farm laborers—hence the name Haymaker's Punch. Think of it as a tangy cousin to ginger beer. This American heritage drink has made a comeback recently, thanks to small-batch Switchel bottlers in Vermont and Bushwick, Brooklyn.

SERVES 8

> 6 cups (1½ L) cold water
>
> 2 tablespoons (30 ml) ginger root, grated
>
> ½ cup (120 ml) maple syrup
>
> ¼ cup (60 ml) molasses
>
> ¼ cup (60 ml) apple cider vinegar
>
> 1½ ounces (45 ml) fresh lemon juice
>
> 1 lemon, sliced, for garnish

Combine the ingredients in a pitcher or large jar and let the flavors meld for at least 2 hours or overnight. Taste it, in case you need to make any adjustments, then strain before serving. Serve in ice-filled highball glasses, garnished with lemon.

MARY POPP-INS
(SHIRLEY TEMPLE)

Pomegranate, citrus, sparkle

- • • • -

The tartness of homemade grenadine makes this a strangely good accompaniment for Mediterranean cuisine, like stuffed grape leaves. It's also excellent with kid food, like a PB&J.

The classic Shirley Temple, a drink served to small beings everywhere, gets a craft update with a bit of extra gleeful customer participation. In the seventeenth century, it was purportedly a common practice to add a "pop-in" flavor shot to a light beer. Re-popularized by the Dead Rabbit Grocery and Grog in New York, we incorporate the fun idea here for added effect—kids and adults alike enjoy the added bit of theater and attention. With homemade grenadine and an umbrella, this is a bit of magic.

1 ounce (30 ml) homemade grenadine (page 244)

3 to 4 ounces (90 to 120 ml) soda water

Lime wedge, for garnish

Cherry, for garnish

Pour grenadine into a shot glass. Add ice to a highball glass and nearly top off with soda. Garnish with an umbrella stuck in the cherry and lime wedge. Let the lucky recipient slowly pour the grenadine from the shot glass into the highball glass before drinking.

VIRGIN BRAMBLE

Herbaceous, berry, citrus

- • • • -

Serve before dinner in the garden at the height of berry season. It pairs well with funky cheeses, pork chops, or roasted chicken.

Featuring blackberries and juniper syrup, this adaptation of Aida Mollenkamp's garden-y sipper riffs off a modern classic, the Bramble (page 178). At a party, try offering both the gin-based Bramble and this nonalcoholic version. It's especially lovely served over crushed ice with its garnish of extra herbs and blackberries. We like to set out a mason jar full of herbs and let partygoers choose from a variety.

3 teaspoons juniper syrup (page 243)

½ ounce (15 ml) fresh lemon juice

6 blackberries

Sprig of tarragon, rosemary, or mint, for muddling

3 ounces (90 ml) soda water

In a rocks glass or highball, stir together juniper syrup and lemon juice. Add the blackberries and a sprig of herbs, then gently muddle. Add ice and top off with soda. Serve with a straw.

BURNING BRANCH

Smoky, caramel, citrus

- ◦ ◦ ◦ -

Try this fireside sipper with toasted almonds and pretzels after work, or pair it with a turkey dinner.

Lapsang Souchong syrup, made from smoked tea, is an excellent replacement for Scotch. In this unusual drink, you get a rich, peaty taste that's brightened by lemon and rounded off with apple cider. During the holidays, this is a perfect nonalcoholic offering since it pairs well with fall flavors.

> 2 ounces (60 ml) apple cider
>
> 2 teaspoons Lapsang Souchong tea syrup (page 243)
>
> ½ ounce (15 ml) fresh lemon juice
>
> Lemon twist, for garnish

Shake ingredients with ice and strain over a single large cube of ice in a rocks glass. To garnish, twist the peel over the surface of the cocktail to express the oil. Then rest it on the edge of the glass.

LIME CORDIAL SODA

Fresh lime, aromatic

- ◦ ◦ ◦ -

Serve these berry-studded sodas at a Fourth of July picnic, alongside grilled chicken and potato salad.

Lime cordial is traditionally used to make a Gimlet (page 113). Here, it makes a bright sparkler that pairs with just about everything—a quiet moment on the porch, a twilight supper in the garden, or an evening of watching fireworks in the park. If you want to make a batch of this soda for taking outdoors, combine it in a glass bottle with a cork stopper. In addition to garnishing the glasses with berries, you can add lime slices or fresh mint.

> ½ ounce (15 ml) lime cordial (page 245)
>
> 4 ounces (120 ml) soda water
>
> Blackberries and blueberries, for garnish

Pour lime cordial into a highball glass. Add ice and soda water. Drop in berries for garnish, and serve with a straw.

BLACK JULEP

Mint, earth, bittersweet

—•–•–•–•—

The ultimate drink to serve with pecan pie, this minty coffee cooler is a dramatic pick-me-up and terrific contrast to sweet flavors.

It is possible to make this drink by muddling mint sprigs with sugar, but a mint syrup melds the flavors together better. The Black Julep is a dramatic combination that lifts a pedestrian cup of coffee into the ethereal, with the mint and sugar teasing out new flavor notes from quality beans. Keep a jar of mint syrup in your fridge door, and you can make them anytime.

½ ounce (15 ml) mint syrup (page 243)

4 ounces (120 ml) coffee, cooled

Mint sprig, for garnish

Stir mint syrup and coffee together in a rocks glass. Add ice and garnish with mint.

PART FOUR

RECIPES FOR SYRUPS, ORGEAT, CORDIAL, GINGER BEER, SHRUBS, BITTERS, TONIC & MORE

SIMPLE SYRUP

Many drinks call for simple syrup to unify flavors and add viscosity to drinks. We like to use organic raw sugar, like Demerara, in place of bleached refined sugar because it has greater depth of flavor. For more about sugar options, check out the sugar note in our pantry list (page 256). Store your simple syrup in a squeeze bottle—a bartender tip that prevents your work space from getting sticky.

For flavored syrups using herbs or fruit, we love the advice of Amy Stewart (aka *The Drunken Botanist*), who recommends heating equal parts sugar and water together, then steeping the herbs or fruit in the hot syrup. Steeping the herbs rather than simmering them with the water and sugar, as many recipes advise—makes for a bright, zesty infusion, rather than a syrup with a cooked taste. You can halve these recipes, or double them, depending on your needs. Covered and refrigerated, these syrups will last for about a month. You can extend their shelf life considerably by adding an ounce of vodka.

MAKES 1½ CUPS (12 OUNCES)

1 cup (200 g) Demerara sugar

1 cup (240 ml) water

Heat the sugar and water in a saucepan over medium heat. Do not boil. Stir until sugar dissolves, about 3 to 5 minutes, then remove the pan from the stove. Cool. Transfer the syrup to a clean bottle or jar. Cover and refrigerate.

Note: If you use plain white granulated sugar, you do not need to heat the mixture on the stove. Simply combine sugar and warm water in a jar, then cover it tightly with a lid, and give it a good shake.

RICH DEMERARA SIMPLE SYRUP

Use in Art of Choke (page 146).

Use a ratio of 2:1 Demerara sugar to water, and follow the recipe instructions above to create a rich, viscous syrup.

RASPBERRY SYRUP

Use in the Clover Club (page 57), Rose Cocktail (page 84), and the Knickerbocker (page 32).

Make a Rich Demerara Syrup (see above) with ½ cup (120 ml) of water and 1 cup (200 g) of Demerara sugar. Add 1½ cups (190 g) of fresh raspberries. Stir. Cover the mixture, and let it rest on the counter for 8 to 12 hours, or overnight. Strain the mixture through a sieve using the back of a large wooden spoon to press down on the berries and extract all the juices. Discard the solids. Transfer the syrup to a clean jar and refrigerate for up to a week.

Note: This syrup is best within a few days when the aroma of fresh raspberries is most intense.

HONEY SYRUP

Use in a Bee's Knees (page 85).

Honey blends with water more easily than sugar and does not need to be heated unless it has crystallized. For the easiest method, combine equal parts honey and warm water in a clean jar or bottle, cover it tightly, and give the mixture a vigorous shake. Then, refrigerate.

HONEY GINGER SYRUP

Use in a Penicillin (page 135) or Barbacoa (page 145).

In a saucepan, combine 1 cup (240 ml) water and 2 inches (5 cm) of peeled fresh ginger root, thinly sliced. Simmer covered for 5 minutes. Remove from heat, strain, and discard ginger. While the mixture is still warm, add a scant cup of honey and stir. Pour into a clean jar or bottle, cover, and refrigerate.

MINT SYRUP

Use in a Mint Julep (page 171).

Follow the Simple Syrup recipe (page 241). Bring the mixture to a simmer, then remove the pan from the heat and add 1 cup (15 g) of loosely packed mint leaves. Gently muddle the leaves against the side of the pan using the back of a wooden spoon. Cover, and allow the mint to steep for 30 minutes to an hour. Strain and pour into a clean jar or bottle. Then, cover and refrigerate.

CINNAMON SYRUP

Use in a Zombie (page 189) or add to iced tea.

Add 3 cinnamon sticks to 1 cup (240 ml) of water, and simmer covered for 10 minutes. Turn off the heat, remove cinnamon sticks from the pan, and stir in 1 cup (200 g) of sugar until it dissolves. Cool. Pour into a clean bottle or jar. Cover and refrigerate.

LAPSANG SOUCHONG TEA SYRUP

Use in a Rob Roy (page 52) or add to Burning Branch.

Pour 1 cup (240 ml) of boiling water over 1 tablespoon (1.5 grams) of Lapsang Souchong tea leaves. Steep for 5 minutes. Strain out tea leaves, and stir in 1 cup of sugar until it dissolves. Cool. Pour into a clean bottle or jar. Cover and refrigerate.

JUNIPER SYRUP

Use in a Juniper and Tonic (page 233).

Follow the recipe for Simple Syrup (page 241), bringing the syrup to a full simmer. Then, remove the syrup from the heat and add 1 tablespoon (1 g) of roughly crushed juniper berries (use a mortar and pestle), 3 loosely torn bay leaves, and a 3-inch (8 cm) sprig of fresh rosemary. Cover, and let steep for 1 hour. Strain the syrup into a clean bottle or jar. Cover and refrigerate.

Note: Additional herbs that can be used: basil, cardamom, peppercorns, sage, lavender, mint.

GRENADINE

Sweet and scarlet, grenadine is what makes a Tequila Sunrise (page 117) rise and what turns a Shirley Temple (page 235) into a grin-inducing mocktail. Unfortunately, most commercial grenadines are nothing more than sugar water and red dye, which is why making it from scratch is preferable. We offer you a simple recipe that can easily be made with POM, a flash-pasteurized juice made from pomegranates, or with freshly squeezed pomegranate juice (use a levered juicer; each fruit yields 2 to 3 ounces (60 to 90 ml). Many grocery stores carry orange flower water in their international foods section.

MAKES 1½ CUPS (12 OUNCES) (356 ML)

   1 cup (8 ounces, or 240 ml) pomegranate juice

   1 cup (200 g) Demerara sugar

   ½ teaspoon fresh lime juice

   2 to 3 drops orange flower water

Pour the juice into a small saucepan and add sugar. Turn the heat to medium-low and stir until the sugar dissolves, about 3 to 4 minutes. Do not boil—you want the flavors to remain fresh, not to taste cooked. When the sugar is dissolved, remove the pan from the heat and stir in lime juice and orange flower water. Cool, then transfer to a clean bottle or jar. Covered, this will last in the refrigerator for about 1 month.

Note: To add to the shelf life of homemade grenadine, drop in an ounce of vodka or bourbon.

ORGEAT

Orgeat is a common ingredient in tiki drinks and several vintage recipes, including the Japanese Cocktail (page 33). Although you can order orgeat syrup online, this is a quick and economical version we've adapted from Kevin Liu. Try a Mai Tai (page 185), a Scorpion Bowl (page 192), or a modern Trinidad Sour (page 142).

MAKES ABOUT 1 CUP (8 OUNCES OR 240 ML)

   ½ cup (100 g) Demerara sugar

   Peel of half a grapefruit

   1 scant cup (220 ml) almond milk (preferably Silk Original)

   8 drops almond extract

   4 drops orange flower water

In a small mixing bowl or measuring cup, macerate sugar and grapefruit peels for 1 hour, so that the oil from the peel seeps into the crystals. After an hour, add almond milk to the sugar mixture and remove the peel (chop-sticks work well). Add almond extract and orange flower water. Stir well or shake the mixture in a jar. It will take several minutes for the sugar to incorporate. Once combined, cover and refrigerate (it will thicken into a syrup). Orgeat will keep for about 1 week.

LIME CORDIAL

Plenty of lime cordial recipes either boil the ingredients or microplane lime zest into simple syrup. Neither method works. Boiling reduces the freshness of the lime flavor considerably, and lime zest, while providing great aroma, does not add enough flavor. It's far better to muddle lime peels in sugar to release their oils, and then add additional lime zest for a wonderfully fresh nose. This recipe makes a robust, unforgettable lime cordial that tastes like Rose's lime juice but without artificial coloring or high-fructose corn syrup! The two additional acids (tartaric and citric) will ratchet up the acidity to the level of Rose's, but you can omit them if you prefer a milder cordial.

Note: Citric acid is available at most super markets in the canning section.

MAKES 2 CUPS (16 OUNCES, OR 475 ML)

8 limes, divided

1 cup (200 g) Demerara sugar

1 cup (240 ml) hot water

½ teaspoon cream of tartar (tartaric acid)

½ teaspoon citric acid

Peel 4 limes so as not to get too much pith (an OXO peeler works better than a typical vegetable peeler here). Muddle peels with 1 cup of sugar. Let rest on the counter for 1 hour to express oils from the peel. Pour in 1 cup of hot (not boiling) water and stir until sugar is dissolved. Juice the 4 peeled limes, and add this to the mixture. Microplane four additional limes and add the zest. Infuse for 15 minutes on the counter, then stir and strain into a clean bottle or jar. Add tartaric and citric acid, then cover and shake. Store in the refrigerator. For the freshest flavor, use this within one week.

FALERNUM

This recipe is an alternative to purchasing commercial falernum, which can be hard to find. Many homemade falernum recipes call for fresh lime juice, but they can turn quickly, even in the refrigerator. A common solution to this problem is to infuse rum with lime zest—but we've noticed that lime zest does not give a lot of flavor; it smells great, but doesn't lend much depth. Instead, we make our falernum starting with oleo saccharum—citrus peels muddled in sugar to release their essential oils—creating a potent simple syrup that we then combine with rum laced with toasted spices. This recipe is terrific in tiki or tiki-inspired drinks, like the Test Pilot (page 187), Three Dots and a Dash (page 187), Rum Runner (page 188), Zombie (page 189), Corn 'n' Oil (page 194), and Chartreuse Swizzle (page 198).

MAKES 3½ CUPS (28 OUNCES OR 828 ML)

FOR THE RUM INFUSION

1 cup (240 ml) rum (use an overproof rum like Wray & Nephew)

40 cloves

1 tablespoon (1 g) allspice berries

15 raw almonds

1½ ounces (43 g) fresh ginger (by weight), or about ¼ cup minced

FOR THE LIME SIMPLE SYRUP

2 cups (400 g) Demerara sugar

1 cup (240 ml) water

6 drops almond extract

8 lime peels

To make the rum infusion, toast the cloves, allspice berries, and almonds in a skillet over medium heat until gently browned. Cool. Then add spices and ginger to the rum. Let infuse covered for 24 hours at room temperature. Strain with a cheesecloth into a jar to combine with the lime syrup.

To make the lime syrup, peel 8 limes so as not to get too much pith (an OXO peeler works better than a typical vegetable peeler here). Muddle peels with 2 cups (400 g) of sugar. Let rest on the counter for 1 hour to express oils from the peel. Pour in 1 cup (140 ml) of hot (not boiling) water and stir until sugar is dissolved. Strain into a jar and add almond extract. Discard peel. Cool.

To make falernum, combine infused rum and lime syrup in a clean bottle or jar. Covered and refrigerated, this will last for several months.

MÉTHODE CHAMPENOISE GINGER BEER

A lot of ginger beer recipes are little more than ginger-flavored punch. We prefer true fermented ginger beers by far, since they have so much more flavor and they're almost as easy to make.

Some recipes call for fermenting ginger beer in glass bottles, but beware that glass can explode. We make our ginger beer in recycled 2-liter plastic soda bottles. They are safer and are helpful because you can squeeze them to test when fermentation is done (when they're firm to the touch, the ginger beer is ready).

During fermentation, you can place the ginger beer in a cooler as an extra precaution, but under a counter works just fine. You will need a juicer to make the fresh ginger juice, or you can purchase it from a juice counter. Just be sure to use it right away, as the flavor dissipates quickly.

MAKES 2 LITERS

1 tablespoon (15 ml) honey

1 cup (200 g) Demerara sugar, divided

¼ teaspoon Champagne yeast (Red Star)

2 ounces (60 ml) fresh lime juice or lemon juice

¾ ounce (22 ml) fresh ginger juice

½ teaspoon cream of tartar

¼ teaspoon cayenne pepper

8 black peppercorns

3 cloves

2 liters filtered water

In a measuring cup, dissolve honey and 1 tablespoon sugar in a shy half cup of warm water, then add the yeast. Pour remaining ingredients into a 2-liter bottle and shake vigorously until the sugar is dissolved.

Add the yeast and sugar mixture. Fill with water half way. Shake again, fill to the top, close securely, and store in a warm, dark place for exactly 48 hours.

Open the bottle slowly and carefully as contents will be under pressure. After opening, keep the ginger beer in the refrigerator and open once or twice a day to relieve additional pressure.

Note: Fermentation is dependent on ambient temperature, so if you put the bottle in a cool basement, it will take longer. Check fermentation by squeezing the bottle; it should be very firm and not give when you press with your thumb.

STRAWBERRY SHRUB

A shrub is a tangy syrup that can be used to flavor cocktails or mocktails—try a splash in soda water or lemonade. Prior to refrigeration, combining fruit with sugar and vinegar was a clever means of capturing the essence of something with a short harvest season, like berries. While commercial shrub varieties are available (we love the shrubs from Tait Farm), it can be gratifying to make it yourself. After experimenting with hot and cold processes, we've fallen for the latter—it retains the freshness of the fruit and tastes less "jammy" than cooked varieties. Keep in mind that you'll need to let the berries macerate in sugar for two days and that a shrub tastes best after it sits in the refrigerator for at least a week or two—the vinegar mellows and the flavors meld.

Note: Granulated sugar works best here since the crystals need to be small enough to dissolve without heat.

MAKES ABOUT 1½ CUPS (12 OUNCES)

2 cups (250 g) fresh strawberries, hulled and sliced

1 cup (200 g) sugar

1 cup (240 ml) Champagne vinegar

Combine berries and sugar in a non-reactive bowl and macerate the fruit, using a muddler or the back of a wooden spoon. Cover the mixture, and let it sit in the fridge for 48 hours, or until the strawberries have released their juices. Stir with a whisk to incorporate any undissolved sugar, then add vinegar. Stir. Strain out the solids and discard them. Transfer the shrub to a clean jar or bottle, and refrigerate for at least a week before using. Refrigerated, a shrub can last up to a year.

SHRUB VARIATIONS

Feel free to substitute raspberries or blackberries for strawberries. You can also add a tablespoon of crushed pink peppercorns for a little kick, or a sprig of fresh herbs, such as rosemary, tarragon, lavender, sage, or mint. Spices like star anise or cloves work well, too, and add a touch of fragrance—crush a few with a mortar and pestle, then toss them in to macerate with the berries and sugar. Just remove the herbs or spices when you strain out the berries.

A note on vinegars: You can make shrubs using other kinds of vinegar or a combination of vinegars, such as rice wine vinegar, white wine vinegar, or other fruit vinegars. Just be aware that if your vinegar is too harsh, it will mask the subtle flavors of the berries. We've found that unfiltered apple cider vinegar works best if it's mixed (1:1) with a light-colored vinegar.

HOW TO USE SHRUBS IN DRINKS

Shrub strength can vary, but here's a general rule of thumb: use ½ ounce (15 ml) of shrub, 2 ounces (60 ml) of spirits, 1 ounce (30 ml) of citrus, and 2 to 3 ounces (60 to 90 ml) of soda water for a shrub cocktail on the rocks. For a shaken cocktail, use ½ ounce (15 ml) shrub, ½ ounce (15 ml) complementary liqueur, 2 ounces (60 ml) of spirit, and a dash of bitters. You can also make a wine spritzer by adding a splash of shrub to equal parts wine and soda water.

HORCHATA

This overnight rice milk drink can be used in our Rumchata (page 201) or to create a nondairy White Russian (page 123). Served without booze, it makes a refreshing nonalcoholic party beverage. It's light, creamy, and laced with cinnamon and vanilla. In Mexico, it's sold at roadside stands and taquerias as a cooling complement to hot weather and spicy foods. To sweeten horchata, you can use simple syrup, sugar, or sweetened condensed milk (this imparts an even creamier texture). We love using leftover horchata to make a coffee-chata—just pour horchata over ice and add a shot of espresso.

MAKES 4½ CUPS (36 OUNCES)

1 cup (185 g) uncooked long-grain white rice

1 small cinnamon stick

4 cups (950 ml) cold water, divided

½ cup (120 ml) simple syrup (page 241)

2 teaspoons vanilla

¼ teaspoon sea salt

Combine rice, cinnamon stick, and 2 cups (475 ml) water in a large jar or pitcher. Cover and let sit for at least 8 hours, or overnight. Blend the rice mixture, including the cinnamon stick, in a blender on high for 15 to 20 seconds, or until the rice has been ground to a sandy consistency. Add the remaining 2 cups of water, and blend a second time, briefly. Strain the rice mixture through a fine-mesh kitchen strainer lined with cheesecloth. You'll need to stir it to help the mixture pass through the cloth. Discard the leftover rice paste. Stir in syrup, vanilla, and salt. Chill until ready to serve.

TONIC WATER (SYRUP)

Making a tonic syrup is a fresh, economical way to create your own tonic water, especially if you want to avoid high-fructose corn syrup. To source some of these ingredients, visit a spice shop or you can find them online (we like dandelionbotanical.com and mountainroseherbs.com). Citric acid powder is available in the canning section of many groceries.

MAKES ABOUT 2 CUPS
(16 OUNCES OR 475 ML)

1 whole lemon peel

1 whole lime peel

1 whole orange peel

2 teaspoons cinchona bark

½ teaspoon allspice berries

1 teaspoon gentian root

2 teaspoons citric acid powder

½ cup (50 g) lemongrass stalk, roughly chopped

⅛ teaspoon sea salt

1½ cups (190 g) sugar

Combine ingredients, except sugar, in a saucepan with 2 cups (475 ml) of water and heat over medium-high heat just until boiling. Turn down the heat to low, cover, and simmer for 15 minutes.

Strain liquid using a coffee filter (or a French press works nicely). Put liquid back on medium heat and stir in sugar until dissolved. Cool. Transfer to a bottle and refrigerate. This will keep for at least 2 weeks.

To make tonic water: Combine ¾ ounces (22 ml) of tonic syrup with 4 ounces (½ cup or 120 ml) of soda water or mineral water.

AROMATIC BITTERS

Making bitters is easy—they are simply infusions of spices, herbs, tree barks, fruit, or other ingredients into high-proof alcohol. Use spirits that are 100 proof or higher, like Everclear, Wray & Nephew rum, or overproof whiskey, such as Wild Turkey 101 or Rittenhouse. Since each herb, spice, or tree bark infuses into alcohol at different rates, a good method for making bitters is to create separate infusions for each ingredient and then combine them. But here we give you a quick-and-dirty, all-in-one recipe that will get you started—and excited—about the world of homemade bitters. The most difficult part of making bitters is procuring the required herbs. There are plenty of online resources (we like dandelionbotanical.com and mountainroseherbs.com). Bitters bottles can be procured online (try specialtybottle.com and cocktailkingdom.com). We like to make two cups of bitters at a time so that it is easy to experiment with a variety of aromatics and bittering agents without ending up with a lifetime supply.

MAKES ABOUT 3 CUPS (24 OUNCES)

2 cups (475 ml) high-proof whiskey (Wild Turkey 101)

2 star anise

2 allspice berries

5 cloves

1 whole cardamom pod

¼ teaspoon coriander seeds

¼ teaspoon quassia bark

¼ teaspoon cassia chips

¼ teaspoon gentian root

1 teaspoon dried lemon peel

1 tablespoon (1 g) dried bitter orange peel

1½ tablespoon (20 g) Demerara sugar

Toast star anise, allspice berries, cloves, cardamom, coriander seeds, quassia bark, cassia chips, and gentian root in a skillet over medium-high heat until they are aromatic (about 5 minutes). In a clean jar, add whiskey and toasted spices plus the lemon and orange peel. Seal and leave on the counter for 2 weeks, shaking once per day.

Strain mixture into a clean jar, reserving spices. Add sugar to whiskey, and shake until dissolved. Steep spices in ½ cup (120 ml) of hot water (just off a boil) for about 8 minutes, strain, and pour spiced water into the whiskey and sugar mixture and stir. Your bitters should keep indefinitely, but it's best to use them within a couple of months while flavors are most potent.

PART FIVE

TOOLS, GLASS-WARE, PANTRY SUGGESTIONS & TECHNIQUES

TOOLS

You may find yourself mixing your first batch of cocktails in a mason jar before you progress to a proper shaker. No harm there. As your interests and technique develops, you'll begin to pick up more bar gear. If you want to flame citrus peel or add fresh nutmeg to a nog, then yes, you will want a Y-peeler and a microplane. Here are the bar tools we could never live without:

bar spoon	citrus press	zester
mixing glass	Y-peeler	funnel
Boston shaker	bamboo skewers	small spray bottle or atomizer
jigger	bottle opener	large-format ice cube trays
julep strainer	wine key	ice bucket
hawthorne strainer	muddler	ice scoop
small sieve	swizzle stick	hand towels
cutting board	squeeze bottle	
paring knife	microplane	

GLASSWARE

You don't need twenty different styles of glasses to set up a respectable home bar. We are cocktail fiends who live in limited spaces, and we've winnowed our glassware down to five basic glass styles. Unless you're fixing tiki drinks, which look sexy in those curvy hurricanes, you don't need a lot of special glassware.

Cocktail or coupe glass (5½ to 6½ ounces or 163 to 192 ml; we love the graceful bird-bath style coupe, even for martinis)

Champagne flute (6 ounces or 180 ml, narrow flutes show off Champagne bubbles)

Rocks glass (5 to 10 ounces or 148 to 300 ml, also known as lowball or old fashioned)

Highball glass (8 to 10 ounces or 240 to 300 ml, perfect for a Collins, fizz, or swizzle)

Irish coffee mug (8 ounces, clear, footed, heat-resistant, good for mulled drinks and toddies)

PANTRY SUGGESTIONS

In addition to stocking quality booze, you'll want fresh ingredients and spices. You may already have many of these staples on hand, but we've put together notes for special items, like eggs and sugar, that appear regularly in this book.

ICE . . . .

Ice is the engine that makes cocktails purr. Needless to say, if you're using expensive spirits, the quality of your water matters, too. We recommend you use filtered water and replenish your ice cube trays fairly often since ice absorbs freezer odors. For minimal cost, buy a large-format silicon square ice cube tray. For crushed ice, it's handy to have a fridge that spews out chips 'n' bits, but you can also use a food processor or opt for an old-fashioned Lewis bag and mallet. If you're throwing a party, and need to pick up pre-made ice, just note that it will melt quickly. To counteract, try filling the shaker a little fuller than normal and shaking for a shorter time.

EGGS . . . .

For flips, nogs, and fizzes, use fresh organic eggs from the farmers' market when you can. Be sure to wash them. If you're concerned about raw egg, use pasteurized egg whites. If you have a compromised immune system, you may want to use powdered egg whites: 2 teaspoons of powder, plus 1 ounce of water will approximate a single white. We measure out ¾ ounce (22 ml) of egg white per drink. Note that old recipes often call for a whole egg white, but today's eggs are larger and can result in a drink that's too eggy. A Grade A large egg today generally yields 1½ (45 ml) ounces of white—so think: one egg equals two drinks.

RAW SUGAR . . . .

Wherever possible, we've cut back the sugar in these recipes. That said, sugar is to bartenders what salt is to chefs—it often adds texture, pulls ingredients together, and lifts drinks into the sublime. From the variety of sugars on the market, we usually opt for organic raw sugar rather than bleached or refined sugar for our simple syrup recipe (page 241). Demerara, turbinado, and Muscovado are examples of raw sugar. They contain a hint of molasses, which we like, especially in dark elixirs. If you want a clear syrup for aesthetic reasons, use white cane sugar.

DEMERARA SUGAR CUBES

Sugar cubes made from organic raw sugar are available at specialty food stores. If you can't find them, substitute 1 teaspoon sugar (preferably Demerara). Sugar cubes figure into several cocktails in this book, such as the Sazerac (page 37) and the Champagne Cocktail (page 205).

HONEY

Recipes like the Bee's Knees (page 85) and Moral Suasion (page 34) call for a honey syrup since pure honey is too thick to dissolve in a cocktail without being diluted. This is usually made with a 1:1 ratio of honey to warm water, but a nice trick is to use 1:1 honey and simple syrup—it brings out honey flavors and dilutes drinks less. We like to use a local light-colored honey for clear cocktails or gin-based cocktails, and we'll ramp up to a darker, more complex honey for whiskey or rum drinks. For our honey-syrup recipe, see page 242.

AGAVE

Despite its popularity in mixed drinks, we rarely use agave due to its heavy processing. (In this book, agave is mentioned in the Oaxaca Old Fashioned, page 139, and the Barbacoa, page 145.) Even though it ranks low on the glycemic index, it contains more fructose than any other sweetener, including high-fructose corn syrup. Beware: when it's labeled "raw," it doesn't mean it isn't processed, due to lax labeling laws.

GRENADINE

Check out our recipe for homemade grenadine (page 244), and avoid buying the fake stuff, which is loaded with red dye and corn syrup. Then make yourself an El Diablo (page 115).

ORGEAT

Commonly found in tiki drinks, like the Mai Tai (page 185) and vintage drinks like the Japanese Cocktail (page 33), orgeat is a syrup made from almonds that first appeared in Jerry Thomas's *The Bar-Tender's Guide* (1862). It tastes a bit like marzipan and gives drinks a wonderful consistency. Now that vintage cocktails are back in vogue, you can find artisan orgeat online from small companies like Small Hand Foods and B.G. Reynolds. It's also easy to make a great-tasting orgeat from scratch (recipe on page 244) using easily sourced ingredients.

HALF-AND-HALF...

In recipes that call for cream, like the Grasshopper (page 229) or Brandy Alexander (page 223), we opt for organic half-and-half. It's lighter and won't coat the roof of your mouth.

GINGER BEER ....

A crucial ingredient in recipes like the Dark 'n' Stormy (page 194), ginger beer is made by a handful of companies, some of our favorites being Blenheim, Boylan, Reed's, and Fever-Tree. Many bars concoct their own versions, making essentially a quick ginger syrup they mix with soda water. For a real fermented recipe that is tasty and far less expensive than anything you can buy, check out ours on page 247. It's a wowing, nearly nonalcoholic beverage.

TONIC WATER ....

For an exceptional Gin and Tonic (page 167), use a tonic water that contains real quinine, like Fever-Tree or Fentimans. Fentimans, from Britain, has been around since 1905 and uses milled quinine bark and cane sugar. You can also use soda water with Jack Rudy small-batch tonic syrup, found in many liquor stores. Or make your own syrup—well worth it and very economical (recipe, page 251).

CARBONATED WATER...

This includes club soda, seltzer, or mineral water. It's worth noting that these differ from one another. Club soda includes additives—usually sodium or potassium, while seltzer is simply water to which carbonation has been added. Mineral water is bottled from a mineral spring and often has finer bubbles than club soda or seltzer.

SPICES ....

Buy small amounts from a spice shop, and store them in tightly sealed containers away from heat so that they don't lose their potency too quickly. Freshly grating or grinding your own spices is always vastly superior to using powders.

CITRUS . . . .

When possible, buy organic citrus fruit. Wash fruits before use. Note that while some bartenders swear by rolling citrus or even microwaving lemons and limes to extract more juice, you get about the same amount of juice any way you go.

OLIVES . . . .

For martinis, we like to buy plump emerald Castelvetranos and store them in dry white vermouth. If there's a jarred olive variety that you like, try pouring out half of the brine and replacing it with dry vermouth and a few extra spices to create your own signature cocktail olive. You can also add a tablespoon of coriander, caraway, or peppercorns (or all three) for added flavor. Toss in a few strands of lemon zest and some chopped jalapeño if you want your olives extra zesty.

CHERRIES. . . . .

Look for Luxardo Gourmet Maraschino Cherries or Amarena cherries imported in syrup—they can be found at specialty food stores. A bartender tip: drain off half the Amarena syrup and replace it with bourbon.

BITTERS . . . .

Keep Angostura, Peychaud's, and orange bitters on hand. They are lovely to drop into a glass of sparkling water as a quick digestif. We offer a recipe for your own in-house version (page 252).

SEA SALT . . . .

Salt is a bold flavor enhancer in drinks such as the Margarita (page 118) or Red Snapper (page 158), but it can be used more subtly to dampen bitterness and accentuate sweetness and sourness. Use a pinch of sea salt to finish drinks (see Harvey Wallbanger, page 128), or you can use 2 to 4 drops of saline solution—1 part salt to 10 parts water.

A NOTE ON STORING BOTTLES

You don't need a fancy cabinet to set up your bar, just somewhere dark and cool (we've used everything from an old desk to a cleaning closet). Most spirits, other than crème liqueurs, will last for years, so you can think of them as long-term investments. However, vermouths or light sherries, once opened, should be stored in the fridge, where they will last for about a month.

TECHNIQUES

STIRRING VS. SHAKING

As a general rule: **Stir** spirit-only drinks. **Shake** any drink with citrus, cream, eggs, and/or muddled ingredients.

A Manhattan (page 41) is *stirred* because it's made up of whiskey and vermouth, which simply need to be blended together. A Ramos Gin Fizz (page 42), the classic egg drink, needs to be *shaken* to emulsify the eggs and citrus.

If you want to explore the value of these techniques, make two martinis. Stir one, shake the other. You'll be able to see and taste remarkable differences. The shaken martini will be cloudy, effervescent (fizzy), and textured with icy shivs, whereas a perfectly stirred martini will be transparent with a texture like velvet.

For more on the timing of these techniques, see our lessons on how to make a perfectly stirred and shaken drink.

Note: Shaken cocktails are strained from the larger, metal half of the shaker with a hawthorne strainer while stirred cocktails are strained from the mixing glass with a julep strainer.

ROLLING A COCKTAIL ....

Rolling is a technique somewhere between shaking and stirring. If a drink needs to be blended but you don't want to flatten the flavors with a true shake, pouring it from one half of the shaker to the other and back again is called "rolling." We mention it with the El Presidente cocktail (page 83), which we believe works wonders for the drink, but it can be used in many applications, including daiquiris and mojitos.

BUILDING A DRINK IN THE GLASS ....

Built drinks are created in the glass in which they are served. They often involve either muddling or the addition of carbonated water.

MUDDLING. ....

The key to muddling is to gently press the ingredients against the side of the glass to release their oils. No need to muddle lime wedges or mint leaves to bits—there's nothing worse than sipping a mojito so overmuddled that the mint catches in your teeth. If you don't have a muddler, you can improvise using the handle of a wooden spoon.

DOUBLE-STRAINING. ....

If a drink contains eggs or seedy berries, sometimes a recipe will call for straining through a second, finer mesh. It can also be used to clear excess ice shivs from a shaken drink. All you need is a small kitchen strainer or tea strainer. Hold it over your cocktail glass as you strain your drink through it from the shaker. To help the liquid pass through the fine mesh, tap the strainer against the shaker.

RINSING (OR WASHING) THE GLASS ....

If a recipe calls for an "absinthe rinse," you can spritz absinthe on the inside of your cocktail glass using an atomizer. Or, simply pour about ¼ ounce (7 ml) of spirit into the chilled glass, whirl it around to coat the insides, and discard any extra drops.

DRY SHAKING ....

Dry shaking helps to emulsify a drink containing egg, which is challenging to incorporate with spirits. For a dry shake, skip the ice and shake the ingredients vigorously for at least 10 to 15 seconds. Then, open the shaker and if things look frothy and well combined, add ice and reshake. Where dry shaking is required in this book, we say so in the recipe.

A NOTE ON SHAKER STYLES

The cobbler shaker is the iconic three-piece shaker of yesteryear, but it can be difficult to get apart when it gets cold. The Boston shaker is simpler in design and has become the professional bartender tool. It has two parts that fit snugly together—a pint glass and a metal shaker bottom.

HOW TO MAKE A SHAKEN DRINK
(THE CORPSE REVIVER NO. 2, PAGE 149)

Chill a cocktail glass.

Set out gin, Cointreau, Cocchi Americano, absinthe, and ¾ ounce fresh lemon juice.

Fill a Boston shaker a little more than half full with ice.

Measure into your shaker: ¾ ounce (22 ml) lemon juice, ¾ ounce (22 ml) Cocchi Americano, ¾ ounce (22 ml) Cointreau, 1 ounce (30 ml) gin.

Cover your shaker (put the metal top over the pint glass at a slight angle). Give the top of it a whack with the heel of your hand to create a seal.

Flip the shaker so the glass side is up. Place one hand on the bottom of the metal tumbler and your other hand securely along the top of the glass.

Shake so that the contents slosh vigorously—you want to incorporate the citrus and aerate the drink to make it effervescent. Shake 8 to 12 seconds.

Place the shaker back on the counter, metal side down. Then, a solid whack on the side of the Boston shaker with the heel of your hand will separate the two parts.

Rinse your chilled glass with absinthe by pouring in about a teaspoon and swirling it around. Then, strain the drink using the hawthorne strainer capped over the shaking tin. Serve immediately.

THE SCIENCE OF THE STIR

Why such exacting directions for a stirred cocktail? Keep this in mind: you're working to reduce the drink temperature to under 40 degrees without making it too watery. A good stir will assure that approximately ¼ of the drink will be melted ice.

HOW TO MAKE A STIRRED DRINK
(THE MANHATTAN, PAGE 41)

Chill a cocktail glass.

Set out rye whiskey, sweet vermouth, Angostura bitters, and cherries. Set out your mixing glass, a bar spoon, and a julep strainer.

Fill your mixing glass about two-thirds full of ice.

Season the ice with 2 dashes of Angostura bitters. Measure 1 ounce (30 ml) of sweet vermouth and 2 ounces (60 ml) of rye whiskey into the mixing glass.

To stir, position the handle of a bar spoon between your second and third fingers. Slowly, move the spoon clockwise for 20 to 30 seconds. Stirring brings the temperature of the drink down and dilutes the spirits with just enough water to open up the aromatics. A gentle hand ensures that you won't incorporate bubbles. You want an ice-cold Manhattan without any froth.

Strain into a chilled cocktail glass.

Garnish with a cherry.

GARNISH TECHNIQUES

HOW TO FLAME A PEEL . . . .

Use a paring knife to cut a strip of orange peel one inch wide, with plenty of pith. Hold the peel between your thumb and forefinger with the orange side facing out. Ready a lighter in your other hand. As you press down on the peel to express orange oil, strike your lighter so that the spray catches fire. Discard the peel, or drop it into your drink—whichever you prefer. Drinks that are good candidates for a flamed peel are spirituous drinks, such as the Negroni (page 91) and the Old Fashioned (page 28). In this book, we use a flamed peel in the Oaxaca Old Fashioned (page 139).

HOW TO MAKE A CITRUS TWIST OR SPIRAL . . . .

For a basic twist, use a Y-peeler or a paring knife to shave off a thin tongue of peel. Try not to shave off a lot of pith. Twist the peel over the top of the glass to release oils, then drop it in the drink or rest it along the rim. For a spiral twist, use a vegetable peeler or a channel knife with a V-shaped blade to groove out a long, thin spiral. You can drape this over the side of the glass, or you can twist the peel around a straw to form a curl, then sling it over the rim.

HOW TO RIM A GLASS WITH CITRUS . . . .

Cut a strip of citrus peel about half an inch wide using a peeler or paring knife. You'll want to use the colored side of the peel, which contains oils, to rim the lip of the glass. Run the peel around the rim, expressing oils as you go. This adds aroma and a burst of flavor to the first sip.

HOW TO CREATE A SUGAR OR SALT RIM. . . . .

Start with a wedge of citrus. Run the wedge along the lip of the glass so that the juice moistens the rim. Invert the glass and dip it into a plate of sugar or salt (usually 1 to 2 tablespoons, or 15 to 30 g). Tap the glass a few times to remove excess granules.

HOW TO SPANK AND FLOAT HERBS. . . . .

When you are working with herb garnishes, like sage, rosemary, mint, or lavender, you can "spank" them to release their essential oils. Then, when you float them on the top of a cocktail, they will send up a gust of lovely aromatics. To spank your herbs, smack them between your palms. It's rather exhilarating.

HOW TO CREATE YOUR OWN DRINKS

NO-FAIL COCKTAIL RATIOS

Making good drinks is fairly easy if you follow basic guidelines and recipes. Making exceptional drinks takes additional skill and practice—like any craft. And making well-developed, entirely new drinks takes all this and a bit of playful ingenuity.

Many bartenders will tell you that inspiration strikes when they are playing around with an interesting new product. By testing and discovering a product's flavor profile, they can discover its affinities for certain other spirits or liqueurs. Enough messing around, and a new cocktail is born.

To keep your bartending playful, try making the same drink multiple different ways in order to explore its features. A trick is to halve a recipe, make the drink the "straight" way, and then, in another shaker, change one feature and make it another way. Do this a few times—over a few days, if necessary—tasting along the way. Be sure to take notes so you can remember what you did!

This kind of experimentation is both

the easiest way to familiarize yourself with products on your shelves, but also ascertain how you prefer your drinks. As you develop your palate, your drink-creating technique will improve as well.

Perhaps the easiest and most common way to construct a "new" drink is to substitute an ingredient or two—or sometimes even three—in a classic recipe and call the result a new name. The famous Red Hook cocktail was created this way, being a Manhattan in which Punt e Mes is substituted for sweet vermouth.

Another common means to a new cocktail is to scan the drink taxonomy (page 54) and use the definitions and features to compose your new sensation.

Of course, the most adventurous method is to build a drink from a blank canvas, much like a Bob Ross painting; you first lay down background color (a base spirit), and then highlight this with modifying liquors or liqueurs. Finally, add splashes and dashes for yet a third or fourth layer—composed of juice, soda, ginger beer, bitters, etc.

To do this, try a ratio of 2:1:1—two ounces of a base spirit, one ounce of sour (think citrus), and one ounce of sweet (think liqueur). Then polish this off with a dash of aromatics such as herbs or bitters. Voilà! Just make sure the ingredients are complementary, and you'll be amazed at how well this works. If you prefer your drinks less sweet or less tart—or both—use a 3:2:1 ratio. After you have worked with both of these, try the more advanced and nuanced ratio of 1½ : ¾ : ¼.

FLAVOR THESAURUS

If you want to experiment with creating your own drink recipes, it's helpful to have a basic understanding of how to combine flavors. We like to start with a seasonal item, usually a fruit as inspiration—then add a complementary flavor and a spirit or two. Use this list of pairing ideas to fuel your creativity as you experiment.

HOW TO WORK WITH FLAVORS

You can use the flavors mentioned in this section to . . .

• Make a syrup (page 239).

• Create a garnish in the form of a peel, sprig, or float (page 264).

• Make your own bitters (page 252).

• Steep an ingredient in a spirit for several days/weeks to create an infusion.

BASE INGREDIENT	COMPLEMENTS	ALCOHOL
LEMON	Rosemary, lavender, thyme, blueberry, strawberry, cucumber	Gin, Vodka, Limoncello
LIME	Mint, lemongrass, ginger, coconut, pineapple, strawberry, raspberry, cranberry	Rum, Tequila, Bourbon, or Vodka
ORANGE	Mint, ginger, hibiscus, coconut, banana, lemon, lime, cranberry, orange bitters	Tequila, Rum, Vodka, Cointreau, Grand Marnier, Aperol
GRAPEFRUIT	Rosemary, mint, sea salt, black pepper, lime, orange, rhubarb	Vodka or Campari
WATERMELON	Mint, basil, sea salt, smoked salt, hibiscus, black pepper, strawberry, lime, cucumber, jalapeño	Rum, Vodka, or Mezcal
PINEAPPLE	Mint, Thai basil, ginger, coconut, orange, strawberry, Angostura bitters	Rum or Vodka
STRAWBERRY	Basil, thyme, freshly brewed green tea, lime, lemon, blueberry, raspberry	Gin, Vodka, or Bubbly
RASPBERRY	Pink peppercorn, rosemary, orange, strawberry, cherry, lime	Gin or Vodka
BLACKBERRY	Sage, black peppercorn, lemon, lime, plum	Gin, Vodka, or Cassis
PEACH/ NECTARINE	Ginger, white pepper, lime, blackberry, blueberry, apple	Rum or Brandy
CHERRY	Clove, cinnamon, freshly brewed black tea, cherry bark bitters	Whiskey or Rye
APPLE	Cinnamon, clove, nutmeg, lemon, orange, Angostura bitters	Applejack, Calvados, Rum, or Bourbon
PEAR	Rosemary, lemongrass, ginger, chamomile, lemon	Gin, Vodka, Pear Brandy, St. Germain
PLUM	Star anise, cinnamon, orange, cherry, peach, black tea	Bourbon or Sherry
CUCUMBER	Rose, dill, lemon, lime, chamomile, celery	Bitters

PART SEVEN

BOOZE GLOSSARY

GIN

Gin gets its English name from genever, or jenever, a distilled malt wine from Holland that was originally flavored with juniper and other botanicals for medicinal purposes and sold in pharmacies. Dutch physician and scientist Franciscus Sylvius is often credited with its creation in the 1700s, but "Geneva" is mentioned as early as the late sixteenth century, when English soldiers brought it back from expeditions in support of Dutch independence. It earned the nickname "Dutch Courage," and gained widespread popularity in Great Britain after William of Orange invaded England in 1688 with a Dutch fleet.

Because it was possible to make without a license, gin became so popular that its overconsumption led to the so-called "Gin Craze" of the first half of the eighteenth century, requiring the government to enact multiple restrictions. England's burgeoning sweet tooth, fueled by sugarcane from its colonies in the Caribbean, led to the production of a sweetened and lighter gin style called "Old Tom." Old Tom was the prevalent gin style during the cocktail's Golden Age, from roughly the 1870s to World War I.

Gin was originally distilled in a pot still, resulting in a maltier taste closer to whiskey, but the invention of the column still in the nineteenth century led to the creation of the cleaner-tasting, lighter London Dry style.

Recently, with America's increasing interest in craft spirits, a new designation has emerged, called "American Western Dry Gin" or "American Dry Gin," which reflects distillers' use of regional botanicals and an attempt to codify quality standards. If you enjoy gin, an exploration into the burgeoning scene can feel like passing through C. S. Lewis's wardrobe into Gin Narnia. You'll find small-batch bottles made from honey, thanks to Caledonia Spirits in Vermont; ethereal gins developed to play up local botanicals, like Sage by Philadelphia's Art in the Age; plus big, branchy evergreen gins like Oregon's Rogue Spruce.

Truly, there is a gin for every predilection.

GIN STYLES AND TASTING NOTES

GENEVER: Malty and complex with soft herbal undertones, sometimes compared to a light Scotch. The smell brings to mind Japanese sake.
(Brands: Bols, Boomsma)

OLD TOM: Round, nuanced, heavy on botanicals, distinctly sweet. There's a slight fruitiness, like fresh peaches.
(Brand: Hayman's)

PLYMOUTH: Astringent, with notes of fresh juniper combined with citrus, making this a choice gin to pair with lime or lemon.
(Brand: Plymouth)

LONDON DRY: Briny, angular, with a sharp finish—a huge blast of juniper. Excellent for martinis; its briny edge loves an olive.
(Brands: Tanqueray, Beefeater, Broker's)

AMERICAN DRY: Various botanicals pop, depending on the terroir. For notes of orange and cardamom, try Aviation from Portland. Greylock, from the Berkshires, highlights lemon, orange, black pepper, and coriander. And the list goes on.
(Brands: Blue Coal, Aviation, St. George, Small's, Junipero, and many more)

RUM

Sugarcane was introduced to the Caribbean Islands in the seventeenth century, where it was discovered that molasses—a byproduct of the sugar-refining process—could be fermented and distilled. Rum today is still made mostly in the Caribbean and aged primarily in oak whiskey or bourbon barrels. There is a dizzying variety, categorized broadly by color, which is related to age. Light (also called white, clear, or silver) is young and crisp; gold (also called amber) is usually aged, and has spice notes like vanilla imparted by wood; and dark (also called black) is aged in charred barrels and often heavily spiced. The color comes from barrel-aging, or from artificial coloring.

Rum became the spirit of choice in the early American colonies, with the first distillery on record in the United States appearing in 1664 on Staten Island. It became the base of many early drinks, only to be supplanted by whiskey and gin later as they became readily available. Interestingly, it returned to popularity during both Prohibition—when bootlegging brought it to speakeasies—and during WWII, when rationing grain for other liquors made rum a viable and inexpensive alternative.

Old cocktail recipes (and some new ones!) will call for rums based on islands, with the expectation that readers will be familiar with the specific flavor profiles of Barbados or Puerto Rican rums versus those of, say, Jamaica or Martinique. The problem with this method today is that many of the old rums have disappeared, or the profile that islands were once known for have been winnowed down to just a few remaining mass-produced bottlings.

Another way to differentiate rums in terms of flavor is to distinguish between rough, funky, pirate-y rums (Wray & Nephew) and mellower, mainstream styles (Bacardi). So-called "pirate" rums are often made in traditional pot stills and exhibit what is called "hogo," from the French *haut goût* (high taste), and have a flavor reminiscent of aged meat.

If you are just starting a bar, three bottles that will make many drinks in this book are listed below:

Light rum: Flor De Caña 4 Yr

Gold rum: Appleton Estate V/X

Black rum: Cruzan Blackstrap

RUM STYLES AND TASTING NOTES

LIGHT (CLEAR, WHITE, SILVER): Light-bodied, crisp, subtle. Think dry sugarcane and vanilla. Wildly versatile, particularly with drinks that feature lime.
(Brands: Flor de Caña 4 Yr, Don Q Cristal, Plantation)

GOLD OR AMBER: Slightly oaky, with flavor notes that can include vanilla, almond, and caramel, making gold a good choice for fruit-based cocktails containing coconut and/or pineapple. Ideal for rum punch.
(Brands: Appleton Special, Appleton V/X, Flor de Caña Gold)

DARK: Mahogany in color from extended aging (at least two years), full-bodied, and heavy on oak and caramel notes. Popular in tiki drinks, especially when mixed with lighter rums to create a layered effect.
(Brands: El Dorado 5 Yr, Zaya 12 Yr, Ron Zacapa 23 Yr)

BLACK: Tar-colored, often due to charred barrels but also from coloring and additional molasses. Heavy flavors of burnt sugar and vanilla. Beware: some exhibit a synthetic taste, particularly those that are spiced.
(Brands: Hamilton Jamaican Pot Still Black Rum, Cruzan Blackstrap)

NAVY STRENGTH OR OVERPROOF: Dark, full-bodied, powerful, often marketed as "151 rum." Frequently used as a float on top of drinks.
(Brands: Hamilton Demerara Overproof, Smith & Cross, Wray & Nephew, Pusser's)

RHUM AGRICOLE: A smooth, intricate class of rums, especially good for sipping. Rhum agricole is fermented and distilled from fresh sugarcane juice, rather than molasses, and has grassy notes. Expect wild variation, from aromas of brown butter to apple and earth.
(Brands: Neisson, Clément)

DEMERARA: Produced in Guyana on the northern coast of South America, these rums are rich and often have a smoky complexity.
(Brands: El Dorado, Hamilton)

SPICED OR FLAVORED: Often highly processed and full of fake flavor. These are to rum as Cheez Whiz is to cheese; they do not appear in this book.

WHISK(E)Y

When referring to grain-based, wood-aged liquor from the United States and Ireland, whiskey is spelled with an "e." In Scotland and Canada—and everywhere else in the world, for that matter—it is whisky with no "e." To confuse things further, there are a few American oddballs, like George Dickel, Maker's Mark, and Old Forester, which also call themselves "whisky.'"

The Irish were probably the first Europeans to distill from fermented grain mash, making whisky for medicinal purposes in monasteries. Whisky is a version of the Gaelic word for "water"—*uisge beatha*. You may see it as the anglicized *usquebaugh* on bottles and bar menus. In the American colonies, whiskey was made with rye in the northeast and with corn farther west. Bourbon County Kentucky lends its name to the unique liquor that must be 51 percent corn and aged for a minimum of two years in new oak barrels (it does not need to be made in Bourbon County).

At one time, the United States probably consumed more rye whiskey than any other kind, which is why so many heritage drinks call for it. Rye was largely wiped out by Prohibition; while distilleries in the west simply unlocked their doors and sprang back into production on Repeal Day, many East Coast rye whiskey distilleries had been sold or repurposed. Rye has seen a major revival in recent years.

WHISK(E)Y STYLES AND TASTING NOTES

BOURBON: Often marked by sweetness or fruitiness. Caramel, charred oak, vanilla.
(Brands: Buffalo Trace, Four Roses, Maker's Mark, Woodford Reserve)

TENNESSEE: Tennessee whiskies (except Prichard's) undergo what's called the Lincoln County process: filtration through maple sugar tree charcoal. The taste is similar to bourbon, but the finish is sometimes longer and cleaner.
(Brands: George Dickel, Prichard's)

IRISH: Once the most popular whiskey in the United States, production was hurt by Prohibition and never fully recovered. Today, there are just a handful of distilleries that produce all of the brands. While there are many varieties of Irish whiskey, the style is most often characterized by toasty honeyed notes.
(Brands: Bushmills, Powers, Tullamore Dew, Red Breast, Jameson)

RYE: Biscuit and caraway notes with maple and oak. Very dry, sometimes walnut flavor.
(Brands: Rittenhouse, Wild Turkey, Sazerac, Old Overholt)

SCOTCH: Scotch gets its smokiness from peat, which is used to dry the malt. There are five (some say six) distinct Scotch regions, each with different characteristics: Islay, Lowland, Campbeltown, Speyside, Highland, and Islands (part of Highlands, but distinct enough that you'll often see it mentioned). There are also blended Scotches, which are mild and can be good for cocktails. In this book, we use Talisker, a hefty Island Scotch, as well as the überpeaty Laphroaig, which is an Islay. Blends like Famous Grouse and Dewar's work for drinks that don't call for strong Scotch characteristics.
(Brands: Talisker, Laphroaig; for blended Scotch: Famous Grouse and Dewar's)

BRANDY

The word "brandy" comes from the Dutch word for "burned wine" (*brandewijn*). It is the name given to spirits distilled from fruit, most commonly grapes. But brandies can be made from apples, pears, apricots, and berries. Sometimes these are called *eau-de-vie*, meaning "water of life.'"

Cocktailians often look for French spirits in this category, namely cognac. Cognac during the Golden Age of cocktails would have been heftier than today's cognac, and French maker Pierre Ferrand has developed a cognac specifically for cocktails with spirits writer David Wondrich. The 1840 formula cognac is slightly higher proof, and appears in such cocktails as the Brandy Crusta (page 27).

In this book we've settled on Pierre Ferrand Ambre for most spirituous drinks in which you can really taste quality brandy or cognac. For drinks that contain serious adulterations—like cream, eggs, coffee, or fruity liqueurs—we use Paul Masson Grande Amber VS.

BRANDY STYLES AND TASTING NOTES

COGNAC/ARMAGNAC: Vanilla, wood, and fruit, such as peaches and pears, depending on the grade and brand.
(Brands: Pierre Ferrand, Tariquet)

CALVADOS: Aromatic and subtle when young, with flavor notes of apple, honey, and baking spices; aged varieties can be dry and taste more like cognac.
(Brands: Boulard, Christian Drouin, Daron)

APPLEJACK: Fresh apple with a spicy finish.
(Brand: Clear Creek)

Note: Confusingly, Laird's Applejack is technically a whiskey.

APRICOT EAU-DE-VIE: Fresh apricot, crushed apricot stone, honeysuckle. This is used to thrilling effect in the Gin Blossom (page 133).
(Brands: Blume Marillen, Clear Creek)

KIRSCHWASSER: Cherry, bitter almond, slight vanilla nose.
(Brands: Clear Creek, Schladerer)

TEQUILA & MEZCAL

Tequila is made from the agave plant, a giant silver-blue succulent with swordlike spikes. To make tequila, the spikes are lopped off and the heart of the plant is steamed (mezcal producers roast the hearts, producing a smoky taste). The hearts are mashed, then fermented. The best tequila is made from 100 percent agave; anything less than 100 percent is a mixture of agave and other sugars (read: a hangover inducer).

Navigating tequilas can be daunting, so it can be helpful to start one's vision quest at a good bar where a few studious pours can quickly show you the difference in smell, taste, and smoothness between the three basic categories.

TEQUILA STYLES AND TASTING NOTES

BLANCO (WHITE) OR PLATA (SILVER): Refers to young tequila bottled right from the still or shortly after distillation. It is icy clear and tends to be grassy and slightly metallic in taste, if not a little harsh. (Brands: El Jimador, Herradura)

ANEJO (OLD): Aged for a minimum of twelve months, often in bourbon barrels. These are fine sipping tequilas, amber in color. In 2006, Tequila Extra Anejo (extra aged) appeared on the market, but as you might imagine these bottles are spendy and therefore not the best for mixed drinks. (Brands: Corralejo, Gran Centenario)

REPOSADO (RESTED): Spends two to eleven months aging in barrels to develop delicate oaky flavors. Its color turns slightly golden, and the taste deepens and softens. (Brands: Corralejo, Cazadores)

MEZCAL: Tequila's more rustic cousin. Its earthy, smoky flavor distinguishes it from tequila, and it can be made from a variety of agave plants, whereas tequila must be made from blue agave. It pairs well with citrus, like orange or pineapple, and it loves spice—like in the Mezcalada (page 160) and the Barbacoa (page 145). (Brand: Del Maguey)

VODKA

Vodka is typically a distillation of grain or potatoes, but is sometimes made with fruit or sugar. It was first produced in the Middle Ages, with its first mention in print in fifteenth-century Poland. Once a rarity on American soil, a sustained campaign by Smirnoff in the '50s (see Moscow Mule, page 122 and the Vesper, page 112) helped its popularity to soar.

Today, it is the most consumed spirit in the United States, pushed by big marketing campaigns selling a variety of flavors. This underscores vodka's versatility; because it is composed of water and ethanol, and thus has a "neutral" flavor, it is the bartender's go-to spirit for creating infusions and tinctures, or as a base for homemade liqueurs.

Vodka is often cited as a major contributor to America's steep cocktail decline from the '60s until the '90s. Despite impressive marketing campaigns by higher priced vodkas, we find Stolichnaya (made from a blend of wheat and rye) to be remarkably good in cocktails.

VODKA STYLES AND TASTING NOTES

WHEAT: The most commonly used grain for vodka. Typified by a very clean flavor and slightly oily texture with citrus notes. (Brands: Grey Goose, Ketel One)

RYE: Most common to Poland, but it is used in some Russian vodkas as well. Aroma can be similar to rye bread with a nice spiciness and a nutty finish. (Brands: Belvedere)

POTATO: Typically Polish, though potato vodka can be found in other countries. Can be rather viscous. (Brands: Chopin, Luksusowa)

CORN: Typically used in western vodkas. Subtle sweet corn notes. (Brands: Tito's, UV)

BARLEY: Rarely used, associated with Finland; black pepper and ginger notes. (Brand: Finlandia)

FLAVORED: A huge category of the vodka market but used with discretion in cocktails due to flavorings that can taste synthetic. (Brands: Stolichnaya, Hangar 1)

APPENDIX

USEFUL EQUIVALENTS FOR MEASURING LIQUIDS

¼ fluid ounce	=	1.5 teaspoons (7 ml)
½ fluid ounce	=	1 tablespoon (15 ml)
¾ fluid ounce	=	1½ tablespoons (22 ml)
1 fluid ounce	=	2 tablespoons (30 ml)
1½ fluid ounces	=	3 tablespoons (45 ml)
2 fluid ounces	=	¼ cup (60 ml)
2½ fluid ounces	=	⅓ cup (79 ml)
3 fluid ounces	=	(89 ml)
4 fluid ounces	=	½ cup (120 ml)
6 fluid ounces	=	¾ cup (175 ml)
8 fluid ounces	=	1 cup (237 ml)
10 fluid ounces	=	1¼ cup (or ½ pint) (296 ml)
1 large egg	=	1 to 1½ ounces of white (30 to 45 ml)
1 lemon	=	about 1½ ounces of juice (45 ml)
1 lime	=	about 1 ounce of juice (30 ml)

USEFUL BOOKS FOR THE AVID COCKTAILER

These books have been invaluable to us during our exploration. We've listed them in the order in which they were published.

The Bon Vivant's Companion, by Jerry Thomas (1862, 1887)

American and Other Drinks, by Leo Engel (1878)

Bartenders' Manual: A Guide for Hotels and Restaurants, by Harry Johnson (1882)

The Flowing Bowl: What and When to Drink, by William Schmidt (1891)

Stuart's Fancy Drinks and How to Mix Them, by Thomas Stuart (1904)

Recipes for Mixed Drinks, by Hugo Ensslin (1917)

The Ideal Bartender, by Tom Bullock (1917)

Harry's ABC's of Mixing Cocktails, by Harry McElhone (1919)

Barflies and Cocktails, by Harry McElhone (1927)

The Savoy Cocktail Book, by Harry Craddock (1930)

The Old Waldorf-Astoria Bar Book, by A. S. Crockett (1935)

Famous New Orleans Drinks and How to Mix 'Em, by Stanley Arthur (1937)

A Gentleman's Companion: Being an Exotic Drinking Book, or, Around the World with Jigger, Beaker and Flask, by Charles H. Baker (1939)

Cocktail Guide and Ladies' Companion, by Crosby Gaige (1941)

The Stork Club Bar Book, by Lucius Beebe (1946)

The Hour: A Cocktail Manifesto, by Bernard DeVoto (1948)

The Official Mixer's Manual, by Patrick Gavin Duffy (1948)

The Fine Art of Mixing Drinks, by David A. Embury (1948)

Bottoms Up, by Ted Saucier (1951)

Martini, Straight Up: The Classic American Cocktail, by Lowell Edmunds (1981)

Straight Up or On the Rocks, by William Grimes (2002)

The Craft of the Cocktail: Everything You Need to Know to Be a Master Bartender, by Dale DeGroff (2002)

Joy of Mixology: The Consummate Guide to the Bartender's Craft, by Gary Regan (2003)

And a Bottle of Rum: A History of the New World in Ten Cocktails, by Wayne Curtis (2006)

The Essential Bartender's Guide: How to Create Truly Great Cocktails, by Robert Hess (2008)

Everyday Drinking: The Distilled Kingsley Amis, by Kingsley Amis (2008)

Big Bartender's Book, by Jeff Mason and Greg Boehm (2009)

Fix the Pumps, by Darcy O'Neil (2009)

Beach Bum Berry Remixed, by Jeff "Beachbum" Berry (2009)

Vintage Spirits and Forgotten Cocktails, by Ted Haigh (2009)

Boozehound: On the Trail of the Rare, the Obscure, and the Overrated in Spirits, by Jason Wilson (2010)

The PDT Cocktail Book, Jim Meehan (2011)

To Have and Have Another: A Hemingway Cocktail Companion, by Philip Greene (2012)

The Drunken Botanist: The Plants That Create the World's Great Drinks, by Amy Stewart (2013)

Craft Cocktails at Home: Offbeat Techniques, Contemporary Crowd-pleasers, and Classics Hacked with Science, by Kevin Liu (2013)

Apothecary Cocktails: Restorative Drinks from Yesterday and Today, by Warren Bobrow (2013)

The Bar Book: Elements of Cocktail Technique, by Jeffrey Morgenthaler (2014)

Death & Co: Modern Classic Cocktails, with More Than 500 Recipes, by David Kaplan, Nick Fauchald, Alex Day (2015)

INDEX

Page numbers in italics indicate photographs.

Hemingway Daiquiri, 62, 102
Hi Ho Cocktail, 20, 103
Highball, 55, 112
Highland Cooler, 162, 172, 174
Hine VSOP cognac
  French Maid, 146
Holiday Cocktails, 217
honey, 17, 257
Honey Ginger Syrup, 242
Honey Syrup, 242
horchata
  recipe for, 250
  Rumchata (Drunken Horchata), 201
horehound tincture
  Rock and Rye, 120
Horse's Neck, 233
Hot (Spiced) Buttered Rum, 215
hot cocktails
  about, 214
  Hot (Spiced) Buttered Rum, 215
  Hot Toddy, 216
  Hot Vietnamese Coffee, 218
  Irish Coffee, 218
  Roasted Apple Toddy, 216
  Smoking Bishop, 220, 221
  Tom and Jerry, 219
Hot Toddy, 216
Hot Vietnamese Coffee, 214, 218
Hotel Nacional, 82, 83
How to Mix Drinks: Or, the Bon Vivant's Companion (Thomas), 23, 98, 131
Hurricane, 118

I

ice, 10, 256
Imbue Bittersweet, 40
Improved Holland Gin Cocktail, 35, 36, 53
Intro to Aperol, 21, 90, 164, 165
Irish Coffee, 218

Irish whiskey
  Irish Coffee, 218
  tasting notes for, 277
  Tipperary Cocktail, 65
Italian Greyhound, 151

J

Jack Rose, 62, 84, 114
Japanese Cocktail, 33, 186
Jasmine, 132
Jersey Cocktail, 136, 174
John Collins, 167
Journalist, The, 94
juice, freshly squeezed, 10
julep, 55
Juliet and Romeo, 139, 208
Jungle Bird, 192, 193, 228
Juniper and Tonic, 162, 231, 233
Juniper Syrup, 243

K

Kahlua
  Black Russian, 123
  Kangaroo Cocktail, 39, 123
Kentucky Buck, 17, 176
Kir, 207
Kir Royale, 207, 208
Kirschwasser
  Rose Cocktail, 84
  Straits Sling, 61
  tasting notes for, 279
Knabenshue, 205, 232
Knickerbocker, 23, 32, 53

L

Lambic Sangria, 136, 175
Laphroaig 10-year Single Malt
  Penicillin, 135
Lapsang Souchong Tea Syrup, 243
Last Tango in Modena, The, 136, 141, 162
Last Word, 21, 79, 85
Leap Year, 38, 73, 208

lemons, 17
light rum
  Daiquiri, 108
  Fog Cutter, 157
  Hotel Nacional, 83
  Hurricane, 118
  Mary Pickford, 80
  Missionary's Downfall, 185
  Navy Grog, 184
  Piña Colada, 196
  Saoco, 199
  Scorpion Bowl, 192
  Between the Sheets, 95
  tasting notes for, 275
  Test Pilot, 187
Lime Cordial, 245
Lime Cordial Soda, 237
Lion's Tail, 108, 163
Literary Cocktails, 114
Little Pink Pearl, 234
London Dry gin
  Fog Cutter, 157
  Gibson, 102
  Gimlet, 113
  Gin Rickey, 161
  Gingin Mule, 133
  Hanky Panky, 73
  Intro to Aperol, 165
  Napoleon, 68
  Pink Lady, 74
  Sky Juice, 201
  tasting notes for, 273
  White Lady, 95
Lone Tree Cocktail, 45
low-proof/no-proof cocktails
  about, 231
  Black Julep, 238
  Burning Branch, 236, 237
  Haymaker's Punch, 234
  Horse's Neck, 233
  Juniper and Tonic, 233
  Lime Cordial Soda, 237

AKNOWLEDGMENTS

Deep gratitude to our editor, Cindy De La Hoz, as well as our agent, Amy Williams, for their guidance and support. A huge thanks to photographer Jason Varney and to designer Joshua McDonnell for bringing these cocktails so vividly to life.

Our heartfelt thanks to friends and professionals who offered their time, talents, and valuable feedback: to consummate reader Jeff Jahnke of Cocktaildudes.com; to Kevin Liu, who gave just the right advice when we needed it; to Ed Hamilton for the excellent rum info and illuminating conversations; to Warren Bobrow, whose gnome knows no bounds; to Chad Vogel, JR Mocanu, and Grant Hurless for their skill, knowledge, and help recipe testing; to Jessica Wohlers for suggesting Raoul's when we needed a lift; and to the many bartenders who have mixed us incredible cocktails over the years, especially Chris Bostick, Micah Melton, Charles Joly, Freddie Sarkis, Phoebe Esmon, and Christian Gaal. Also, hats off to the gents at Bittercube, Nick Kosevich and Ira Klopowitz, as well as the awesome Little Wisco crew in New York.

We're also indebted to the many cocktail writers before us, whose books and articles slaked our thirst for knowledge and fed our imaginations: William Grimes, Kingsley Amis, Lowell Edmunds, Bernard DeVoto, Charles H. Baker, Dale DeGroff, David Embury, Craig Claiborne, Gary Regan, Jeff "Beachbum" Berry, Ted Haigh, Paul Clarke, Paul Harrington, Caroline Pardilla, Lauren Viera, Philip Collins, Jeffrey Morgenthaler, Jim Meehan, Camper English, Tony Conigliaro, Steven Raichlen, Amy Stewart, David Wondrich, William Schmidt, Jason Wilson, Robert Simonson, Darcy O'Neil, François Chartier, Greg Seider, Katie Loeb, Matt Robold, Robert Hess, Erik Ellestad, Jamie Boudreau, Dinah Sanders, Maggie Savarino, Andrew F. Smith, Philip Greene, Wayne Curtis, Jeff Masson, Greg Boehm, and Paul Pacult.

For their support of our writerly endeavors, thanks to Dean Robbins and Linda Falkenstein of *Isthmus Newspaper*, the artists' community at Yaddo, and colleagues at Saint Joseph's University in Philadelphia.

To our friends and family, thank you for enduring countless drink trials, sticky kitchens, and broken glassware, especially our partners, Patricia Davis and Todd Stregiel.